This book makes available five classic studies of the organization of behavior in face-to-face interaction. It includes Adam Kendon's well-known study of gaze direction in interaction, his study of greetings, of the interactional functions of facial expression and of the spatial organization of naturally occurring interaction, as recorded by means of film or videotape. They represent some of the best work undertaken within the "natural history" tradition of interaction studies, as originally formulated in the work of Bateson, Birdwhistell and Goffman. Chapter 2, written especially for this publication, provides an historical and theoretical discussion of this tradition, and a final chapter takes up the theme of the organization of attention in interaction. The introduction provides details of the circumstances of how each paper came to be written. Each of the papers reprinted is also accompanied by a short postscript, placing the work in the context of more recent research.

Several of the papers presented in this volume, although widely referred to, have long been difficult to obtain. Their re-publication will be warmly welcomed by all students and teachers who are concerned with face-to-face interaction.

Studies in Interactional Sociolinguistics

*General Editor: John J. Gumperz*

# Conducting interaction
## Patterns of behavior in focused encounters

Companions to this volume

*Discourse strategies* by John J. Gumperz
*Language and social identity* edited by John J. Gumperz
*The social construction of literacy* edited by Jenny Cook-Gumperz
*Politeness: some universals in language use* by Penelope Brown and
    Stephen C. Levinson
*Discourse markers* by Deborah Schiffrin
*Talking voices: repetition, dialogue, and imagery in conversational discourse* by Deborah Tannen

# Conducting interaction

Patterns of behavior in focused encounters

ADAM KENDON

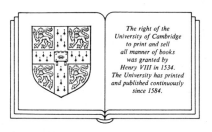

The right of the
University of Cambridge
to print and sell
all manner of books
was granted by
Henry VIII in 1534.
The University has printed
and published continuously
since 1584.

Cambridge University Press

*Cambridge*
*New York*   *Port Chester*
*Melbourne*   *Sydney*

Published by the Press Syndicate of the University of Cambridge
The Pitt Building, Trumpington Street, Cambridge CB2 1RP
40 West 20th Street, New York, NY 10011, USA
10 Stamford Road, Oakleigh, Melbourne 3166, Australia

First published 1990

Printed in Great Britain at the University Press, Cambridge

*British Library cataloguing in publication data*
Kendon, Adam
Conducting interaction: patterns of behavior in focused
encounters – (Studies in interactional sociolinguistics; 7).
1. Social interactions
I. Title II. Series
302

*Library of Congress cataloguing in publication data*
Kendon, Adam.
Conducting interaction: patterns of behavior in focused
encounters / Adam Kendon.
    p.     cm. – (Studies in interactional sociolinguistics; 7)
ISBN 0-521-38036-7. – ISBN 0-521-38938-0 (pbk.)
1. Conversation. 2. Social interaction. 3. Interpersonal
communication. I. Title. II. Series.
P95.45.K46 1990
302.3'46–dc 20     90–1410 CIP

ISBN 0 521 38036 7 hardback
ISBN 0 521 38938 0 paperback

WD

# Contents

# Preface

The papers reprinted in this book may be seen as responses to Erving Goffman's (1967, pp. 1–3) call for a study of the "ultimate behavioral materials" of interaction. These papers deal, in some detail, with what he referred to as the "small behaviors" of interaction. That is, they deal with "the glances, gestures, positionings and verbal statements" that constitute the stuff of face-to-face encounters. Goffman believed that their study would make possible both a description of "the natural units of interaction" and an understanding of the "normative order prevailing within and between these units." He argued that, in order to understand how people routinely achieve order in their interactions with one another, "we need to identify the countless patterns and natural sequences of behavior occurring whenever persons come into one another's immediate presence." It is just this that is attempted by five of the papers republished here (Chapters 3–7).

For the theoretical and methodological outlook that governs these studies I am indebted not only to Erving Goffman, but, as well, to Gregory Bateson, Ray Birdwhistell and Albert Scheflen. Bateson, Birdwhistell and Scheflen showed the value of a "natural history" approach to the study of interaction and they showed what may be derived from the detailed examination of specimens of it, as these may be collected by means of film or video-tape. The five studies reprinted here all follow this method, which is sometimes referred to as "Context Analysis." In Chapter 2, I discuss the antecedents of this approach, and how they combined to form this method of investigation. I discuss the place of Context Analysis in the study of social interaction, as this has developed in social science generally, and I show the nature of the influence of such diverse lines of work as interpersonal psychiatry, information theory, cybernetics, and structural (descriptive) linguistics, as these were brought to bear in the development of the method.

Finally, Chapter 8 considers some of the implications of findings reported by Context Analysis and seeks to provide some behavioral grounding for the theoretical work on "framing" that was developed first by Bateson and, later, by Goffman. It is a contribution to a theory of how participants in focused interaction organize and regulate the coordination of each other's attention.

Chapters 3–8 first appeared in print between 1967 and 1985. Original place of publication is acknowledged in a footnote, in each case. Five of these papers (Chapters 3–7) were also published together in 1977 by the Peter De Ridder Press and the Research Center for Language and Semiotic Studies, Indiana University, in a collection entitled *Studies in the Behavior of Social Interaction*. Except for Chapter 5, where I have rewritten a small section which had become completely outdated, the papers are reprinted here without alteration. However, where appropriate, I have added a short postscript to indicate what work related to the topic of the paper has been published since it originally appeared. The Introduction (Chapter 1) is a rewritten version of the Introduction to the 1977 collection. Chapter 2, although it draws upon a previously published paper (Kendon 1982), has been specially written for the present volume and includes a good deal of new material. Frederick Erickson read these two newly written chapters in draft form and his detailed suggestions, where I have tried to follow them, have led to significant improvements.

In the 1977 collection I acknowledged a special debt to Albert Scheflen. I count myself especially fortunate in having been able to work closely with him over a number of years. The work of Chapters 4–7 was directly facilitated by him, both intellectually and administratively. I should like to repeat, once again, my expression of indebtedness to Andrew Ferber for his collaboration with me on the work of Chapter 6 and for allowing me to make free use of it and of the materials on which it is based. Robert McMillan and Robert Deutsch contributed significantly to the work of Chapter 7. Discussions with Matthew Ciolek were also important for this Chapter and he helped me with the illustrations. William Condon gave me a very thorough introduction to his work and methods. Chapter 4 was a direct outcome of my work with him. Dr. Henry Brosin was director of Western Pennsylvania Psychiatric Institute in Pittsburgh at the time I did this work and I remember with much appreciation his kindness in facilitating my stay at that institution. At Oxford, Dr. E. R. W. F. Crossman first suggested that I should work with films of social interaction. My early attempts at film analysis were done in collaboration with Professor J. Ex of Nijmegen. I still remember how valuable the discussions were which we had. Michael Argyle has taken an interest in my work over the years and has always been encouraging. He remains a good friend.

Finally, I would like to thank Professor John Gumperz for suggesting that this collection of papers should be reissued in his Interactional Sociolinguistics Series.

# 1

---

# Introduction

Occasions of interaction are, most of the time, ordered affairs. When two people greet one another, when several sustain a conversation, when a committee meets to conduct its business, when people pass one another on the street, most of the time these are ordered occasions in the sense that they "come off" in an unnoticed fashion. We may remember being pleased or disturbed on meeting our acquaintance, we may recall the value of what passed in the conversation, of the business accomplished in the committee meeting, but such memories generally do not include details about how these events were organized. We tend not to recall the spatial organization of the event, how we decided when it was our turn to speak, how we organized ourselves when we did so and how the others showed that they did, or did not understand what we said. Yet, to engage in a greeting, to sustain a conversation, to pass another on the street, requires of us both an ability to recognize the nature of a given interaction situation and to receive and interpret information from others in the light of this, and to produce acts of maneuver, orientation and utterance that will at once further our private purposes and serve so as not to disrupt, distract or otherwise render the situation socially impossible. Participants in such events must be able to act "appropriately": in greeting, for instance, we rarely hesitate about just what should be said or done, in passing another on the street we each keep going, confident in the assumption that the other will take no more interest in us than we in them and confident that the other sees us as well as we see them, and so can steer by us smoothly.

Most of the time this orderliness of face-to-face interaction is unquestioned. Occasionally, however, we experience encounters in which something goes wrong, in which, somehow, what went forward was not "appropriate": a *faux pas* was committed or a "brick" was dropped. Many people also have acquaintances who are somehow "awkward," or who, worse than this, seem somehow routinely unable to cope with encounters and always cause extensive interactional trouble. Such instances of awkwardness, or our acquaintance with interactional troublemakers, make us realize, from time to time, that routine interactional smoothness is not something that comes automatically. Rather, it appears as something people are more or less capable of. Further, as anyone who has reared children knows, it is something that must be learned. If we reflect on such realizations we may be led to raise questions about what people need to know to interact smoothly in everyday life, what the sources of information are that they must rely upon for this, and how such information is interpreted.

These kinds of questions have come in for an increasing amount of systematic investigation in recent years. In psychiatry there have been attempts to reformulate issues of psychopathology in terms of defective abilities in interaction, there has been a widespread development of concern with the management of interpersonal relations, and there have been more technical concerns with procedures of interviewing, and the like. The issue of cultural differences in interaction practices has also been raised, because of the difficulties this can create when persons of different cultural backgrounds must do business with one another. In social and cultural anthropology there have been attempts to formulate the concept of "culture" in interactional terms. In sociology there is the viewpoint of "interactionism" in which individual personality and social structure are regarded as the product of interaction processes. The more recent ethnomethodological critique, in raising fundamental issues about the nature of "social facts" and how they are constructed, has also led to an interest in examining, in detail, the interactive processes through which such "facts" are created and sustained. The most conspicuous outgrowth of this is Conversation Analysis, which seeks to describe the detailed orderliness with which people relate their utterances to one another in conversation. In linguistics, there have been extensive developments, in sociolinguistics, ethnography of communication and discourse analysis, for example, in which language is looked at in terms of how it is used in interaction. Further, there are students of language who argue that, if language is an instrument of interaction, its structure will be shaped as much by the requirements of its use, as it is by extremely general, abstract, "pre-wired" grammatical constraints. In addition, some linguists realize, along with others with related interests, that if spoken language is to be accounted for, this must be in terms of its relationships with other modes of communication. The communicative functions so often assigned to language can be, and often are, accomplished by non-linguistic means and the reverse is also the case. The embeddedness of spoken utterance in the whole configuration of behavior in interaction demands examination, therefore (see, for example, Poyatos 1983, Arndt and Janney 1987).

To an increasing degree, thus, investigations into interaction are raising the question as to how people accomplish it. More and more, issues such as how interactions between people get started in the first place, how the status of interactional participant is entered into or relinquished, what it takes for someone in an encounter to know what relevance the actions of others have for him and what is required, on his part, to ensure that his actions have relevance for others, are coming to be focused upon. It is this sort of study of interaction that concerns us in this book. All of the papers here reprinted are inquiries into the details of just what interactants actually do when they interact with one another: where they look, when they speak or remain silent, how they move, how they manage their faces, how they orient to one another and how they position themselves spatially. It is out of such concrete observable behaviors that particular events of interaction are fashioned, and if we are to come to an understanding of how people manage to sustain encounters with one another we must understand the organization and import of everything that they do.

The way this approach to the study of interaction developed is discussed in some detail in Chapter 2. I myself first came to it through a reading of two of Goffman's earliest papers, "On face-work" (Goffman 1955) and "Alienation from interaction" (Goffman 1957), while an Advanced Student at the Institute (now Department) of Experimental Psychology at Oxford. In these papers Goffman showed how occasions of interaction could be treated as such, and he pointed out that participants enter into elaborate systems of cooperation with one another, effectively allowing their behavior to be governed by the requirements of the interaction system they had entered into. He suggested how the behavior of people in interaction could be looked upon from the point of view of how it functions in the interaction system, rather than from the point of view of how it furthers or reveals an individual's current intentions, or gives expressions to aspects of his particular personality.

The analysis offered in these papers suggested to me that the individual, when engaged in face-to-face interaction, could be regarded as if engaged in a skilled performance, analogous to the way in which the driver of a car or the pilot of an airplane is engaged in a skilled performance, in which the operator must continuously organize his behavior so that it is patterned to meet the complex demands of the situation and still keep the car on the road or the plane on course. In a face-to-face encounter the participant is faced with the necessity of sustaining a complex organization of his behavior which can meet the fluctuations of the situation and maintain him as a fully incorporated participant. He has to mount a performance which can match the standards set by the jointly negotiated working consensus of the encounter. This will include the maintenance of an appropriate appearance and manner, a proper handling of moment-to-moment details such as the negotiation of the turn-taking rules operative in the situation, and an appropriate management of the content of his talk, so that it is fitted properly to the current topic jointly being sustained. An interactant, thus, must constantly be attentive to the relationship between his performance and that of others in the encounter and adjust his performance in relation to this. An occasion of interaction such as a conversation, thus, may be looked upon as an occasion in which the participants enter into a complex system of relationships which nonetheless may be understood in terms of general principles which are discoverable and generally applicable, even though the course of any specific encounter is unique (cf. Kendon 1963, Argyle and Kendon 1967).

In my initial attempts to analyze the interrelatedness of behavior in interaction, I confined myself to working with the temporal patterning of utterances, as this may be measured by means of Chapple's technique of interaction chronography (Chapple 1940, Kendon 1963). However, in 1963, in response to suggestions made by E. R. W. F. Crossman at Oxford, who had done considerable work in the analysis of manual skills, I began to look at films of two-person conversations. It became apparent at once that there were complex patterns and regularities of behavior, and that the interactants were guiding their behavior, each in relation to the other, in respect to many of them at once.

Soon after beginning work on films of conversations I became aware of the work of Scheflen (1963, 1964) and Birdwhistell (1952 and subsequent unpublished papers). The "behavior systems" approach (Scheflen 1973) and its methodological corollary, Context Analysis (Scheflen 1964, 1966, 1973, Bär 1974), that these workers were developing, which also emphasized the detailed analysis of filmed specimens of interaction (cf. Kendon 1979), clearly provided an appropriate framework for the line of inquiry I was following.

The first of the studies reprinted (Chapter 3) is concerned with the way in which participants in interaction pattern their direction of gaze in relation to one another and in relation to their utterances. It deals with a number of different questions, but a main theme addressed in the paper is the way in which gaze direction in conversation can serve at once, for the actor, as a way in which he manages what aspect of the interaction situation he receives information from but, at the same time, it serves to provide information to coparticipants about how his attention is being distributed. The suggestion is made that how the display of the direction of visual attention is coordinated in relation to who is speaking in a conversation may play an important role in the process by which utterance coordination in conversation is achieved.

This study, completed in 1965 but not published until 1967, and which was done while I was at Oxford, was directly inspired by the approach to the analysis of perceptuo-motor skills that had been worked out at Cambridge in the preceding decades by F. C. Bartlett (1947), Kenneth Craik (1947, 1948), Russell Davis (1948) and A. T. Welford (see Welford 1968 for an overview of this work). The idea that gaze direction in interaction should be analyzed derived directly from the idea that the understanding of the relationship between sensory input and motor output is crucial for the understanding of the organization of perceptuo-motor skills. The way in which a skilled operator patterns his targets of visual attention as he carries out his task is thus an important datum (Crossman 1956). If engaging in conversation is looked upon as a skilled task, then the targets of a conversationalist's visual attention could be relevant in the same way. During the same period, also at Oxford, Michael Argyle undertook his own first studies on gaze direction in interaction (Argyle and Dean 1965) while Ralph Exline of the University of Delaware, perhaps the first student of social interaction to pay attention to gaze (Exline 1961), was a visiting scholar at Oxford. The other pioneer of gaze-direction studies who should be mentioned is Gerhard Nielsen (1964), some of whose findings on looking in relation to utterances in conversation anticipated those reported later in the study we have here reprinted.

Films or video-tapes of occasions of face-to-face interaction permit the behavior of the participants to be inspected repeatedly so that it may be analyzed in great detail. When one first begins to undertake such detailed inspection one cannot help but be struck by the intricacy with which participants' behavior is coordinated. It becomes apparent that participants come to sustain systems of relationship which integrate many different aspects of their behavior. A particularly striking demonstration of this was provided by William Condon (Condon and Ogston 1966, 1967) who undertook extremely detailed studies of the way in which movement is organized in relation to speech, not only within a single individual, but also between individuals. Condon has shown that conversationalists can become synchronous in their movements, entering into a continuous and jointly sustained "dance."

During 1966–7, through the good offices of Albert Scheflen and Henry Brosin, I was given the opportunity to work with Condon in Pittsburgh. I am very much indebted to him for the extensive introduction to his work that he gave me. Chapter 4 is a direct consequence of this. It consists of a detailed examination of the relationship between the speech and bodily movements of a speaker–listener pair (termed in the paper here reprinted an "interactional axis," though a better term for it would be an "utterance exchange axis," since it is specifically around the task of exchanging spoken utterances that the behavior observed is organized) within the context of an ongoing focused gathering containing eleven participants. The paper demonstrates how, as an utterance exchange axis is established in this situation, the two individuals involved come to move in synchrony with one another, and it suggests that the synchronization of movement that obtains plays an important part in the maintenance of coordinated attention. The phenomenon of behavioral synchrony between participants in interaction and its functioning is discussed in several other papers in this volume also. In Chapter 6, where greeting interactions are discussed, the question of how a greeting is initiated is investigated. An example is described of a synchronous relationship being established between two individuals as a prelude to their becoming mutually engaged in a salutational exchange. Synchronous relationships in spatial–orientational maneuvering are also referred to in Chapter 7, where examples are described that suggest that it is through entering into a shared rhythm of movement that new participants become incorporated as full-fledged participants in ongoing interactional events. Its significance in the process of attentional and affective attunement is also discussed in the final chapter.

Chapter 5 is a reprint of a paper in which an attempt is made to analyze the organization of what is here called a "kissing round." It is an analysis of a film of a young couple sitting together on a bench in a large urban park. An important feature of this paper is its treatment of the behavior of the face from an interactional point of view, rather than regarding it solely from the point of view of how it displays emotions, the most usual way in which the face is considered (Fridland, Ekman and Oster 1987 is the latest comprehensive review of work from this viewpoint). As is clearly illustrated in the example analyzed in this chapter, the face has an important role to play in regulating the interaction. Thus in this paper it appears that the variable behavior observed in the face of the female is coordinated in a highly ordered manner with the approaches and withdrawals of her male partner. This coordination is such as to suggest that her face is here functioning as a regulator of his behavior. The implication is, thus, that the various smiles, frowns, "surprise" expressions and so on, that occur in this interaction are not significant only as symptoms of feeling but also as displays of interactive intent and, as such, serve as forewarnings, and hence as regulators of the other's behavior.

Another theme of Chapter 5 is the way in which an established interactional routine is changed. The kissing round treated in this paper, like the interactional axis treated in the one that precedes it, is a routine of interaction that takes place within the frame of a more inclusive system of relationship. The interactional axis is but one of many such episodes that occur within the frame of a more inclusive episode, the discussion session. Similarly, the "kissing round" is an episode within the episode of "sitting together," which in turn is an episode within the "afternoon walk" which the couple in question were engaged in. One problem that arises is that of how an ongoing routine of interaction is terminated while at the same time the more inclusive interactional frame which contains it is preserved. In the kissing round analyzed in Chapter 5 several phases could be distinguished in terms of who was taking the initiative in approaching the other. A question that is raised and discussed is how one phase of the interaction within the round is changed to another phase, without the more inclusive frame, that of the "kissing round" as a whole, being altered. Such "contained" routine changes must be accomplished jointly, and they involve devices whereby each participant is forewarned of the other's next mode of interaction before the present mode is actually changed.

This question of how participants inform one another of the context in terms of which their current actions should be interpreted, and the importance of this for the accomplishment of smooth interaction has received attention in the work of several others. The classic discussion is by Bateson (1955, 1956) where he raised the question as to how participants label or frame each other's behavior (as "play" or not, for instance) and advanced his concept of "metacommunication." Hall (1964) observed how, in a number of ways, people in interaction adumbrate or foreshadow their future course of action even as they carry out current action, and he showed that smooth interaction would not be possible without this. Gumperz has drawn attention to what he calls "contextualization cues" (Gumperz 1982). These are features of the form of any activity that conveys a message, that contribute to how participants interpret the nature of current activity for which the message is relevant, and to how the semantic content of the message itself is to be understood. Gumperz has discussed this mainly in relation to how the linguistic form of spoken utterances functions in this way, but the concept can clearly be extended to other aspects of behavior in interaction, as has been done by Erickson and Schultz (1982). McDermott, Gospodinoff and Aron (1978) also address the issue of how participants in interaction come to share a common context for the interpretation of one another's action. The issue is discussed further in the present collection in Chapter 8.

The first three studies reprinted are all concerned with the organization of sub-systems of behavioral relationships within a more inclusive system of behavioral relationship. Chapter 6, in which greeting interactions are examined, attempts to deal with a complete interactional event. This paper, written in collaboration with Andrew Ferber, was done while I was associated with Albert Scheflen at Bronx State Hospital (now Bronx Psychiatric Center) in New York. Scheflen, in his work on the organization of communication behavior in psychotherapy (Scheflen 1973), had dealt with a complete interactional event and in doing so had shown how it could be organized at several different levels, and that it had a programmatic structure. He was able to show how several features of behavior in the event could be seen as marking the steps and phases of the program. He suggested that such behavior functions in maintaining the alignment of the participants within the various phases of the program. To develop this work further would require the study of other complete interactional events and the greeting offered itself as a possible candidate because it is short, and thus easily collected and examined, routine and relatively simple in structure, and yet at the same time it involves all aspects of behavior in its organization. There are other reasons for studying greetings as well, of course, including the fact that they are important in the management of social relationships and also that they are widespread, and so offer an excellent unit of interaction with which to undertake comparative studies of human communicative behavior.

The paper reprinted here represents an examination of some seventy examples of greeting encounters, most of them recorded in a film made at an open-air birthday party. An account of their organization as an interactional event is given and a description is made of the various elements of behavior observed in them. It will be apparent from the analysis that though the greeting transactions examined vary one from another, they do so within the limits of a kind of program for a greeting event which serves as a framework structuring them. The several stages of the program are found to be marked by specific actions which may have the function of cueing the participants as to which stage of the program has been reached, so making possible coordinated progress to the next phase. Thus, in all greetings there is a phase in which the two individuals sight one another and give each other some indication that they will engage in a greeting encounter with one another. This may be followed by a coordinated change in their spatial–orientational relationship, explicit gestures of "distance salutation" may then be exchanged and this may then be followed by further steps, leading to "close salutation" (such as a handshake). If this occurs, prior to the close salutation a phase can be observed in which the participants negotiate the kind of close salutational enactment they will engage in together.

An important theoretical and methodological issue that became apparent as the work on the greeting examples proceeded was the question of the units in terms of which the analysis was to be conducted. For example, what was to count as a greeting event? At the outset, our grasp of the greeting event as a well-bounded interactional event was intuitive. In examining the birthday party film it was easy enough to locate all the instances where people shook hands, embraced, or in some other way exchanged salutations with one another. What was problematic was to decide when to begin the analysis and when to bring it to an end. Behavior is continuous. Could any means be found of defining an interactional event such as a greeting in terms of changes or boundaries in the behavior flow?

We began by trying to define the start of the greeting by looking for the earliest point at which "greeting behavior" could be identified. However, this immediately led to difficulties, for it was by no means clear what should count as "greeting behavior." Perhaps the first moment at which one of the participants begins to lift his arm in preparation for the handshake could be considered the beginning, but what about an exchange of glances that occurred prior to this? Sometimes such an exchange appears to be accompanied by some gesture of the head or face, at other times it does not. Is either to be counted as part of the "greeting" or only the first variety? If only the first, how are we to decide what is a "gesture" and what is not?

It became apparent that this approach, in which behavior is classified in terms of whether or not it could be said to belong to the category of "greeting," could only be carried on by arbitrary decision. As an alternative, we began to search for a means of segmenting the behavior in terms of contrasting patterns of organization and to see whether we could establish any criteria for separating that period of time during which the close salutation occurred from adjacent phases of the flow of behavior, simply in terms of the manifest features of the behavioral organization itself. It became obvious at an early stage that we would have to recognize that there is no "absolute" unit of behavioral organization. We found that in order to establish the boundaries of the segment of behavior we wished to analyze in detail, it was best to begin by searching for patterns of organization at the most inclusive levels first.

An answer to the problem of defining in structural terms the unit to be analyzed developed when we observed that in every case, shortly after a close salutation was completed, or sometimes during its enactment, the participants both stepped away from the spot on the ground where they were standing and changed their bodily orientation to one another. Scheflen's work on the hierarchical organization of posture and orientation in interaction (Scheflen 1964, 1973) had already alerted us to the idea that bodily orientation often provides a "frame" for activity, and it became apparent that when people were engaged in a close salutation they always established a spatial and orientational relationship within which the salutation was enacted. Further, this spatial orientational relationship was invariably altered upon the completion of the salutation. Thus one rather obvious inclusive level of organization in terms of which subsequent joint activity could be contrasted with the salutational exchange was that of the spatial or orientational relationships that were sustained. The change in this to a new one, thus, became the point at which the participants began the spatial orientational movement which culminated in the frame within which the salutation was enacted.

The work on the structure of greeting encounters reported in Chapter 6 pointed us toward a conceptualization of the structure of behavior in terms of levels of organization. It also suggested criteria by which an "interactional event" might be defined in terms of observable behavioral organization. "Interaction" can be regarded as occurring whenever there is observable interdependence between the behavior of two or more individuals. Such interdependence may occur, however, in respect to any level of behavioral organization. An "interactional event," thus, is any boundable instance of behavioral interdependence. The "handshake" when considered as such an event, for instance, must nevertheless be seen to occur within the framework of a more enduring event, specifiable in terms of whole-body spatial–orientational maneuverings and arrangements. For the purposes of our study of greetings we chose to consider units of interaction defined at the level of behavioral organization and all that occurred within them. For the purposes of other kinds of analysis, we might have chosen an interactional event at some less inclusive level of organization – as we have, in effect, in the studies of "interactional axes" and of the "kissing round." On the other hand, for some other purposes we might find it expedient to define a unit that is even more inclusive than the one we used for the greetings study.

The spatial–orientational "frame" which the two participants in a salutation create and within which they perform the salutation, can be seen as the means the participants have of "bracketing" such an enactment. After the salutation, the spatial–orientational "frame" is changed, as we have said. Commonly the two individuals will remain together for a while and engage in conversation. Here, then, a new activity, "talk," is "bracketed" by a new spatial–orientational frame. Such spatial–orientational relationships, which are sustained only by the cooperation of the participants, may be regarded as systems of behavioral inter-relations at the level of spatial–orientational arrangement and they are characteristic of many kinds of occasions when two or more individuals are engaged in utterance exchanges or other kinds of focused interaction. Such systems we have termed "F-formation" systems. Chapter 7 outlines some of the characteristics of such systems.

It will be noted that the F-formation system is an example of a unit of behavioral organization at the interactional level. In the greetings study, the outer limits of the complex of behavior that was studied were defined in terms of the spatial–orientational behavior of the two participants separately. The analysis was begun when the first of the two participants began his maneuver and it was only ended when the last participant changed to a new spatial–orientational phase. In the case of the F-formation system, however, what we are concerned with is the system of cooperative relations itself. As will be clear from Chapter 7, so long as these relationships are sustained, so long do we have the same unit of interactional behavior, notwithstanding the fact that the actual individuals who are participating in the system may change. It will be seen, thus, that we may arrive at a way of thinking of transindividual systems of behavior which nevertheless have a concrete existence. We may at once avoid postulating abstract concepts which are in danger of becoming reified, while at the same time we may see how "entities" such as encounters, social occasions, and so forth, can indeed be identified in terms of systems of behavioral relations.

As we have already mentioned, it is suggested that the F-formation system provides one way in which participants in interaction can inform one another that they are sharing a common attentional perspective. It is through entering into and sustaining an F-formation system that participants can give overt evidence that they have come to share a working consensus, at least at some level. The importance of this, and the fact that behavior in interaction should be looked at from the point of view of how it contributes to this "framing" of the event, was identified as a central issue in the study of interaction by Erving Goffman. As will be apparent, this issue is an important theme in several of the papers reprinted here (most notably in Chapters 4 and 5, as well as Chapter 7). It seemed appropriate, thus, to include as the final paper in this collection one which discusses it directly. This paper (Chapter 8), first published in 1985, provides a re-statement of the problem of "frame attunement" in interaction and offers a summary of several of the ways in which this is achieved. Particular emphasis is given to the question of the way in which participants differentially interpret each other's behavior in terms of levels of "intentionality" and "communicative relevance."

It directs us to the question of how participants in interaction attend to and process each other's flow of action and suggests how the social organization of this process is central to what makes "frame attunement" possible.

# 2

## Some context for Context Analysis: a view of the origins of structural studies of face-to-face interaction

As we stated in the introduction, an important influence governing the approach to the study of interaction taken in the papers reprinted in this volume, has derived from the work of Ray Birdwhistell and Albert Scheflen, as well as that of Erving Goffman. The approach we have taken is sometimes referred to as the *structural* approach (Duncan 1969). It has been given this name because it proposes to provide an account of how, in terms of behavior, occasions of interaction are organized. Each interactional event, it is assumed, is not created *de novo*, but is fashioned as the participants draw from repertoires of behavioral practices (units of language, gesture, orientation, posture and spacing, and the like) that are widely shared and follow certain organizing principles that are commonly adhered to, within any given communication community. It maintains that communication in interaction is a continuous, multichannel process and it seeks to provide descriptions of the structural characteristics of the communication systems employed in interaction.

The methodology associated with the particular development of the structural study of interaction that has been most influential for the work reprinted here has been termed "Context Analysis" (Scheflen 1963). It has been called this because of the emphasis it places on the importance of examining the behavior of people in interaction in the contexts in which they occur. It is maintained that a given act, be it a glance at the other person, a shift in posture or a remark about the weather, has no intrinsic meaning. Such acts can only be understood when taken in relation to one another. It makes little sense to count them up and sort them out in an effort to understand the significance of other-directed gaze, postural restlessness or weather conversation unless one has a clear understanding of the place such acts have in the overall structure of the interactional events in which they occur. Further, it will be seen that this approach stresses the importance of an integrated approach to the study of interaction. It refuses to assume that any particular modality of communication is more salient than another. Its aim is to show how all aspects of the actions of the participants are interrelated.

In this chapter I shall discuss some of the considerations that gave rise to this approach. I shall show that it derives from a combination of ideas from interpersonal psychiatry, anthropology, information theory, cybernetics, and structural linguistics, which came about as a result of a specific collaboration. After a brief history of this, I will describe the contribution of each of these different disciplines, and I shall also discuss the influence of certain other work, such as that of Pike and Goffman. In concluding the chapter I will take note of work that bears on a structural understanding of interaction, but which emerged somewhat separately. I refer here, in particular, to certain work in anthropological linguistics and to Conversation Analysis.

## The collaboration at Palo Alto

We can establish a beginning point for the particular amalgam of interpersonal psychiatry, anthropology, cybernetics and structural (i.e. descriptive, pre-generative) linguistics that gave rise to Context Analysis, at the Center for Advanced Study in the Behavioral Sciences, in Palo Alto, California, in 1955. In the fall of that year, several psychiatrists, anthropologists and linguists began regular discussions that led to a joint analysis of an actual strip of interaction that had been recorded on film. This collaboration, which has been described in detail by Leeds-Hurwitz (1987), included the psychiatrists Frieda Fromm-Reichmann and Henry Brosin, the anthropologists Gregory Bateson and Ray Bird-whistell, and the anthropological linguists, Charles Hockett and Norman McQuown. However, precursors of this amalgamation of thinking from different disciplines around the problem of interaction can be found in the joint work of Bateson and Mead (Bateson and Mead 1942), of Bateson and Ruesch (Ruesch and Bateson 1951), and in the work of the Josiah Macy Jr. Foundation conferences on cybernetics (von Foerster, et al. 1949–53). Albert Scheflen, who came to this approach through his collaboration with Birdwhistell which began in 1959 (Scheflen 1973, p. 9) has provided the most explicit methodologi-cal statements (e.g. Scheflen 1966) and his work on the organization of interaction in a psychotherapy session (Scheflen 1973) remains the most fully developed example of the application of this approach. Discussions of the approach may also be found in McQuown (1971a), McDermott and Roth (1978), Kendon (1979, 1982), Thomas (1980), Heilman (1979), and Sigman (1987).

The collaborative work in which we find the beginnings of Context Analysis started in 1955 when Frieda Fromm-Reichmann, an interpersonal psychiatrist, persuaded Norman McQuown, an anthropological linguist, to undertake a micro-linguistic transcription of a recording of a psychiatric interview. Fromm-Reichmann's hope was that such an analysis might provide the basis for an explicit account of the cues she relied upon for the intuitive clinical judgments she made. She hoped that such explicit descriptions would be useful from the point of view of training other clinicians (Bateson 1958). Fromm-Reichmann and McQuown were both Fellows at the Institute for the Advanced Study of the Behavioral Sciences at Palo Alto, California. This made it easy for their initial discussions to draw in others. These included the psychiatrist Henry Brosin, the linguist Charles Hockett and the anthropologist Alfred Kroeber, among others. As discussion proceeded it was realized that visual as well as vocal cues would have to be studied. McQuown knew of Birdwhistell's work in kinesics (Birdwhistell 1952) and was able to arrange for Birdwhistell to attend one of their seminars, since he was visiting Gregory Bateson as a consultant. Bateson, an anthropologist trained in the British tradition (Lipset 1980), was at that time involved in the study of family interaction in collaboration with several psychiatrists at the Veterans Administration Hospital in Palo Alto. The work he was then doing led to the formulation of his well-known "double bind" hypothesis on the origin of schizophrenia (Bateson, Jackson, Haley and Weakland 1956). Bateson was active in making films of families in interaction, both in their own homes and in therapy sessions. When Birdwhistell visited the seminar at the Center, Bateson also attended, and he agreed to supply a film that the group could study. The film that was made (the so-called "Doris" film – see Bateson 1956 in Film References) was not a film of psychotherapy, but a film in which Bateson was conversing with a woman known as Doris, a woman who, with her family, was participating in the program of psychotherapy with which Bateson was involved. As Bateson (1958) has noted, the fact that this film was used rather than a psychotherapy film, was influential in broadening the work of the Palo Alto group toward more general issues in the analysis of interaction.

The aim of the group, as it came to be formulated, was to analyze the "Doris" film with a view to establishing how all the different aspects of behavior that could be observed were organized and how they articulated with one another. It was through the work that was jointly done on this project that several of the ideas central to the Context Analysis point of view came to be formulated. The work that this group did was never published, although the manuscript is available from the Regenstein Library in Chicago (McQuown 1971). Several of the individual participants went on to publish work which showed the influence of this collaboration and drew on some of its findings. These include Birdwhistell (1970), Hockett (1960), Pittinger, Hockett and Danehy (1960).

It should be stressed that the collaboration which took place at Palo Alto was possible because a pattern of collaboration between the disciplines of psychiatry, anthropology and anthropological linguistics had already been established. Bateson's collaborative work with Ruesch, which has already been noted, could be regarded as a continuation of a tradition that had already begun with Edward Sapir (e.g. Sapir 1951 [1927]) and continued by Ruth Benedict, Margaret Mead, Abram Kardiner, among others, in the development of "culture and personality" studies in anthropology (Harris 1968). What was special about the Palo Alto collaboration was that it brought psychiatry, anthropology, information theory and cybernetics, and structural linguistics into relationship with one another in a particularly focused way around the analysis of a specific piece of actual interaction.

## Interpersonal psychiatry

The Palo Alto collaboration was initiated by Frieda Fromm-Reichmann, as we have seen. She had been trained as a psychoanalyst in Germany, but became interested in therapy with schizophrenics. When she moved to the United States she came into contact with Harry Stack Sullivan who, at that time, was a leading exponent of the approach known as Interpersonal Psychiatry. Her own ideas and those of Sullivan had much in common and they collaborated closely (Gunst 1982).

Interpersonal psychiatry, which began to be established from 1920 onward, views psychiatric disorder not as a condition of the individual, as does organically oriented psychiatry or classical psychoanalysis, but in terms of patterning in interpersonal relationships. Therapy is seen as a process of *interaction* between patient and therapist and success in therapy is formulated in terms of bringing about changes in the way in which disturbed individuals manage their interactions with others. Accordingly, psychiatrists of the interpersonal persuasion came to focus their interest upon the patient–therapist *relationship* and the interaction process that created this. The process of therapy itself was seen as interactive. The idea that the therapist could be a kind of passive mirror, as in the classical psychoanalytic tradition, reflecting back to the patient his own unconscious processes, was thought highly misleading.

The most influential figure in this development in psychiatry is probably Harry Stack Sullivan. However, there is no doubt that it developed with especial vigor because of the development of the interactionist tradition in the social sciences in the United States in which the starting point for understanding human beings was to be the observation of actions and their consequences, rather than an analysis of processes deemed to be internal to the individual. The unique personality of each individual was seen not as the source of action but as an *outcome* of the way in which people engage in interaction with one another. Within this movement of thought it is not "selves" that interact, it is interaction that produces selves (Held-Weiss 1984). Sullivan himself took much interest in social science (Sullivan 1964, Mullahy 1952) and he was especially influenced by the work of George Herbert Mead. In 1926 he met Edward Sapir, the anthropological linguist who was a colleague of Mead's at Chicago, and they became firm friends (Perry 1982, Chs. 28–29, Darnell 1990, Ch. 15). Edward Sapir undoubtedly had much influence on Sullivan's thinking, and Sullivan also influenced Sapir. Sapir, as we shall see below, is an important figure in the history of the development we are tracing. He not only played an important role in developing the methodology of structural linguistics. He was also important because of his interest in the relationship between language and culture and because of his suggestion that it would be fruitful to extend the techniques of linguistic analysis beyond the boundaries of speech.

The kind of detailed, explicit understanding of the process of the psychiatric interview that was being sought by Fromm-Reichmann and others required the development of a theoretical framework in terms of which the interaction process could be richly conceptualized. It also required the development of methods of observation which, though rigorous and repeatable, would nevertheless permit one to be open to all of the details and nuances of action and not determine, in advance, what would be recorded. These requirements were met as a result of three developments.

These were, the application of information theory and cybernetics in the conceptualization of the interaction process; the use of the natural history approach combined with the use of cinematography; and the use of methods and concepts from structural linguistics in the recording and representation of data.

Information theory and cybernetics, when adapted as a framework for the understanding of interaction, led to a comprehensive conception of how behavior could function as communication and it led to wholly new modes of observation and inquiry.

The natural history approach proposed detailed description of whatever could be observed in an interaction. Since what was sought for was an understanding of the natural orderliness of interaction, observation must be in terms of what is there to be observed, not in terms of pre-established category systems. To decide what will be measured and counted before this is done will prevent the very understanding that is sought. It was the adoption of this approach that led to the need for the use of specimens of interaction, acquired by the (then available) technique of sound-synchronized cinematographic recording.

The application of transcription techniques derived from descriptive linguistics not only provided a detailed systematic method of transcribing speech, but this also directly inspired methods of dealing with such aspects of behavior in interaction as body motion, spacing and posture. It led to an orientation toward the search for structural units within these communicative modalities and to a recognition that these units participated in, and were themselves to be defined in terms of, multiple levels of organization. It also reinforced an approach in which the interactional event became the observational unit and the analysis focused upon the parts of which such events were composed and on how these parts were organized in relation to one another within the whole.

The role each of these developments played in the emergence of Context Analysis will be discussed in greater detail below. First, however, the development of the study of social interaction in sociology and related disciplines in the United States will be sketched. This development has been extensive, and it led to a great deal of quantitative and experimental work on interaction that was dominant for many decades. Although this had little direct influence on the development of Context

Analysis, it is important to refer to it here for it is this tradition which, to some extent, workers who later became important in the development of Context Analysis, such as Scheflen and Goffman, sought to differentiate themselves from. These workers felt that most of this work in social interaction not only failed to address fundamental questions about the process of interaction itself but, also, that it relied upon techniques of observation that could not do justice to its complexities.

## The interactionist tradition

The interactionist tradition in American social science began with the introduction to America of the work of Georg Simmel, the German social philosopher who sought to define the subject matter of sociology as the study of the forms of interaction; and with the work of the Americans C. H. Cooley, and G. H. Mead, who were more psychological in their orientation and were especially interested in the problem of the origin of the self. Simmel, whose work began to be influential in the United States from 1905 onwards (Levine 1971), explicitly identified interaction as the distinct subject matter of sociology. He emphasized that it is only through the way in which individuals interact with one another that society is possible. Simmel wrote that "Society is merely the name for a number of individuals connected by interaction" (Simmel 1950, p. 10) and he argued that "if society is conceived as interaction among individuals, the description of the forms of interaction is the science of society in its strictest and most essential sense" (1950, 21–22). C. H. Cooley argued in his *Social Organization* (1909, p. 30) that "human nature comes into existence. Man does not have it at birth; he cannot acquire it except through fellowship, and it decays in isolation." In developing his well-known concept of the "looking glass self," furthermore, Cooley (1902) had argued that individuals developed a sense of "self" in the process of interaction with others, the imagined reactions of others to proposed actions becoming the source of the sentiments of the self. Cooley (1909) also introduced the concept of the "primary group," which he defined as those people with whom the individual had repeated face-to-face contact, such as his immediate family or the others with whom he worked. For Cooley the primary group was the level of social organization that must be looked at if the processes of socialization were to be understood, for it was through interaction at the level of the primary group that people acquired their values and their sense of self and individuality. George Herbert Mead, under the influence of his work with William James and John Dewey, developed similar views, arguing that it is interaction that produces selves. As he put it, "selves must be accounted for in terms of the social process, and in terms of communication" (Mead 1934, p. 49). Social interaction, thus, was established rather early in the history of social science in America as of central importance.

The theoretical importance given to the process of interaction in American sociology led to the extensive development of empirical studies that focused on interaction. The concept of the "primary group" led, first of all, to field studies of various kinds of face-to-face groups, such as street corner gangs (Whyte 1943) and groups of workers in industry (Roethlisberger and Dickson 1939). The processes characteristic of small or primary groups were also taken up by psychologists. For example the Gestalt psychologist, Kurt Lewin, first at MIT and later at Michigan, inspired studies of "group dynamics." An important early study, carried out in collaboration with Lippitt and White (Lewin, Lippitt and White 1939), showed that very different kinds of behavior could be expected of members of a group who were led by an "authoritarian" leader as compared to one led by someone with a "democratic" style. This work, carried out with after-school activity clubs for eleven-year-old boys, showed that it was possible to experiment with groups. Studies of groups in laboratory settings soon followed. Such work led to a need for increasingly detailed observation of interaction. A number of category systems were developed in terms of which the "acts" of the participants could be classified according to a predetermined set of categories (see Heyns and Lippitt 1954 for a review). This method provided quantitative protocols that could be subjected to statistical analysis. One of the most widely used was the system developed by Bales (1950) known as Interaction Process Analysis. This system was extensively used in studies of phenomena such as the solving of problems by groups, the development of roles, the nature of leadership and followership, and the like. These studies were almost always conducted with groups of strangers, typically college students, brought into an observation room for the purposes of the study, although studies of interaction in similar circumstances between people who already had an established social relationship, such as married couples or parents and their children, were also undertaken (e.g. Strodtbeck 1951, 1954). The number of studies of this sort is very large. Hare, Borgatta and Bales (1955) and Hare (1962) provide comprehensive surveys.

Another early attempt to deal systematically with the details of behavior in face-to-face interaction was developed by Eliot Chapple. Chapple, a social anthropologist who had worked with Lloyd Warner on the "Yankee City" series of studies, was impressed with the "functionalist" approach to the analysis of social structure, but he was also impressed with the criticism that the "functional relationships" that were claimed to obtain within a society or group such as "solidarity," "superordination" or "subordination," and the like, were described only in literary, impressionistic terms and were not based on quantitative, verifiable observations (Chapple 1940a, pp. 5–6). He proposed the view that social relationships of any sort are built out of, and sustained by interactions between individuals and he suggested that they could be analyzed in terms of the amount of time individuals spent in interaction with one another, how periods of interaction were distributed in time, and in terms of how, within any period of interaction, the acts of which the interaction was made up were distributed in time and distributed between the participants. He devised methods for measuring these various aspects of interaction and proposed that "human relations" could, thus, be "measured," and that a quantitative science of society would thus become possible (Chapple 1940a, Chapple and Coon 1942).

In developing this work, Chapple devised an "interaction chronograph" by which units of behavior he termed *actions* could be recorded by an observer and their temporal parameters assessed. An "action," for Chapple, in talking situations, comprises the duration of time an individual spends in active speech or gesture (or both). The frequency and duration of actions, and also of the periods between actions, or interactions, may be measured within occasions of interaction, and various quantitative indices of the individual's interactive performance may be extracted. These have been found to be predictive of how the individual may behave across a variety of interactive situations (Chapple and Lindemann 1942, Chapple and Donald 1947, Matarazzo, Saslow and Matarazzo 1956, Kendon 1963) and Chapple developed "interaction chronography" into a technique for assessing individual differences in interactional behavior. This had a number of applications in psychiatry and management consulting. Reviews of

Chapple's approach and the wider outlook of which it is a part may be found in Arensberg (1972) and Collins and Collins (1973).

Notwithstanding these developments in the detailed observation of interaction, as noted above, they had little influence on the line of development we are tracing here. So far as the work in "small-group" sociology and social psychology is concerned, this appears to be because, in the first place, those who developed the structural approach to the study of interaction were anthropologists, linguists or clinical psychiatrists by training, who did not have contact with "small-group" sociology and psychology. However, to the extent that they did know about or have contact with these traditions, this had little impact because the style of research was quite different from the style of research in either anthropology or linguistics. It was not attractive to clinical psychiatrists, either. The highly experimental and artificial character of much of the work was not consonant with the ethnographic orientation of anthropology and anthropological linguistics, and the observation techniques employed, using pre-established category systems, were also counter to the more open, probing, flexible and reflective style of observation characteristic of those with a clinical or anthropological orientation. Structural linguists, furthermore, sought ways in which the data of spoken language could be fully described. An approach that defined what was to be observed in advance would not be congenial. Furthermore, the level of observation was, of course, quite different.

Chapple's work, although explicitly interactionist and developed within the discipline of anthropology, also did not have very much influence and his work remained isolated for many years (Arensberg 1982). His view that social relationships must be seen as sustained through patterns of interaction between people was congenial to the structural view of interaction and the ethnographic character of his early work would have been compatible. However, his insistence on a single dimension in terms of which "action" and "inaction" was to be measured, without paying attention to the different kinds of actions that people produce and the various levels at which action in interaction is organized, and his simplistic formulation of the interaction process as a matter of patterned alternation between the actions of participants (e.g. Chapple 1940a, p. 24) seemed to leave out too much of what appeared important in interaction.

Context Analysis, then, developed as a mode of approach to the phenomena of social interaction that was distinct from the approach

developed more widely in social science. As we have indicated, this is
because of the application of ideas from information theory and cybernetics, the use of a "natural history" style of observation which derived
from anthropology, and the use of ideas from structural linguistics. The
importance of each of these will now be discussed in more detail.

### Information theory and cybernetics

Information theory was developed to provide a way of measuring the
amount of information that may be transmitted through a channel.
Information, according to this theory, is conceived as a measure of the
relationship between a given signal and the possible number of different
signals that could have been sent. Thus it will be very much easier to predict which state a signalling device will be in at any given time if it can
be in only one of two states than if it can be in, say, one of ten different
states. The easier it is to predict the state of the device, the less information a given signal, upon receipt, is said to convey. Information, then,
is measured as the reciprocal of predictability.

Here, what I would like to point out is that the concept of information developed in this theory is entirely general: it can be applied to
*anything whatever*. Once you have made a selection from among the
flux of phenomena as to what, for you, is to count as message, then you
can, in principle, at least, apply this theory. Theoretically, any instance
where you have something that has a repertoire of different states, if you
have a receiver trying to predict what state it might be in, could be
analyzed in this way. This contributed to the idea that *all* detectable
aspects of behavior can be approached through information theory.
That is to say, any aspect of behavior that can be received by another
can be regarded as potentially informative in this sense. All aspects of
behavior can therefore be of interest from a communicational viewpoint. As Warren Weaver put it in the popular exposition of information theory that he published in collaboration with Claude Shannon
in 1949:

> The word *communication* will be used here in a very broad sense to include all
> of the procedures by which one mind may affect another. This, of course,
> involves not only written and oral speech, but also music, the pictorial arts, the
> theatre, the ballet, and in fact all human behavior. (Shannon and Weaver 1949,
> p. 95)

At the time this was a significant broadening of the sense of what could be regarded as "communication." It helped to open a great many people's eyes to the idea that communication between people involves far more than just what they say to one another.

Information theorists like Claude Shannon were interested in designing communication systems, such as telephone systems which could transmit the maximum of information with the minimum of loss. It was recognized that when signals were transmitted over a channel, events in the channel itself could interfere with what was received at the other end. If these events were random, they would be referred to as "noise." Since, in all real transmission channels there are always random events of some kind that produce alterations in the signals that are initiated, it became necessary, in developing ways of measuring the information capacity of a channel, to build in a measure of the ratio of signal to noise and, further, to devise ways of reducing this.

From the point of view of understanding how this idea also was important in shaping the outlook of Context Analysis, it is important to see that "noise" and "signal" are purely relative terms. "Noise," in fact, is simply *unwanted* signal. To use an example suggested by Charles Hockett, from the point of view of someone watching television, the "snow" or other patterns that sometimes occur that break up the picture is "noise." For the repairman, however, the interfering events on the TV screen constitute signals, for it is these that tell him what he must do to get rid of them. Or again, in a crowded room, Mr. Jones's speech is noise if you are trying to hear what Mr. Smith is trying to say, but if you switch your attention to Mr. Jones, then Smith's talk is noise. What is "signal" and what is "noise," thus, depends upon the frame of reference that is used at the time. Since, however, people regularly operate with multiple frames of reference, they are oriented to a multiplicity of signals. As Hockett says: "Perhaps somewhere in the web of human communicative behavior there is a residuum of 'pure' noise – activity of no communicative relevance at all – but one putative example after another seems to vanish upon sufficiently close scrutiny. The fruitful working assumption is that any act of one human being which can be detected by the sense of any other – or by those of the actor himself – is communicative" (Hockett 1977, p. 115).

Insights from information theory also led to the realization that messages function communicatively in more than one way simultaneously. Furthermore, the function of messages can only be understood in terms of their contextual relations. Shannon and Weaver had shown that every message that is transmitted can be looked upon as serving both as a report, in virtue of it being a consequence of an event at some previous moment in time, and as a command or stimulus for what is to follow. Bateson (in Ruesch and Bateson 1951) developed this further and showed that, in any communication system, including, of course, human interaction, there must be provision for a type of communication which permits the participants to calibrate the way in which they interpret each other's messages. Bateson showed that, at the same time as $p$ sends a message, he must also send information about what constitutes the boundaries of the message he is sending and what sort of message it is. Such instructional communication, which he called *metacommunication* (Bateson 1955) is found both in the nature of a given message and in how it is embedded within a context of other messages. Messages, thus, have "meanings" at multiple levels simultaneously. It eventually came to be seen that what message is regarded as "meta" to another is a purely relative matter. What is "message" and qualifying "metamessage" cannot be identified in any absolute sense. As one of Bateson's collaborators, Jay Haley, expressed it some years later: "There was no 'message' but only metamessages qualifying one another" (Haley 1976, p. 65, as quoted by Rawlins 1987). This means that, in the study of interaction, we must see that the behavior observed functions communicatively at more than one level simultaneously, and that because of the necessarily embedded character of anything that is focused upon, to understand how it is functioning in the interaction we must look at this embedding as well.

The importance of information theory for the development of Context Analysis, it will be seen, thus, lay not in the application of the mathematical formulae derived to measure rate of information transmission, channel capacity, signal-to-noise ratio and its relationship to redundancy, and so on, but in the fact that it allowed theorists to see that all aspects of behavior in a situation of co-presence must be considered at least, potentially, to have a role in the communication process. As Birdwhistell puts it in one of his essays, the greatest utility of information theory "has come from the fact that it serves to desentimentalize the message process. With such an outline of our universe of investigation [i.e. of the phenomena of communication], we are freed to tackle problems which had not been seen before" (Birdwhistell 1970, p. 69).

At the same time as information theory was being developed, ideas were also emerging concerning the way in which the flow of information within systems controlled their operation. This eventually came to be formulated as a general theory of self-regulating systems, named *cybernetics* and largely pioneered by Norbert Wiener (1948). This also had an important impact on the development of Context Analysis. Cybernetics developed initially out of a need to find a way to design an anti-aircraft gun that could automatically track its moving target. The central idea here is that the system controlling the output of the device was directed by information about the consequences of this output. This information is *fed back* to the controlling mechanism.

As with information theory, it was the generality of this idea that gave it its importance. As Wiener and others saw, their analysis made possible a new understanding of such self-regulating entities as organisms (Rosenblueth, Wiener and Bigelow 1943). They could be understood as negative feedback devices or cybernetic systems. It was quickly seen that the same thinking could be applied to the phenomena of interpersonal relations and the interaction that mediates them. As with information theory, the ideas of cybernetics were developed at such a high level of generality that they could readily be applied far beyond the context of their original development.

The application of these ideas to the study of human interaction – especially as it was undertaken by Jurgen Ruesch and Gregory Bateson (1951, Ruesch 1972) and further developed through the Josiah Macy Jr. conferences on cybernetics and group processes (von Foerster, Mead and Teuber 1949–53, Schaffner 1956; see also Heims 1975, 1977) – led to a re-orientation in how interaction was to be studied. With a perspective on interaction informed by ideas from cybernetic theory, participants are not looked upon as "respondents" but are recognized as actors with aims. A comparison might be made with a study one might make of driving skills. Drivers are assumed to have a number of aims – to get from A to B, to keep on the road while doing so, and, at middle levels between these goals, to deal with the various segments of the journey in a fashion that will serve their overall goal. In studying driving from this point of view we become interested in the relationship between the information the driver takes in and how his actions are guided by this – and, furthermore, it is recognized that the actions the driver takes may themselves control the kinds of information he receives. Likewise, in interaction, the participants may be looked upon as steering a course in relation to one another.

This has a number of consequences for how interaction is studied of which the two following are among the most important:

*First*, as soon as *p* and *q*'s actions are not seen as linked in sequential chains, but are regarded as produced under each other's guidance, one's investigatory interest shifts to include the study of what *p* and *q* are both doing at the same time. One comes to recognize that what a person may be saying, for example, *while he is saying it*, may be shaped by information he is taking in from his recipient; and by the same token, how the recipient is behaving, where he is placing his headnods, his smiles and frowns, and how he is patterning his visual attention, may also be shaped by, even as it is shaping, the activity of the speaker. One is encouraged, thus, to look at the ongoing behavioral relationship *between p* and *q*, rather than first looking at what *p* does and then looking at what *q* does.

*Second*, adopting this perspective makes one realize that maintaining a steady state in an interaction is as much a matter for investigation as are phenomena of change. Hence one becomes interested in the *regulatory* aspects of communication in interaction. For instance, in the study of psychotherapy, viewing patient–therapist interaction from a systemic perspective directed attention to an analysis of the *constant* features of the therapist and patient's behavior. It drew attention to the importance of considering how it was that patient and therapist followed the same program of activity at each session and how they regulated each other so that they would do this.

## The natural history approach and the role of cinematography

Given the approach to the study of interaction that ideas from information theory and cybernetics inspire, it will be seen that a descriptive approach, in which naturally occurring instances of interaction are examined for what they can reveal about the organization of the process, is the most appropriate method. If we take the point of view that all aspects of observable behavior can play a role in communication, if we regard the simultaneous interrelationships of the behavior of participants as significant, if we regard stability in an interaction situation to be in as much need of explanation as change and if we recognize that how participants interpret each other's flow of action depends upon how the various aspects of action are patterned in relation to one another, it is natural that we should require as full a *description* as possible of the behavior that can be observed in an interaction. This, it will be clear, can only be achieved if we have *specimens* of interaction available to us for study. Such specimens can only be obtained through the use of audio-visual recording technology.

It was precisely the kinds of theoretical considerations just outlined that led those who were developing Context Analysis to turn to sound-film recordings of interaction as a source of data. It was not that the availability of sound-film recording technology brought about the development of Context Analysis. Such technology had already been around for several decades. It was the emergence of a particular theoretical orientation toward the study of interaction that motivated the choice of such technology (Kendon 1979).

The natural history approach that was adopted by the Palo Alto group was by no means new in the study of social behavior. There had already been many ethnographic studies of interaction by sociologists, the linguists involved were of an anthropological and descriptive orientation for whom gathering field data for later analysis was a cardinal component of their methodology. Birdwhistell had been trained as a cultural anthropologist for whom observation in the field was also natural.

The same was true of Bateson; however, there are some additional considerations that must be mentioned in his case. His father, William Bateson, was a leading biologist and Bateson had grown up thoroughly imbued with the attitudes of the natural historian. He well appreciated the value of specimens and in turning to the use of film in his anthropological work, as he did systematically in his work with Margaret Mead in Bali (Bateson and Mead 1942), he was turning to a method that offered the only way in which the specific behavioral events from which his anthropological descriptions were derived could be captured and set before the observer, much as a naturalist might capture and set out for inspection the specimens upon which taxonomic descriptions are based. Both Bateson and Mead believed that the cultural patterning of behavior which they were interested in could not be convincingly described in words. They felt that by using photographs and films, on the other hand, they could compare the pattern and form of behavior directly.

As Harris (1968), among many others, has pointed out, photographs and films do not provide quite the objective record that Bateson and Mead appeared to have believed. Not only must the material photographed be interpreted, the very act of taking a photograph or taking a shot of cinefilm is an interpretative act, because, necessarily, it is selective. Because, in recording behavior on film, the investigator must decide what to include and when to start and stop filming; whether he acknowledges it or not, his theoretical biases enter unavoidably into the creation of the behavior specimen.

Furthermore, because the photographic image is two-dimensional and because the camera's angle of view is restricted and inflexible, the temptation in recording behavior on film is to employ film-making techniques, including the use of camera movement, change of camera angle and, in editing, the subsequent juxtaposition of originally separate slots into new sequences. These techniques serve as means by which the film maker can strive to overcome the limited view that the camera provides and one can give the viewer a sense of continuity of action and a sense of a coherent world that one feels one inhabits or witnesses, almost as if one is present.

Such techniques, of course, make the cinematographic record into a frankly interpretative document. Nevertheless, there is some justice to the claim that the camera can be used to create specimens of interaction that do make possible the discovery of facts about behavioral organization which cannot be done by other means. If the inherent limitations of the cinematographic record are fully acknowledged and if one makes one's choice of camera position and angle as explicitly linked as possible to the kind of specimen one is trying to capture, one is able to get *true* specimens. As Sandall (1978) has pointed out, any photographic or cinematographic shot always contains far more information than can possibly be foreseen – at least if it is a shot of the uncontrived world of daily life – and it provides, thus, a genuine "field" for exploration within which real discoveries can be made about what happened out in the world when the shutter was open. Even the most interpretatively constructed piece of cinema (e.g. Vertov's *Man with a Movie Camera*) can also be employed as a source of data about how the world was when the film was made – in the case of Vertov's film, for instance, what the streetcars of Moscow were like, what clothes people wore, how they walked, and many other things.

Accordingly, a sophisticated understanding of the nature of the cinematographic shot allows it to be used as a means of getting genuinely objective behavior records. In filming for the sake of getting a record that will allow one to do a detailed analysis of the organization of behavior in interaction, for instance, one must aim to keep the angle of view consistent with capturing material relevant to the kinds of behavior one wishes to study. If one is looking at interaction, then the whole bodies of all the participants in the interaction must be kept in frame at all times, as far as possible. Furthermore, one should avoid allowing one's preconceptions about what constitutes an interactional event to guide when the camera is turned on and when it is turned off. In filming greetings, for example (as in Chapter 6), we found it a good rule to start the camera well in advance of when a greeting was likely to occur (this was possible, in this case, because we could see people approaching the site of the social occasion before they entered it) and to keep the camera rolling until well after what seemed to us, naively, to be "the greeting" was well over. The issue of how an interactional event begins, how people alter their behavior as they come into one another's presence was *not* something we could know without analyzing filmed records, but these records could not, of course, be obtained, if one's presuppositions were allowed, unthinkingly, to govern what was being filmed.

This understanding of the limits and subjective character of cinematography and the way in which, by working within these limits, one can nevertheless overcome them and acquire useful specimens for analysis, was not something that was arrived at all at once. Bateson's experience with using photography in Bali notwithstanding, it is obvious when one looks today at the films he made for the purposes of studying interaction in families that a high degree of intuitive variable selectivity in shooting was permitted. In the "Doris" film that was used in the Palo Alto collaboration, for instance, a great proportion of the film is shot in medium close-up, the camera focusing exclusively on "Doris" so that very little analysis of her interaction with Bateson is in fact possible. The principles of behavior specimen filming were developed slowly over the subsequent decade (see Van Vlack 1966 and the discussions of filming technique in Scheflen 1973). It came about as the subjective possibilities of the cinematographic medium came to be more fully realized. Only by an explicit recognition of the subjective and selective nature of photographic image can its thoroughly objective, specimen-capturing possibilities be realized.

## Structural linguistics

Further progress could not be made in the analysis of recordings of inter-action, however, in the absence of a method of description. Detailed study of specimens of interaction require some means of conceptualiz-ing and describing the patterning of activity that can be observed in them. The orientation that was adopted in the development of tran-scription methods used in Context Analysis was explicitly that of struc-tural linguistics. The communicational analysis of interaction that was to be undertaken proposed that the participants were to be regarded as making use of shared communication codes. An understanding of the organization of the interaction could only be arrived at if these codes were known. Spoken language had received explicit analysis as a com-munication code by linguists. A detailed understanding of its structural elements and the way these were organized at various levels had been developed and methods of transcription had been devised in conjunc-tion with this. What was undertaken in the development of Context Analysis was the extension of these methods of analysis to other aspects of behavior in interaction.

The idea that such an extension could be undertaken was first put forward explicitly by Edward Sapir (e.g. Sapir 1927, in Mandelbaum 1951), as already mentioned. Sapir was an important pioneer in the development of the study of Native North American languages and he always maintained that language should be regarded as but one among many culturally patterned communication systems. For example, in a widely read article, "The unconscious patterning of behavior in society," which was published in 1927 in a symposium on *The Uncon-scious*, Sapir set out to show that behavior could be approached from two points of view: the individual or psycho-physiological and the social. He points out, for instance, that the activity of breathing is typi-cally thought of as a strictly individual activity, governed by the physi-ological requirements of the individual's need to gain oxygen and expel carbon dioxide. However, there are styles of breathing that may be taught and which are held to be appropriate in particular circumstances. As he puts it:

the regularized breathing of the Hindu Yogi, the subdued breathing of those who are in the presence of a recently deceased companion laid away in a coffin and surrounded by all of the ritual and funeral observances, the style of breath-ing which one learns from an operatic singer who gives lessons on the proper control of the voice are, every one of them, capable of isolation as socialized modes of conduct that have a definite place in the history of human culture. (1927, p. 546)

He goes on to show that the cultural patterning of all aspects of behavior is recognized by members of the society, insofar as they are able to notice when things are not done right, but that, most of the time, people are not conscious of the rules they are following in their conduct. His main illustrations come from language – showing, for instance, that speakers of English have no explicit knowledge of the rules for forming plurals, though they follow a consistent pattern in doing so, which is different from the way plurals are formed in other languages. He says that the study of language illustrates unconscious patterning of behavior most clearly, but there are others that do so too. He draws attention in particular to gesture. He says:

Gestures are hard to classify and it is difficult to make a conscious separation between that in gesture which is of merely individual origin and that which is referable to the habits of the group as a whole. In spite of these difficulties of conscious analysis, we respond to gestures with an extreme alertness and, one might almost say, in accordance with an elaborate and secret code that is written nowhere, known by none, and understood by all. [Further on in the same passage he adds:] Like everything else in human conduct, gesture roots in the reactive necessities of the organism, but the laws of gesture, the unwritten code of gestured messages and responses, is the anonymous work of an elaborate social tradition. (ibid., p. 556)

The implications are thus clear that all aspects of our behavior can be approached as if they are patterned as languages are patterned. The possibility that we might, by using techniques similar to those used for the analysis of the structure of language, make explicit the nature of these patterns is thus raised. Sapir did not himself undertake any work in which non-linguistic behavior was analyzed using structural methods. Several of his students and younger colleagues did so, however, in turn influencing several others. Thus G. L. Trager (1958) extended linguistic methods to the analysis of voice qualities and other aspects of speech that are, in his term (which has since become current), *paralinguistic*; Edward Hall (1959, 1968), an anthropologist who collaborated with Trager, extended the linguistic approach to the analysis of the role of space in interaction under the rubric of *proxemics*; Ray Birdwhistell (1952), who, again under Trager's influence, undertook to analyze body motion behavior from this point of view, suggesting the notion of *kinesics*; and Kenneth Pike (1954–69, 1967), who extended the methods of linguistic analysis to the study of the organization of whole occasions of interaction.

The application of these extensions of structural linguistic methods to the description of all aspects of behavior in interaction has several consequences. Two are singled out here. First, as already pointed out, there is a working assumption that, just as the spoken utterances of the participants employ the *customary* units of a particular language, so the other aspects of their behavior have a customary structure to them. This will apply to everything, from the way they manage their bodies as they sit down, how they change posture, and how they move their heads, to the details of their hand movements and how they manage artifacts like cigarettes or cups of coffee. That is, the participants engage in actions which are drawn from repertoires of recurrent forms of behavior and these are patterned according to customary, quasi-grammatical rules. An important aim of the method of Context Analysis is to provide an account of the recurrent behavioral forms that are employed in inter- action and the rules that govern how they are employed.

This means that, in examining the behavior in the specimens gathered, one seeks out recurrent patterns in terms of units of behavior that are relevant for the communication system that is in operation. In transcribing speech, for instance, one can transcribe in terms of phonemes and morphemes, which are structural units of the linguistic code, rather than in terms of, say, sound frequencies or lip and tongue movements. In the same way, in looking at head movements in an inter- action, one does not attempt to plot out every deviation of head position from the vertical, every degree of rotation or tilt, as these occur as con- tinuous movements. Rather, one seeks to note recurrent patterns of movement which function equivalently or in contrast to one another. Some of these are immediately recognizable as "headnods" or "head- shakes." Others may be detected only after repeated viewing, as when one comes to notice that a speaker may tend to end a spoken utterance with a head tilt of a particular sort, whenever he asks a question; or how there may be a cycle of head orientation changes just before the speaker speaks each time he asks a question.

Second, it is supposed that the structural units of behavior which are being sought for the participants' behavior may be recognized at several different levels of organization. Units at one level, furthermore, may themselves participate as components of units at higher, more inclusive levels. In the structural analysis of language this principle of hierarchical organization is central. Phonemes are components of morphemes; morphemes are constituents of clauses; clauses are constituents of sentences; and so on. In the same way, recurrent patterns of changes in head orientation, say, may combine to form an extended cycle of head movements which, on repeated observation, is found to span recurrent units of action such as asking questions. Within the course of a given interaction participants may engage in a series of shifts in bodily posture, but, throughout, these posture shifts are within a certain range and within a certain spatial location. This range and location then itself may contrast with another range and location for some other, quite different kind of interactional activity. Eventually, this mode of thinking was extended to a consideration of interactional events as a whole. These became objects of study rather than individuals, and these were conceived of as having an organization in terms of parts, articulated in relation to one another at several different levels. This, however, was not accomplished by the original pioneers of the Palo Alto collaboration but is a later development which will now be discussed.

### Interactional event structure: the influence of Pike and Goffman

The work of the original pioneers of Context Analysis, at least as it may be gathered from a reading of the *Natural History of an Interview* and some of the early publications, is oriented very much toward the individual within the interaction. Although Birdwhistell, especially, had some conception of the interactional occasion as a system of behavioral relationships, he did not clearly articulate a notion of how such a system might be structured. Furthermore, there is little in the way of an attempt to characterize different kinds of interactional events and to consider how communicative behavior might be organized differently from one kind of circumstance to another. Furthermore, interest was virtually confined to situations in which talk is the main activity and, on the whole, analysis proceeded at increasingly microscopic levels. A consideration of the structure of interactional events and their relationship to social occasions is, however, a distinctive characteristic of later work in the structural approach. It came about through the influence of the work of Kenneth Pike and Erving Goffman.

Pike, as already mentioned, sought to extend the methods of structural linguistic analysis to the analysis of social occasions (1954–60, 1967). Thus, he analyzed a church service, a football game event and a family breakfast to show how such occasions could be viewed as being structured both in terms of their sequential organization as a succession of "slots" but also in terms of the units of behavior that served to fill the "slots" which, Pike suggested, could be thought of in terms of the linguistic units that fill the "slots" in a sentence. Thus, in the case of the church service, Pike showed how the whole event could be analyzed in terms of a programmatic arrangement of units such as "hymn," "offering," "sermon," and the like and that these "slots" served to specify what class of unit could occur. Within the class "hymn," for example, a particular set of songs can occur but not one from another class, say "ballad."

This approach to the social occasion, in which it is understood as having a programmatic structure, and the idea that one could, in analyzing them, extend concepts derived from the analysis of the structure of sentences, influenced Albert Scheflen's thinking in his treatment of the psychotherapy session as an interactional event. His most distinctive contribution to the development of Context Analysis perhaps lies in this – in his recognition of the programmatic structure of events such as psychotherapy sessions and his identification of some of the features of the behavior of the participants by which the various steps and stages of such events can be recognized. According to Scheflen (1973), an occasion of interaction such as a psychotherapy session has a customary structure to it. It has an opening phase, a middle phase and a closing phase, for example, but these phases themselves may be analyzed in terms of a sequential organization of subphases. All of these phases of the encounter may be directly observed in terms of spatial and postural configurations of the participants. Thus the event as a whole extends during the time that the participants are assembled together in the same room, for example. Within that assemblage, different postural configurations may be observed which are changed and sustained as the activity in the interaction changes or is sustained. Phases in which the therapist is listening to the patient's explanation of his feelings and fears are characterized by postural configurations and bodily orientations that are different from those that may be observed when the therapist is offering an interpretation and the patient is listening. Participants may shift from a postural configuration characteristic of one phase to one that is characteristic of another and this may serve as part of the process by which participants inform one another of their orientation to the ongoing activity in the interaction and whether, for example, there is to be a change of phase. Scheflen's observations of psychotherapy sessions led him to see how repetitive they were, in structural terms, and he came to regard them as highly institutionalized interactional occasions with a good deal of the sequencing of what went on in them as if it were organized in advance, according to a program.

Structural analysis that extends to the level of the complete event and which might, as in the analysis of an occasion such as a picnic or a market day, consider the relationship of small interactional events to the larger occasion in which they occur is a natural extension of the approach of Context Analysis. It has not been undertaken extensively, however. Besides Pike, who provided one sort of conceptual framework for analyses of this sort, mention should also be made of the work of Roger Barker whose treatment of "psychological ecology" (Barker and Wright 1951) included detailed study of "behavior settings" which show the structure that social occasions can have. Goffman, also, discussed the concept of the "social occasion" (see Goffman 1953, pp. 127–35) and, especially in his *Behavior in Public Places* (Goffman 1963), provided the beginnings of a natural history of social occasions and the interactional events which occur within them. It might be added here that this work, along with that of Scheflen already mentioned, has been especially influential in my own work on greetings (Chapter 6) and the spatial organization of encounters (Chapter 7).

We shall now discuss the contribution of Erving Goffman in more detail. Scheflen and those who preceded him in the development of Context Analysis were not at first influenced by Goffman's work, but they certainly recognized its relevance when it became known. His influence became greatest somewhat later, but it has profoundly affected those who might be considered to be in the third generation of Context Analysis, as well as those in other traditions of work, such as Ethnography of Communication and Conversation Analysis.

We pointed out in the introduction that Goffman had argued, as early as 1957, that face-to-face interaction deserves to be studied for its own sake. In fact, Goffman first expressed his interest in the study of face-to-face interaction in his Ph.D. thesis, which was completed in 1953 (Goffman 1953). In this work he examined the generic character of interaction practices, using an ethnographic study he had undertaken in a Shetland Island community as the source of most of his examples.

In his thesis he states that the aim of his research was to "isolate and record recurrent practices of what is usually called face-to-face interaction" (p. 1). He was especially concerned to describe those "social practices whose formulation an analysis might help to build a systematic framework useful in studying interaction throughout our society" (ibid., p. 1). He proposed that face-to-face interaction constituted a species of *social order*, a position he maintained throughout his career. By this he meant that a pervasive set of norms could be described which governs all occasions in which people must communicate with one another. It is this completely general set of norms that is the focus of Goffman's interest. Goffman states that he attempted to abstract from the diverse comings and goings of interaction "the orderliness that is common to all of them, the orderliness that obtains by virtue of the fact that those present are engaged in spoken communication" (ibid., p. 345). Goffman uses the term "spoken communication" here, it will be noted, and elsewhere he refers to "spoken conversation." However, even in his thesis he did not mean to confine his observations to this sort of interaction alone and in his published work he speaks simply of "interaction." He makes it clear that whenever people are co-present they inevitably engage in some kind of exchange of information and, in virtue of this, are engaged in interaction, whether or not they are speaking (e.g. Goffman 1963, pp. 13ff.). Goffman sought to establish the nature of the "interaction order" as it operated in all circumstances of co-presence, not just those in which talk was featured, and, of course, he is well known for his analyses of the communicative significance of clothing, gesture, ecological placement, and the like, as well as the particularly spoken aspects of interaction. In his thesis Goffman justifies the attention to the interaction order in terms of its functional value in making communication possible. Communication is, after all, a fundamental condition of any society. For Goffman the question became: what are the underlying practices that govern *all* communication occasions, and what are the fundamental sets of expectations and norms that govern them? *This* becomes the goal of Goffman's studies of interaction practices.

Such an orientation leads one to look at the details of everyday interaction because the underlying interaction order occurs everywhere and must be manifested in all instances of communication, not just in selected events. The *same* underlying principles must apply, whether you are engaged in unloading goods from a ship to the docks, relaying information of a critical nature to a distant neighbor via someone else's telephone, or chatting about the doings at the Hotel (to refer to examples Goffman uses in his thesis). If the underlying arrangements in the one case are to be demonstrated as applying in the other, details of interactive practice inevitably become the focus of one's attention. Otherwise, the comparisons through which the general principles of interaction practice can be discerned cannot be made.

Goffman was aware of the distinctive character of his interest in interaction. A review of the prefaces he wrote to his several published books shows that, in each case, although in a slightly different way, he sought to demonstrate that his approach to interaction was not to be considered the same as that encountered in the work of others in sociology (Kendon 1988). He recognized, of course, that face-to-face interaction had been much studied but, in his view, it was never studied as a phenomenon in its own right, but always as a means to illuminate something else. As he put it in the preface to *Relations in Public* (1971) "interaction practices have been used to illuminate other things, but themselves are treated as though they did not need to be defined or were not worth defining. Yet the nicest use for these events is the explication of their own generic character" (Goffman 1971, p. ix).

Goffman saw the study of the interaction order, as he conceived it, as a development within the framework of existing sociological tradition. As the opening quotation in his thesis shows (Goffman 1953, p. iv), as well as discussions in his published work, he drew heavily upon Simmel for the view that society is constituted and maintained through interaction practices and, as Collins (1981, 1988), among others, has shown, he drew upon Durkheim for his belief in the norms of conduct as comprising a kind of external framework into which participants must fit their actions (see also Gonos 1977) and for his analysis of social encounters as rituals (see especially Goffman 1956). Notwithstanding this, Goffman's interest in the practices of interaction, especially in describing just how participants manage actual events in everyday settings, was quite innovative at the time he began to publish. Goffman's acute analytic descriptive attention to the details of interaction, and his conceptualization of the systemic, ritual character of everyday encounters, gave a sense of fresh discovery and created a quite new way of thinking about interaction.

Goffman, in his various publications, especially in those prior to 1974 (including Goffman 1955, 1957, 1961, 1963, 1971), provided a set of interrelated concepts in terms of which the phenomena of face-to-face interaction may be approached. He provided an initial framework in terms of which the management and exchange of information among co-present individuals could be understood, he offered the beginnings of a taxonomy of interactive situations and showed how the organization of action within them could be interpreted. He provided a perspective in terms of which such diverse interactional phenomena as the orderliness of pedestrian traffic, of denizens of waiting rooms, of users of merry-go-rounds, of gamesters, as well as of conversationalists, could be described. He encouraged a kind of natural history of face-to-face interaction and its circumstances.

## Ethology

One other line of work that has been, and to some extent continues to be, influential for work being done on human interaction from a structural point of view, is ethology. This is best defined as the biological study of behavior. That is to say, in ethology behavior is studied in the framework of Darwinian evolutionary theory. This means that behavior is viewed from the point of view of its adaptive functioning. In an ethological study, in consequence, one is concerned with the way in which observable behavior serves to relate the animal to its environment and to the other animals with which it is associated. The manifest forms of behavior are, thus, the starting point in any ethological study, and the interest is in working from this manifest form outward, as it were, to see how the behavior functions in sustaining the animal in its world.

In this respect, it will be seen, ethology's emphasis has some similarities to the structural approach considered here. Like the structural approach, ethology is much interested in the manifest forms of behavior. It lays great emphasis on watching and describing patterns of action. And, like the structural approach, it insists upon examining behavior in the context of its natural setting. In attempting to work out the function of behavior patterns, ethology, again like the structural approach to human interaction, seeks to examine how units of behavior are patterned in context. Ethology differs, however, not so much because it has mostly been concerned with animal rather than human behavior (there is a fairly vigorous "human ethology" movement – see von Cranach, Foppa, Lepenies and Ploog 1979 and Eibl-Eibesfeldt 1989 for important products of this), but because of the theoretical context in which its investigations are set. The interest of ethology, as I have said, is ultimately in understanding how behavioral forms can be accounted for by Darwinian evolutionary theory. The interest of the structural approach is more narrow. Its concern is to display the structures into which human behavior is patterned and to consider how these structures function in the construction of interactional events. It does not necessarily have, as ethology does, the ultimate ambition of accounting for the behaviors it describes in terms of how they originated in evolution. The methodological orientation of much ethology (at least of the naturalistic, field observational sort) has much in common with the structural approach, however. This has been recognized by several authors in this tradition, including Goffman. Indeed, in his preface to *Relations in Public* he suggested that we use the term "interaction ethology" for studies which describe how behavior in interaction is organized. He writes (p. xvii),

[ethologists] have developed a field discipline that leads them to study animal conduct in very close detail and with a measure of control on preconception. In consequence, they have developed the ability to cut into the flow of apparently haphazard animal activity at its articulations and to isolate natural patterns. Once these behavioral sequences are pointed out to the observer, his seeing is changed. So ethologists provide an inspiration.

Goffman continues, however, that ethologists "are quick to apply a Darwinian frame" which can result in some "very unsophisticated statements . . . But if we politely disattend this feature of ethology, its value for us as a model stands clear."

The essays reprinted in this book exemplify quite well what Goffman appears to have meant by "interaction ethology." However, as will be apparent to the reader, in several of them the "Darwinian frame" has not always been disattended quite to the extent that, perhaps, Goffman would have recommended. Chapter 5 (on "kissing") and, especially, Chapter 6 (on "Greetings") discuss the findings in relation to questions about the human universality of the behavior patterns described and, briefly, their possible adaptive significance. It remains our own view that cultural comparative studies of interaction practices should be given a very high priority. Such comparisons, to be undertaken effectively, require that the practices being compared be understood in terms of the place they have within the cultures in question. Nonetheless, there are patterns of interaction that do seem to have the same form in widely separated cultures and if these can be well established there seems no reason not to consider them in terms of their biological evolutionary significance.

## Context analysis and other structural studies of interaction: concluding observations

From the foregoing outline, we see that a distinctive approach to the analysis of social interaction emerged as a result of the collaborative application of ideas from several different disciplines. Information theory showed that the concept of "message" was entirely general, hence any aspect of behavior could be thought of in communicational terms. Cybernetics concepts showed how interactions could be thought of as information exchange systems. This encouraged the study of the way in which the behavior of participants in interaction was co-occurrent. It also showed that stability in interactional relationships was as much in need of explanation as change. Since the kind of study of interaction this encouraged required that complete information about it be available, audio-visual recording technology became a necessity of such research. This, however, confronted investigators with the need for methods of conceptualizing and transcribing the behavioral flow in all its complexity. The methods and orientation of structural linguistics were adopted as an answer to this. This, however, directed researchers to search for behavioral patterns which could be treated as structural units of the communicational system. It also encouraged the view that behavior is organized at multiple levels simultaneously.

The work undertaken by the members of the Palo Alto group and their colleagues and others who they influenced, both collectively and separately, was, for the most part, micro-analytic and it tended to concentrate on analyzing very small strips of behavior recorded within encounters. Scheflen, however, undertook a comparative study of psychotherapy sessions and this led him to think about the organization of the interactional event as a whole. He drew on the work of Pike in this thinking, as we have seen and, somewhat later, on the work of Goffman. These influences extended the structural view of interaction to consider how whole events might be organized, as well as looking at details of interaction within events.

There are several investigators who have followed Scheflen's lead here. For example, McDermott and his associates have undertaken detailed analyses of interactional events in the First Grade classroom.

They have studied a "reading group" and have shown how the task of reading proceeds in several episodes, each one differentiated in terms of the spatial–orientational organization of the children and teacher which, it appears, frames different patterns of participation organization (McDermott, Gospodinoff and Aron 1978, McDermott and Gospodinoff 1979). Erickson (Erickson 1975, 1979, Erickson and Schultz 1982) has undertaken a detailed study of counseling interviews in which he demonstrated the phasic structure of such events and showed the ways in which the participants keep one another oriented to a given phase of the event or bring about change from one phase to the next through a variety of means, both linguistic and kinesic, including posture and orientation. In this respect, his work is a direct extension of that of Scheflen. In the same study, Erickson compared interviews in which the participants were of the same or of different cultural backgrounds and through detailed analysis of the rhythmic patterning of utterance, examining spoken and kinesic components in their conjoint organization, he was able to show that sources of "trouble" in interviews, where the participants were of different cultural background, could be traced to differences in certain aspects of interactional practice. Together with several associates, Erickson has extended the structural analysis of interaction to the elementary school classroom and the family dinnertime. In this work he has shown how social occasions may be compared in terms of differences in the patterning of speaker–addressee relationship. He has shown how this is established, regulated and changed through proxemic, orientational, postural and spoken activities, both in terms of what is said and done and in terms of the rhythmic organization of such doings (Erickson 1982, Erickson and Schultz 1981, Schultz and Florio 1979, Schultz, Florio and Erickson 1982).

Structural analyses of face-to-face interaction, which have developed findings that both complement those of the Context Analysis tradition and converge with them, have been done both in linguistics and in what is known as Conversation Analysis. In both of these lines of work, in contrast to Context Analysis, the spoken component of interaction has been the point of departure. This has been for different reasons in each case. For the linguists who study interaction, the spoken component has received the most attention because it was certain linguistic questions that prompted their attention to interaction. In Conversation Analysis the starting point was an interest in studying the procedures of everyday interaction and spoken interaction was studied because this was the easiest to record. For both of these developments, however, the work of Erving Goffman has been important and the work of some of those who were directly involved in the development of Context Analysis has also had some influence. Although both these lines of work have had different origins, and although they have developed somewhat independently of one another and, in large part, separately from work in Context Analysis, there are certainly more connections between them than might be apparent at first sight.

The interest in the study of interaction that has come about within linguistics may be derived from a persistent concern among some linguists with *variation* in language (cf. Gumperz 1982a). Although this was, for a time, somewhat eclipsed by interests in "universal grammar" which seemed especially important following the impact of the work of Noam Chomsky (1957), the view that language is a social creation, and that a study of its dialectical and stylistic variations is central to any understanding of it, has persisted. As the study of the way social factors affect language structure and use became more detailed, it became apparent that how people choose to speak – what dialect they employ, or what speech register – can only be understood in the context of the interactional events within which the speaking that is studied takes place. In what has come to be known as "sociolinguistics" there has been an increasing concern with understanding the "speech event" as a structural unit. Studies such as those inspired by Hymes's concept of "ethnography of communication" (Hymes 1974, 1964, Gumperz and Hymes 1964, 1972) – see the papers by Phillips, Reisman, Irvine, and Sherzer in Bauman and Sherzer (1974) as examples; or, more recently, work such as that by Schiffren (1977, 1987) – are witness to this.

Even more pertinent is the work of Gumperz (1964, 1982a, 1982b, Blom and Gumperz 1972) which he has distinguished as "interactional sociolinguistics." Here it has been shown that differences in dialect, style and register are differences that may be at the command of participants in interaction and may be used by them as part of the way in which they manage their participation in interaction. Strategies of self-presentation, the way in which the situational definition of social occasion is negotiated, and the way in which participants manage transitions from one phase of an interaction to another, all can involve the use of different linguistic forms. Modes of speaking, whether in terms of style, register, dialect or language thus, are not only to be understood in terms of regional origin, group affiliation or relative social status of the speaker that they may index. They must also be understood as resources at the command of participants to be used by them as discourse strategies within interactional events. The realization that such features of language can only be understood if the way in which participants manage interactions can be understood has led to an examination of interaction which has many features in common with the approach arrived at through Context Analysis.

In Conversation Analysis, also, the starting point has been *spoken* interaction, as already mentioned. Unlike linguistically oriented studies of interaction, however, this emphasis on talk developed in the first place for practical reasons. Conversation Analysis originated in sociology, not linguistics, and talk was seized upon for study mainly because it was an aspect of human social action that could readily be recorded. For example, Schegloff and Sacks (1973, pp. 289–90) state that their work in Conversation Analysis is to be seen as "part of a program of work undertaken . . . to explore the possibility of achieving a naturalistic observational discipline that could deal with the details of social action(s) rigorously, empirically and formally." They add that their focus on conversational materials "is not because of any special interest in language"; however, as Conversation Analysis has developed, it has been mainly concerned with the properties of how conversations, as such, are organized, and in only a few cases, to be noted below, have students in this tradition actually undertaken to look at social actions other than talk or to look at how talk and other kinds of social action are interrelated.

Conversation Analysis, so-called, originated in Sacks's work with Garfinkel (Schegloff 1989). It is often considered a branch of ethnomethodology; however, it differs from this insofar as it is more firmly oriented toward the organization of talk, or interaction, as an activity, whereas ethnomethodology proper has a more cognitive outlook, with an emphasis upon the analysis of the grounds upon which everyday activities are carried out. Conversation Analysis began with Harvey Sacks's lectures in California in 1964 and with the appearance of Schegloff's paper on telephone conversation openings in 1968 (Schegloff 1968). One of the first (and still one of the best) programmatic statements of the enterprise is to be found in Schegloff and Sacks (1973). Another excellent statement, also written early on in the development of the approach, but which was not published until much later, is by Moerman and Sacks (in Moerman 1988). Subsequent landmarks in the development of this line of analysis include the paper on turn taking (Sacks, Schegloff and Jefferson 1974), papers on "adjacency pair" organization and "side sequences" (Jefferson 1972, Schegloff 1972), timing in turn taking (Jefferson 1974), repair (Schegloff, Jefferson and Sacks 1977, Schegloff 1979), the conversational management of assessments (Pomerantz 1984), topic (Button and Casey 1984, Jefferson 1984) and narrative (Sacks 1974, Goodwin 1984). This is but a sampling of the achievements of this line of work. Major collections of papers include Sudnow (1972), Schenkein (1978) and Atkinson and Heritage (1985). Reviews of the work have been published by Levinson (1983), West and Zimmerman (1982), Heritage (1984) and Sigman, Sullivan and Wendell (1987). Moerman's (1988) studies of the organization of conversations among Thai is an important step toward developing a cultural comparative dimension to this work which, hitherto, has been carried out entirely with English speakers (mostly in the United States but also in Britain).

Notwithstanding the central place of *spoken* interaction in the *œuvres* of Conversation Analysis, and although it had a very different starting point, it will be apparent that Conversation Analysis approaches the phenomena of human interaction in very much the same way as Context Analysis. Both Context Analysis and Conversation Analysis insist on the study of specimens of interaction that actually occurred. Neither uses contrived data nor do they employ experiment. Both are oriented to the discovery of the organization that is displayed in the specimens and what is found there is taken to exemplify the various ways in which people organize interaction. Statistical analyses are not employed because the underlying assumption is that participants in interaction are not the victims of external pushes and pulls of motivation and circumstance. They are, rather, creatures capable of employing strategies of action and follow shared principles to do so. If order can be demonstrated in the examination of just a few specimens of interaction, this is taken to be one of the orders that humans employ in interaction. The frequency with which it occurs is not taken as an index of the firmness with which its reality can be believed in.

Neither Conversation Analysis nor Context Analysis employs pre-established categories of observation but, in both approaches, there is a continual willingness to review the typifications in terms of which the specimens are described. In Conversation Analysis the aim is to estab-

lish the principles that are governing the conduct of the conversationalists as they exchange turns at talk and what these principles are can be
established by inspecting how the conversationalists themselves deal
with each other's utterances. By the same token, the units or acts in
terms of which the participants are dealing with one another may be
established by examining how they respond to one another.

To illustrate this point, consider how absence of talk in a conversation, or silence, is treated. If $p$ is speaking, then ceases to speak and
then resumes speaking again, without any turn by $q$, or any other evidence that $q$ found this unusual or an interruption in what was going
on, this can be evidence that the "pause" in $p$'s speech was heard as an
integral part of $p$'s turn (a pause while he is working out just how to put
something, for instance) and should be treated differently than a case
where such an absence of speech is followed, after a while, by a querying
response by $q$. In such a case, $q$ treats $p$ as if he had "broken off" his turn
and had not "finished." Silences in conversation, thus, are handled by
the analyst in terms of how the participants themselves are observed to
handle them. Different kinds of silences (pauses, failures to respond,
breaking off in the middle of a turn, etc.) are established in terms of how
the conversationalists themselves treat them. To approach silences in
talk with a categorization of them constructed in advance of observation and independently of how participants deal with them would be
to miss their significance completely. A very similar procedure is
followed in Context Analysis where great attention is paid to how the
participants orient to and deal with the various patterned aspects of
behavior each displays. For example, the significance of shifting postures, changing gaze patterns or the sequencing of spatial maneuver,
gesture, facial display and spoken utterance in a greeting, can only be
established in terms of how the participants themselves appear to be
dealing with them. Externally developed categorizations cannot reveal
the interactional significance of what people do in relation to one
another.

Conversation Analysis has remained mainly preoccupied with problems having to do with the organization of talk, as we have seen.
Nevertheless, there are some workers in this tradition who have taken
other aspects of interaction into account as well. Schegloff (1984) has
reported observations on the relationship between gestures and turns at
talk and Goodwin (1981) has considered the way in which participants
employ gaze direction, bodily orientation and posture in the construc-

tion of speaker-recipient relations within and between turns and turn sequences in conversation. His work points toward a more comprehensive approach to the study of interaction, which has been developed further by Heath (1986). Drawing partly on Goodwin's work and on the work of Scheflen, as well as others in Conversation Analysis, he has published an analysis of doctor-patient interaction in medical interviews which treats within a single conceptual framework both the talk, and the ecological and kinesic aspects of the interaction.

In studying the medical examination, Heath was dealing with an interaction in which much of what takes place involves the manipulation and inspection of objects, such as the patient's body or medical records and much of the talk that occurs is done as part of such activities. Heath was thus forced, by the nature of the material he chose to study, to look beyond the structure of talk alone to consider talk–object–manipulation as an integrated package. But Heath goes further than this, for he examines the entire structure of the encounter, from the way it begins, when the patient enters the consulting room, to the way in which the ending is negotiated and the patient finally departs. In this respect, in particular, his work differs from what has been so characteristic of Conversation Analysis hitherto which has given so much attention to the local organization of conversational sequence. As Scheflen recognized, and as is clear from Heath's treatment, turn-by-turn sequences often (perhaps always) take place within the frame of an "encounter," that is, within the frame of some event which can be considered to have an organizational structure above the level of the turn-by-turn sequence. Medical consultations and psychiatric interviews unquestionably have agendas which govern the structure and timing of much that goes on within them. This may also be true of afternoon telephone chats between housewives and interaction at the dinner table. It is this possibility that Scheflen, following Pike, had raised and it is notable that Heath also tackles this issue. In Heath's treatment of the various stages of the encounter, his discussion of the way in which patient and doctor jointly negotiate the successively different frames of attention, he provides analyses which are completely compatible with those offered by Scheflen. Heath's work shows clearly how an integration of the findings and procedures of Context Analysis, on the one hand, and Conversation Analysis, on the other, may be achieved.

# 3

## Some functions of gaze direction in two-person conversation

### Introduction

An awareness of the social significance of gaze direction is very old. Tomkins (1963) provides a review of some of the early writers on this topic, and quotes one reference to it from a clay tablet from a civilization in Iraq of the Third Millennium B.C. More recently it has been the object of systematic inquiry. Sartre (1956) has provided an exceptionally brilliant description of the experience of being looked at, and he suggests that it is through our experience of the Look that we most directly apprehend another person as a being with consciousness and intentions of his own. Other writers have commented not only upon the power of the Look, but also upon the almost mysterious quality of the mutual gaze in which, as Simmel (1924) has described it, one enters with another into the most pure and intimate kind of direct relationship that is possible. Other writers have discussed the expressiveness of the glance or gaze, noting how there seems to be a whole "vocabulary" mediated by it (see, for example, Ortega y Gasset 1957 or Ogden 1961).

Within the last few years, these phenomena have received the attention of experimental psychologists. Thus Wardwell (1960) has made systematic observations on how the behavior of children in a test situation was affected by whether or not they were being looked at. Gibson and Pick (1963) have reported an experimental analysis of the individual's perception of where another is looking, and they have shown that people are remarkably sensitive to this. Exline and his colleagues, in a series of studies (Exline et al. 1961, Exline 1963, Exline, Gray and Schuette 1965, Exline and Winters 1965), and Argyle and Dean (1965)

First published in *Acta Psychologica*, 26 (1967), 22–63. Reprinted by permission of North-Holland Publishing Co., Amsterdam.

have explored some aspects of the phenomenon of the factors that are associated with the amount of mutual gaze an individual seeks to engage in.

All these investigators, however, appear to have been concerned mainly with the relationship between habits of looking and other characteristics of the looker or, by manipulating the subject's reaction to their co-interactor, they have observed variations in the amount which he looks. They have not attempted any analysis of its function within ongoing social interaction, although the interest in it that they evince implies that they believe it to be of importance in this context. Only two authors have considered direction of gaze from this point of view. Goffman (1963) has drawn together the observations of a number of writers to suggest that direction of gaze plays a crucial role in the initiation and maintenance of social encounters. He points out that where an individual is looking is an important indicator of his social accessibility. This is because, whether or not a person is willing to have his eye "caught," whether or not, that is, he is willing to look back into the eyes of someone who is already looking at him, is one of the principal signals by which people indicate to each other their willingness to begin an encounter. It seems that it is through the mutually held gaze that two people commonly establish their "openness" to one another's communications.

Goffman goes on to describe how, when two or more people have agreed to engage in interaction, they position themselves in what he described as "an eye-to-eye ecological huddle," which "tends to be carefully maintained, maximizing the opportunity to monitor one another's mutual perceivings" (Goffman 1963, p. 95). It would appear that it is through the continued maintenance of this positioning in relation to one another, and through the intermittent mutual gazes, that each participant expresses his continued commitment to it. Direction of gaze, thus, serves in part as a signal by which the interactants regulate their basic orientations to one another.

Gerhard Nielsen (1964) has also considered the role of gaze direction in social interaction. From an analysis of sound-film records of two-person discussions, and of comments which the participants made later, when they had been made aware of their own particular habits of looking, Nielsen concluded that direction of gaze has a number of different functions, which he describes mainly from the point of view of what someone can signal to another by changing his direction of gaze, while talking with them.

The study to be reported here is exploratory. Our main aim is to contribute to the almost non-existent literature on the natural history of gaze direction as it occurs within the context of ongoing conversation between two people. In particular we have looked at the relationship between direction of gaze and the occurrence of utterances. On the basis of the relationships we shall describe, we shall offer some suggestions as to the function of gaze direction, both as an act of perception by which one interactant can monitor the behavior of the other, and as an expressive sign and regulatory signal by which he may influence the behavior of the other.

## The material gathered and the procedures for analysis

The data to be discussed in this paper have been drawn from sound and film records of parts of seven two-person conversations, involving thirteen individuals in all, three of whom were female, and all of whom were undergraduates at the University of Oxford. Each pair, the members of which were in all cases previously unacquainted, were left together for half an hour with the instruction to "get to know one another." The conversations were recorded on magnetic tape, and two parts of it were filmed. The subjects sat across a table, facing one another (about three and a half feet between them) and to one side of them, on the table, a mirror was placed in such a way that the camera, which was placed eight feet away behind a screen, could photograph both subjects in full face, one directly and one in the mirror. The film was shot at the rate of two frames a second (so that several minutes of film could be shot at once), and a special piece of apparatus was attached to send in a signal to the tape recorder each time a frame was taken. In this way a fairly precise coordination between the film and the sound record could be made.[1]

The subjects were fully informed of the set-up beforehand. This was done in the hope that their suspicions and curiosities would be allayed so that, during the conversation, they would not have to worry too

[1] This coordinating device was designed and constructed by Dr. E. R. F. W. Crossman.

much about what was going on. In fact few of the subjects had difficulty with the situation, and in some cases they became very involved with one another and enjoyed the conversation very much. On being questioned afterwards, all of them stated that there was some initial awkwardness, but they quickly came to accept the situation, and were not disturbed by the knowledge that they were being recorded or by the presence of the apparatus.

The analyses to be reported here are based on a study of five-minute samples from six of the conversations, all of them taken from the last ten minutes of it. The sample from the seventh conversation was in two parts. One was seven minutes long, and the other nine minutes, taken from the first and last ten minutes of the conversation respectively.

The films were transcribed, frame by frame, by means of a positional notation using pictographic symbols (Ex and Kendon 1964). With this notation not only was direction of gaze recorded for each frame, but also details of the facial expression, the position of the head, the hands and arms, and the trunk. The words uttered, if any, within the half-second interval elapsing between each frame and the one following, were written in against each frame transcription. All of the analyses to be reported here were done from these transcripts. Limitations in the projection apparatus available did not make it possible to do the analyses directly from the films.

No formal reliability studies were made of the work of the transcribers. The transcription of one of the films was done by Dr. J. Ex, and the author, who worked in close collaboration, each concentrating on only one of the subjects, but nonetheless in continual consultation. Four further films were transcribed by the author and a research assistant again working in close consultation. In all cases, what was aimed at was a transcription on which the transcribers were in complete agreement. Two further films were transcribed by the author for direction of gaze only. Since the author worked on the transcriptions of all the films studied for this paper, at least they have been done according to a consistent method, though of course other transcribers might have used slightly different criteria in making their transcriptions. Also, since this part of the work was purely descriptive, and no interpretation was involved, it is thought likely that discrepancies between different transcribers would be quite small.

**Results of the analyses**

*Proportion of time spent looking and not looking at q*[2]

The proportion of the available time that *p* spends looking at *q* when in conversation with him is a matter of considerable variation. In the examples studied here (see Tables 1a and 1b), this varies from 28% to over 70% of the time. An even greater range has been reported by Nielsen (1964), who based his observations on ten-minute samples of conversation. Nielsen also reports that *p* spends less time looking while he is speaking than while he is listening, a finding which the present observations, as well as those of Exline (1963) confirm.[3]

In the present data, in eleven cases out of fourteen, *p* spends less than half his speaking time looking at *q*, and in nine cases he spends more than half of his listening time in looking at *q*. Once again great variation is to be observed in the figures. Thus there are subjects who spend as much as 65% of their speaking time in looking at *q*, or as little as 20% of it. Or there are subjects who look at *q* while they are listening for only 30% of listening time, or they look for over 80% of it.

So far as the average length of *q*-gaze is concerned, there is a similar variability, though again there is a consistency in the differences in average length of *q*-gazes during silence as compared to those during speaking. Thus, with two exceptions, the mean *q*-gaze is longer during silence than during speaking, and during silence the *q*-gazes tend to be longer than the *a*-gazes, whereas the reverse is the case during speaking. Insofar as it is possible to speak of a typical pattern, it would appear to be this: during listening, *p* looks at *q* with fairly long *q*-gazes, broken by very brief *a*-gazes, whereas during speaking he alternates between *q*- and *a*-gazes being longer than those that occur during listening.

[2] In this paper, *p* will be used to designate the individual who is being discussed, and *q* will be used to designate the person he is in interaction with. We shall speak of *q*-gaze, when *p* is looking at *q*, and of *a*-gaze when *p* is not looking at him.
[3] In an unpublished study of a seven-person seminar (Weisbrod 1965) subjects were found to spend over 70% of their time looking at others, but only 47% of their time looking at speakers. It is possible that here, where to whom one is speaking may be signalled by to whom one is looking, the high proportion of speaking time accompanied by looking is associated with the need in a multiperson gathering to make it clear to whom one is speaking. The rather low proportion of time that *p*'s spent looking while listening may have had to do with the fact that in a seminar some time would be spent in making notes or referring to books, an activity that would be carried out while not speaking.

Table 1a. *Proportion of time spent looking at interlocutor for thirteen subjects in seven two-person conversations*

|  | Proportion of time spent in $q$-directed gaze | | | Proportion of time spent in $a$-directed gaze | | |
|---|---|---|---|---|---|---|
| Subject | Overall | During long utterances | During silence | Overall | During long utterances | During silence |
| RB (male) | 52.9 | 34.3 | 81.0 | 47.0 | 65.7 | 19.0 |
| JS (female) | 45.4 | 26.9 | 63.5 | 54.7 | 73.1 | 36.5 |
| *JH (female) | 65.8 | 57.5 | 79.0 | 34.2 | 42.5 | 21.0 |
| *NL (male) | 62.7 | 46.8 | 82.2 | 37.3 | 53.2 | 17.8 |
| SJ (male) | 29.0 | 20.7 | 39.3 | 71.0 | 79.3 | 60.7 |
| W (male) | 31.8 | 27.6 | 34.8 | 68.2 | 72.4 | 65.2 |
| JS (male) | 43.0 | 41.1 | 58.9 | 57.0 | 55.0 | 45.0 |
| WJ (male) | 69.0 | 42.4 | 57.6 | 31.0 | 58.6 | 41.4 |
| TG (male) | 28.7 | 22.0 | 32.0 | 71.3 | 78.0 | 68.0 |
| VM (female) | 44.4 | 39.2 | 52.3 | 55.6 | 60.8 | 47.7 |
| KA (male) | 71.2 | 62.0 | 76.8 | 28.8 | 38.0 | 23.2 |
| T (male) | 62.7 | 67.8 | 56.8 | 36.2 | 32.2 | 43.2 |
| KA (male) | 49.1 | 41.6 | 48.7 | 51.0 | 58.4 | 51.3 |
| W (male) | 36.2 | 31.0 | 44.0 | 63.8 | 69.0 | 56.0 |

*Figures based on a 16-minute sample. In all other cases the sample is 5 min. long.

Figures are also given for the proportion of time spent in mutual gaze (Table 1c). They will merely be noted here, since the phenomenon of mutual gaze is the object of an investigation reported in a later section of this chapter. It will be seen here that there is considerable variation from dyad to dyad, both in the proportion of time spent in mutual gaze, and in the proportion of $p$'s $q$-gaze that is taken up with mutual gaze. Mutual gazes tend to be quite short, lasting for little more than a second as a rule.

Some rank order correlations between some of these measures are presented in Table 2. None of them are very high, though a few reach significance at the 5% level of confidence. Thus there is some tendency for $p$'s with long $q$-gazes to have short $a$-gazes, and vice versa (rho = −0.53). It also appears that the *rate* at which $p$ changes his direction of

Table 1b. *Mean length of glances for thirteen subjects in seven two-person conversations*

| | Mean length of q-directed gaze (in half-sec) | | | Mean length of away-gaze (in half-sec) | | |
| Subject | Overall | During long utterances | During silence | Overall | During long utterances | During silence |
|---|---|---|---|---|---|---|
| RB (male) | 4.04 | 2.57 | 6.75 | 3.59 | 4.55 | 1.73 |
| JS (female) | 4.12 | 2.33 | 5.68 | 4.89 | 6.25 | 3.37 |
| *JH (female) | 5.72 | 3.35 | 4.24 | 2.97 | 3.46 | 1.64 |
| *NL (male) | 4.90 | 2.68 | 7.93 | 2.93 | 2.85 | 2.61 |
| SJ (male) | 2.10 | 1.94 | 2.24 | 5.14 | 6.62 | 2.98 |
| W (male) | 2.24 | 2.08 | 2.28 | 4.80 | 4.56 | 5.36 |
| JS (male) | 2.84 | 2.41 | 2.76 | 3.80 | 3.09 | 3.05 |
| WJ (male) | 3.86 | 2.75 | 4.47 | 1.74 | 1.80 | 1.56 |
| TG (male) | 3.66 | 2.44 | 2.85 | 9.09 | 4..00 | 5.45 |
| VM (female) | 3.52 | 2.48 | 3.61 | 4.46 | 3.98 | 3.25 |
| KA (male) | 7.04 | 4.56 | 7.13 | 3.08 | 3.13 | 2.04 |
| T (male) | 7.98 | 7.32 | 5.00 | 4.51 | 3.55 | 4.83 |
| KA (male) | 4.04 | 3.94 | 3.47 | 3.74 | 4.38 | 3.14 |
| W (male) | 3.04 | 2.96 | 3.56 | 5.22 | 6.44 | 3.80 |

*Figures based on a 16-minute sample. In all other cases the sample is 5 min. long.

gaze depends more upon the length of his *a*-gazes, than upon the length of his *q*-gazes. That is, whereas if *q*-gazes are long, his rate of gaze direction is bound to be slow, he may have either long or short *a*-gazes when his *q*-gazes are short.

Secondly, correlations between the length of *q*- and *a*-gazes during speaking and listening are presented. Here it is to be observed that there is some tendency for *p*'s *q*-gazes during listening and speaking to be positively related. This implies that how much on the average they look during either speaking or listening is interrelated and that while whether or not they are speaking or listening affects the length of *q*- and *a*-gazes, it does not do so independently of an overriding looking tendency which can be considered separate from the utterance structure of the social performance.

Table 1c. *Amount of time spent in mutual-gaze (eye-contact) during
five minutes from five two-person conversations*

| | Proportion of time occupied by mutual gaze ($1/2$ sec) | Mean length of mutual gaze ($1/2$ sec) | Proportion of $p$'s $q$-gaze which is mutual with $q$ | Proportion of time occupied by mutual not looking | Mean length of mutual not looking |
|---|---|---|---|---|---|
| RB JS | 22.7 | 2.00 | 43.2 50.8 | 23.5 | 2.43 |
| *JH *NL | 38.43 | 2.80 | 59.0 61.9 | 10.0 | 1.59 |
| SJ W | 9.83 | 1.44 | 34.4 31.3 | 49.0 | 3.13 |
| JS WJ | 30.0 | 1.91 | 70.0 43.6 | 18.7 | 1.49 |
| TG VM | 11.85 | 1.73 | 44.1 26.9 | 39.8 | 3.32 |

*Based on a 16-minute sample.

Table 2. *Rank order correlation coefficients between selected measures
of q-gaze and a-gaze variables*

| | | $r_s$ $p$ |
|---|---|---|
| Rate of change of gaze-direction | & mean length of $q$-gaze | +.19 $p$>.05 |
| Rate of change of gaze-direction | & mean length of $a$-gaze | +.58 $p$<.05 |
| Mean length of $q$-gaze | & mean length of $a$-gaze | −.53 $p$<.05 |
| Mean $q$-gaze during speech | & mean $a$-gaze during speech | −.43 $p$>.05 |
| Mean $q$-gaze during speech | & mean $q$-gaze during listening | +.52 $p$<.05 |
| Mean $q$-gaze during speech | & mean $a$-gaze during listening | −.40 $p$>.05 |
| Mean $a$-gaze during speech | & mean $q$-gaze during listening | +.40 $p$>.05 |
| Mean $a$-gaze during speech | & mean $a$-gaze during listening | +.48 $p$>.05 |
| Mean $a$-gaze during listening | & mean $q$-gaze during listening | −.42 $p$>.05 |
| Percent $a$-gaze during speech | & percent $a$-gaze during listening | +.62 $p$<.05 |
| Percent $q$-gaze during speech | & percent $a$-gaze during listening | +.61 $p$<.05 |
| $p$'s mean $q$-gaze | & $q$'s mean $q$-gaze | +.87 $p$<.01 |
| $p$'s rate of change of gaze-direction | & $q$'s rate of change of gaze-direction | +1.00 $p$>.01 |

The most noteworthy observation to be made from these overall figures, however, is that the mean length of $p$'s $q$-gaze, and also the rate at which $p$ changes his direction of gaze, is directly and closely related to his partner's average $q$-gaze and rate of change of gaze direction. Thus the rank order correlation between the rate of change of gaze direction over the seven pairs is 1.00, and between average length of $q$-gaze it is 0.87, which is significant beyond the 1% level of confidence. Thus in terms of how long at a time $p$ looks at $q$, and $q$ looks at $p$, it seems as if each dyad comes to a kind of "agreement" whereby each looks at the other for a particular length of time, on the average, though for how long at a time each looks at the other depends upon the dyad. This is clearly illustrated in the case of KA, who took part in two conversations. With WT his mean $q$-gaze was 7.04 half-seconds[4] and that of his partner was 7.98 half-seconds. When with TW, whose mean $q$-gaze was 3.04 half-seconds, his mean $q$-gaze was only 4.04 half-seconds.

This finding raises the question as to how far the variability in the figures reported here (and those reported by Nielsen) reflect stable individual differences in how much a person looks or does not look at his co-interactor. It clearly suggests that how much $p$ will look at $q$ will depend to an important extent upon factors specific to the dyad he is in. There remains the possibility, however, that though people may all adjust their looking behavior in accord with situationally specific factors, each will do this to an extent and in a way that is characteristic of him. Certainly, the findings reported by Exline, that individual differences in measures of "need affiliation" and in responses to Schutz's FIRO Scale are related to individual differences in the amount a person looks at another interaction (Exline 1963, Exline and Winters 1965), would suggest that there are stable individual differences, but of their nature we have no knowledge.

### Direction of gaze in relation to utterance occurrence

It has emerged that an important source of variability in the amount $p$ looks during the course of a conversation is the amount that he speaks, since it was found that the pattern of $p$'s looking behavior during speaking was quite different from that found during listening. It appeared that

---

[4] The half-second is the unit of time-measurement employed throughout this paper, since each frame of the film was separated from its successor by a half-second.

whereas during silence $p$ looks in long gazes at $q$, while speaking he alternated between $q$- and $a$-gazes more equal in length. Since it is through the utterance, primarily, that $p$ seeks to pursue his projects in the encounter, whether these concern the material being dealt with in it, or the relationship he has with the other participants, perceptual activity in relation to the occurrence of utterances has considerable interest, for we may expect that it plays a part in the guidance of $p$'s behavior in the encounter. We shall see also that it may play a part in the guidance of $q$'s behavior.

*(i)   Beginning and ending of long utterances.* First of all, we shall consider how gaze direction changes as $p$ begins and as he ends a long utterance. A long utterance, for present purposes, is any utterance that lasts for five seconds or more. Such utterances typically require that $q$ be silent while $p$ is speaking. Shorter utterances are often produced during the other person's utterance, and they tend to fall into the class distinguished by Ogden and Richards (1947) as "emotive" or, by Soskin and John (1963) as "relational." They are, that is, immediate reactions to the other person's ongoing behavior. They do not involve any planning phase. In their lexical form they suggest that they are always old and well-established speech habits. Long utterances by contrast always always involve a certain amount of advance planning, even if it is a matter of selecting from among a number of alternatives, of which a number of well-rehearsed phrases shall be used (cf. discussion in Goldman-Eisler 1958).

In Fig. 1 a diagram is presented, giving an example of a typical long utterance exchange, showing not only changes in gaze direction, but changes in the position of the head and in certain aspects of the facial posture as well. It will be seen first that as NL ends his utterance, the fluctuations in the position of his head come to an end and he holds his head in a pose little different from the erect position, he looks up at JH before he finishes speaking, and goes on looking at her after he has finished. JH behaves rather differently. Up to 362 and for quite a long period before this, she combined looking at NL with a fairly fixed head posture, one in which she has her head cocked slightly to one side and tilted forward. At 361 she utters a faint "mm," and at 362 she drops her eyelids over her eyes, tilting her head forward in the next frame. She continues to look down, even after she begins to speak at 366. Her head position shows marked changes. This looking away, and other changes, which

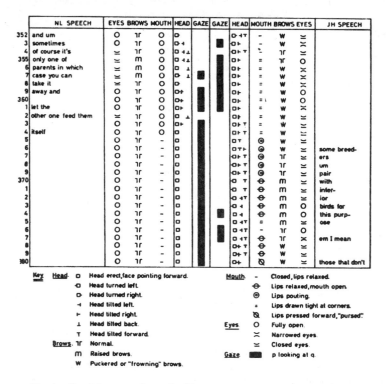

Fig. 1  Partial extract from the film-transcript showing a long utterance exchange.

occur before she begins to speak, coincide with the beginning of the last phrase of NL's utterance, at the point at which, it may be presumed, JH has realized NL is going to finish. Thus it seems that JH is already showing that she is ready to talk before she actually begins to. And NL, looking steadily at JH before he finishes speaking, is in a position to pick up this advance warning, that she has already, in this case, accepted his offer of the floor.

This example provides all the elements that we have found to occur in many long utterance exchanges. Such exchanges occur quite often in conversations when people are exchanging points of view, comparing experiences or, as in the particular case used for illustration, exploring one another's knowledge of something. When individual cases of this sort are examined, it is found that there is usually some change in the auditor's behavior before he actually begins to speak, and the person

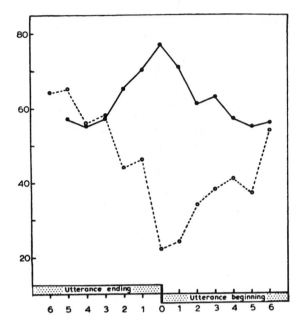

Figure 2    Direction of gaze and the beginning and ending of long utterances. Frequency of $q$-directed gaze at successive half-second intervals
before and after the beginning (broken line) and ending (continuous line)
of long utterances. Pooled data from ten individuals, based on sixty-eight
utterances.

who is bringing a long utterance to an end does so by assuming a characteristic head posture (which is different for different individuals), and by
looking steadily at the auditor, before he actually finishes speaking.
Such changes in behavior which precede the utterance itself clearly
make it possible for each participant to anticipate how the other is going
to deal with the actual point of change of speaker role, perhaps facilitating the achievement of smoother or more "adjusted" changeovers than
might otherwise occur.

The element which has been found to be most typical, and to occur
most commonly, is a certain pattern of changes in direction of gaze.
Data on this for all of the samples analyzed for this study are presented
in Fig. 2. Here the percentage frequency of $q$-gaze for each half-second
is plotted, for three seconds preceding the beginning and the end of the
utterance, and for three seconds following its beginning or following its
end.

Table 3. *Number of utterances which displayed the patterns of gaze direction portrayed in Fig. 2*

|      | Number of utterances beginning with a-gaze | Number of utterance beginnings | Number of utterances ending with q-gaze | Number of utterance endings |
|------|------|------|------|------|
| RB   | 3    | 10   | 4    | 10   |
| JS   | 4    | 4    | 1    | 4    |
| JH   | 8    | 10   | 9    | 12   |
| NL   | 15   | 12   | 16   | 16   |
| SJ   | 8    | 8    | 6    | 8    |
| W    | 2    | 6    | 5    | 6    |
| WJ   | 1    | 3    | 5    | 5    |
| JS   | 5    | 5    | 3    | 4    |
| TG   | 2    | 2    | 2    | 2    |
| VM   | 8    | 8    | 6    | 8    |
| KA   | 5    | 7    | 5    | 7    |
| T    | 4    | 6    | 6    | 6    |
| KA   | 4    | 5    | 2    | 5    |
| TRW  | 4    | 4    | 2    | 4    |
| Total | 73  | 90   | 72   | 97   |

As will be apparent, there is a very clear and quite consistent pattern, namely, that p tends to look away as he begins a long utterance, and in many cases somewhat in advance of it; and that he looks up at his interlocutor as the end of the long utterance approaches, usually during the last phase, and he continues to look thereafter. In Table 3 the total number of utterances examined for each individual is given, and, as the numerator of this total, the total number of utterances which p begins by looking away from his interlocutor, and the number that he ends by looking up at him has been recorded. It will be seen that of the ninety-five utterances for which beginnings could be observed, over 70% of them were begun with an a-gaze, and that there are only three individuals for whom less than half of their utterances do not begin in this way; and of the ninety-seven utterances for which endings could be observed, there were four individuals for whom less than half of their long utterances ended with a q-gaze.

This relationship may be understood from two points of view. In looking away at the beginning of an utterance, p is shutting out one important source of input from his interlocutor, and it may be that he is actually withdrawing his attention from him, as he concentrates on planning what he is going to say.[5] When he approaches the end of his utterance he is approaching what might be called a choice-point in the interaction sequence. This is a point at which subsequent action he might take will depend largely upon how his interlocutor is behaving. We expect, thus, that $p$ will seek information about his interlocutor at such points and, therefore, that he will look at him, as indeed we have found.

From another point of view it should be observed that insofar as looking away at the beginning of an utterance, and looking back as it ends, are regular occurrences, these changes in direction of gaze can come to function as signals to $p$'s interlocutor, marking points of significant change in his stream of behavior, and, further, may be exploited by $p$ to regulate $q$'s behavior. Thus, in looking away as he begins an utterance, or before he begins it, in many cases, $p$ may be seen by $q$ to be about to be engaged in an action, and $p$ may indeed look away to forestall any response from $q$. Similarly, in looking up as he ends an utterance $q$ can perceive that $p$ is not ceasing to talk yet still giving him his attention,[6] and in giving his attention in this way, $q$ can perceive that $p$ now expects some response from him. From $p$'s point of view then, $p$ may be said to be "offering" $q$ the floor, for in looking steadily at him he indicates that he is now "open" to his actions, whatever they may be.

In an attempt to corroborate the last part of this interpretation, namely that looking up at the ends of long utterances functions for $q$ as a signal that $p$ is ready for a response from him, we examined the latency with which $q$'s utterances followed those of $p$'s where $p$ did not look up as he ended his utterance. If the interpretation is correct we should expect that in these cases, where $p$ does not look up, $q$'s latencies should

[5]  We imply here that paying attention to one's interlocutor and planning what to say are incompatible activities. Analyses of the relationship between sensory input and motor action in serial tasks such as tracking, and studies of selective listening to speech, support the hypothesis that the human being is to be regarded as capable of dealing with only limited amounts of information at once, and this imposes upon him the necessity of distributing his attention among the several facets of the situation where his activity depends upon processing large amounts of information from several sources simultaneously. This is likely to be the case in social interaction. See the discussion in Broadbent (1958) and Welford (1960).

[6]  We make the assumption here that to perceive the direction of an individual's attention we rely largely upon the direction in which he is looking. Wardwell(1960) has partly confirmed this assumption though she shows that direction of gaze taken alone is not sufficient. See also the discussion in Heider (1958) and Goffman (1963).

Table 4. *A comparison between* q'*s responses to* p, *when* q *ends his utterances looking, and when he ends them without looking at* q. *Data from two conversations only, including all utterances*

|  | q fails to respond or pauses before responding | q responds without a pause | Total |
|---|---|---|---|
| p ends utterance |  |  |  |
| looking | 10 | 24 | 34 |
| not looking | 29 | 12 | 41 |

be greater than where he does do this. Table 4 presents a comparison of $q$'s responses following utterances ended with a $q$-gaze with those following utterances ended with an $a$-gaze. These results are taken from two conversations (these were the only two in which a sufficient number of the two kinds of utterance endings occurred to enable a proper comparison to be made). It will be seen that of those utterances which ended with an extended look, 29% were followed by either no response or by a delayed response from $q$; but of those that ended without $p$ looking up, 71% were followed by either a delayed response or by no response ($x^2 = 13.38$, $df\,1$, $p > .001$).

*(ii)   Gaze direction during long utterances.* We have seen that $p$ tends to look at $q$ more while he is listening than while he is speaking, and we have seen too that his $q$-glances during speech tend to be shorter than those observed during listening. It is of some interest to inquire whether there is any association between the structure of $p$'s speech and where he is looking as he produces it. From the work of Goldman-Eisler (1958), and of Maclay and Osgood (1959), we know something of the significance in changes in rate of speech, and of the occurrence of hesitations and fluent passages. Should a consistent association emerge between direction of gaze and these structural aspects of the utterance, this may add to our understanding of the role of visual information in the regulation of utterance production.

(a) *Speed of speech and direction of gaze.* Earlier it was suggested that $p$ looked away at the beginning of an extended utterance because such an utterance would require planning, and that $p$ would not be able both to plan what he had to say and monitor $q$'s behavior simultaneously. As

Goldman-Eisler (1954) has shown, although the actual rate of articulation remains remarkably constant and highly characteristic for a given individual, there are large variations in overall speech rate and these are a function of the amount of hesitation that occurs in the utterance. She has further shown (Goldman-Eisler 1958) that hesitations tend to precede novel combinations of words, and that they are also more common during speech expressing abstractive and interpretive thought, than during speech in which $p$ is merely describing something (Goldman-Eisler 1961). This leads her to the suggestion that hesitations occur when there is a lag between the organizational processes by which speech is produced, and actual verbal output. Thus periods of fluent speech correspond to the running off of well-organized phrases, or of phrases that are pre-learned (as, for example, in conventionalized phrases or repeated phrases that form part of an individual's habit of speech), whereas unfluent speech corresponds to the interruption of the processes of speech production by organizing processes (Goldman-Eisler 1958). If the suggestion made earlier is correct, we should expect that $p$ will be less likely to look at $q$ during those periods when he is engaged in organizing his speech, that is, during periods of hesitant speech, than he will when he is speaking fluently, running off a well-organized phrase. We have, therefore, compared the rate of speech production (measured as the number of syllables per half-second) during those portions of the utterance when he is not looking at him. The results are presented in Table 5. The speech rates have been computed for ninety-two different speech stretches taken from eight different individuals. It will be seen first that for all individuals the speech rate is higher during looking than it is during not looking. Second, that for all individuals more than half of the speech stretches examined, and for all of them together, three-quarters of the speech stretches display faster speaking during looking than during not looking.

It should be noted that this analysis is confined to long utterances, in which only stretches of continuous speech have been considered. Where, as is often the case, a long utterance consists of two or three units of speech separated by a clear phrase boundary pause, these have been treated separately.

(b) *Fluent speech, hesitant speech and pausing, and direction of gaze.* For the purposes of the present analysis the utterance has been considered to consist of a series of phrases (identifiable as complete grammatical units), each phrase separated from the one that follows it by a

Table 5. *Speech rates and direction of gaze**

| Subject | Mean speech rate while looking in syllables per half-second | Mean speech rate while not looking in syllables per half-second | Number of stretches of continuous speech where speech rate was faster while looking than while not looking | Number of stretches of continuous speech where speech rate was slower while looking than while not looking |
|---|---|---|---|---|
| RB | 2.4 | 2.1 | 8 | 2 |
| JS | 2.6 | 2.0 | 3 | 1 |
| JH | 2.3 | 1.7 | 14 | 4 |
| NL | 2.3 | 1.9 | 16 | 10 |
| SJ | 3.0 | 2.3 | 9 | 4 |
| W | 2.4 | 2.0 | 4 | 0 |
| JS | 2.7 | 2.2 | 5 | 2 |
| WJ | 2.8 | 2.4 | 8 | 1 |
| Overall mean | 2.5 | 2.03 | 67 (72.8%) | 24 (26.2%) |

*The dyads TG/VM, KA/TRW and KA/T have been omitted because they did not offer a sufficient number of long stretches of continuous speech for comparison.

short pause, the phrase boundary pause. Within these phrases there are likely to be variations in the fluency with which words are produced. There may be actual breaks in word production (unfilled hesitations), or the break in word production may be filled by a "hesitation noise" ("um" or "uh," for example), $p$ may break off in mid phrase and repeat what he has just said, or he may retrace his steps, as it were, and correct the phrase he has just produced. These varieties of hesitation have been distinguished by Maclay and Osgood (1959), but for present purposes they have been considered together as "hesitant speech." Besides this, "fluent speech," "phrase ending," "phrase pausing," and "phrase beginning" have been distinguished. For each half-second of every long utterance, whether $p$ was looking at $q$ or whether he was not has been noted against the structure of the utterance prevailing at the time. The results are presented in Table 6.

This shows, first, that $p$ tends to look at $q$ during fluent speech much

Table 6. *Direction of gaze and its association with certain aspects of the structure of long utterances*

| | RB | JS | W | SJ | JS | WJ | JH | NL | Total |
|---|---|---|---|---|---|---|---|---|---|
| Total amount of fluent speech | 227 | 63 | 119 | 203 | 185 | 175 | 547 | 591 | 2112 |
| Amount of fluent speech with $q$-gaze | 117 | 17 | 27 | 40 | 97 | 118 | 345 | 294 | 1055 |
| Proportion of fluent speech with $q$-gaze (%) | 51.5 | 26.9 | 22.7 | 19.7 | 52.4 | 67.4 | 62.8 | 49.7 | 50 |
| Total amount of hesitant speech | 74 | 18 | 31 | 123 | 100 | 35 | 82 | 149 | 612 |
| Amount of hesitant speech with $q$-gaze | 21 | 4 | 8 | 13 | 22 | 8 | 13 | 35 | 124 |
| Proportion of hesitant speech with $q$-gaze (%) | 28.4 | 22.2 | 25.8 | 10.6 | 22 | 22.9 | 15.9 | 23.5 | 20.3 |
| Number of phrase endings | 34 | 3 | 19 | 25 | 14 | 25 | 62 | 70 | 252 |
| Number of phrase endings with $q$-gaze | 18 | 0 | 5 | 8 | 9 | 23 | 47 | 50 | 150 |
| Proportion of phrase endings with $q$-gaze (%) | 52.9 | 0 | 26.3 | 32 | 64.3 | 92 | 75.8 | 71.4 | 63.5 |
| Amount of phrase pausing | 29 | 3 | 14 | 36 | 15 | 28 | 51 | 50 | 226 |
| Amount of phrase pausing with $q$-gaze | 9 | 0 | 6 | 11 | 5 | 18 | 29 | 26 | 104 |
| Proportion of phrase pausings with $q$-gaze (%) | 31.0 | 0 | 42.9 | 30.6 | 33 | 64.2 | 56.9 | 52 | 46.0 |
| Number of phrase beginnings | 20 | 2 | 11 | 20 | 9 | 21 | 40 | 53 | 176 |
| Number of phrase beginnings with $q$-gaze | 7 | 0 | 1 | 1 | 5 | 12 | 12 | 15 | 53 |
| Proportion of phrase beginnings with $q$-gaze (%) | 35.0 | 0 | 9 | 5 | 55.6 | 57.1 | 30 | 28.3 | 30.1 |

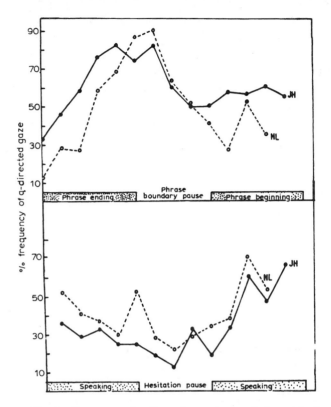

Fig. 3   Frequency of $q$-directed gazes in association with phrase boundary pauses (upper figure) and within phrase hesitations (lower figure). Total sample: forty-eight phrase boundary pauses and forty-three hesitation pauses.

more than he does during hesitant speech (50% of the time spent speaking fluently, as compared to only 20.3% of the time spent speaking hesitantly). This finding, of course, coincides with the one reported in the previous section, insofar as fluent speech tends to be fast compared to hesitant speech. Secondly, the table shows that $p$ is more likely to be looking at $q$ at the moment that he ends a phrase than he is when he resumes speaking after the phrase boundary pause.

What appears to be a typical pattern of gaze-direction change in association with the occurrence of phrase boundary pausing, as compared to hesitation, may be seen clearly from the diagram in Fig. 3, where a plot is presented of the percent frequency with which $p$ was found to be looking at $q$ at each successive half-second preceding, during and following a phrase boundary pause (upper graph), and a hesitation (lower graph), for two individuals, based upon 16 minutes of conversation. It will be seen that this figure illustrates graphically what the figures in Table 6 also show, namely that phrase boundary pauses and hesitation pauses differ sharply in how $p$ distributes his gaze when they occur. In the former, $p$ looks at $q$ as he comes to the end of the phrase, he continues to look during the phrase (though the longer the pause lasts the less likely he is to be looking) and then, as the next phrase begins, the tendency is for $p$ to look away again. Hesitations, in contrast, are marked by a decline in the extent to which $p$ looks at $q$ and, unlike the phrase boundary pause, $p$ tends to look back at $q$ as he begins speaking fluently again. The hesitations once over, $p$ has worked out a phrase to express what he wants to say, and he can run it off, watching $q$'s response to it as he does so.

Phrases, in the sense in which they are referred to here, comprise the minimally meaningful units of an utterance, they are grammatically complete, and it might be said that they constitute the packages in which the speaker ties up what he has to say, and evidence from memory span experiments, in which subjects were asked to repeat as much as possible from a passage of speech they had just heard, suggests that this packaging of information assists the listener in his assimilation of the material (Moyra Williams, personal communication). The gaze that is associated with, as it were, the delivery of each phrase, can be seen to have both a checking function for the speaker, in that it is at these points that he is free to check upon how what he is saying is being received by the listener, and it may also have a signalling function for the listener, insofar as it marks the boundary of these information packages. It also, we may suppose, marks the points at which $p$ is looking for an accompaniment response from $q$.

Evidence that the speaker does indeed get some response at these points in his utterance is provided by an analysis of the distribution of accompaniment signals in relation to certain aspects of the speaker's utterance structure. In Table 7 we have recorded, for each occurrence of an accompaniment signal, what the speaker was doing at the time of the signal. It will be seen that the highest proportion of them (48%) occur during the phrase boundary pause, and that extremely few occur at the point at which speech is resumed after such a pause. Compared with the number that would be expected to occur, if accompaniment signals

Table 7. *Distribution of accompaniment signals in relation to certain aspects of the structure of the speaker's speech*

| | Number of accompaniment signals that occurred during | | | | |
|---|---|---|---|---|---|
| | Fluent speech | Hesitant speech | Phrase ending | Phrase pausing | Speech resumption |
| | 2 | 1 | 1 | 6 | 0 |
| | 2 | 4 | 8 | 2 | 0 |
| | 2 | 1 | 1 | 5 | 0 |
| | 8 | 9 | 0 | 14 | 1 |
| | 1 | 1 | 0 | 1 | 1 |
| | 0 | 1 | 0 | 7 | 0 |
| | 6 | 2 | 1 | 12 | 0 |
| | 2 | 4 | 3 | 15 | 2 |
| Observed totals | 23 | 23 | 14 | 62 | 4 |
| Expected totals* | 90 | 26 | 10.8 | 9.7 | 7.6 |

*Calculated on the assumption that they occur at equal time intervals during the speaker's speech without regard to the structure of the speech.

were produced without any relation to the structure of the speaker's speech, it will be seen that far fewer than would be expected occur during fluent speech, and far more of them occur during phrase boundary pauses.

We may now see something of the part that gaze direction plays for the interactants in regulating each other's behavior. In withdrawing his gaze, p is able to concentrate on the organization of the utterance and at the same time, by looking away, he signals his intention to continue to hold the floor, and thereby forestall any attempt at action from his interlocutor. In looking up, which we have seen that he does briefly at phrase endings, and for a longer time at the ends of his utterances, he can at once check on how his interlocutor is responding to what he is saying, and signal to him that he is looking for some response from him. And for his interlocutor, these intermittent glances serve as signals to him, as to when p wants a response from him.

*(iii) Gaze direction in relation to the occurrence of short utterances.*
Long utterances, as we have said, are those utterances which, for their effective production, demand that the speaker "holds the floor" for their duration, and that the listener listens. Such utterances, which last

for at least five seconds, and usually for much more than this, involve some degree of planning and organization, and they cannot be responded to properly until they are completed. Short utterances, in contrast, which include accompaniment signals, attempted interruptions, exclamations and short questions, and short answers to questions, have in common that they are simple in their content and that they do not in themselves involve the speaker's claim to the floor, though they may be either a request for the floor, or they may be an advance indication of the speaker's intention to take the floor. For the purposes of the following discussion, we have considered short utterances as falling into the groups mentioned above.

(a) *Accompaniment signals.* These are the short utterances that the listener produces as an accompaniment to a speaker, when the speaker is speaking at length. There is some evidence to suggest that the speaker does rely upon them for guidance as to how what he is saying is being received by his listener,[7] but very little has been done in the way of classifying the wide variety of forms which accompaniment signals take, or in examining possible differences in their functions. Birdwhistell (1962) reports an investigation of headnods, which are usually coincident with vocalized accompaniment signals, in which he distinguishes between the single, double, and triple headnod, and describes how each of these different sorts of headnods have different consequences for the way the speaker organizes his performance. For example, where the single headnod occurs in rapid succession during the course of a phrase within the speaker's utterance, the speaker may slow up and hesitate. Where it occurs in association with the points of stress in his speech, he will continue. From examples such as these, it is clear that the auditor can exert a fairly detailed control over the speaker's behavior by the kind of headnods he produces, and how he places them in relation to certain aspects of the structure of his interlocutor's speech. The same is no doubt equally true of verbalized accompaniment signals. Fries (1952) has noted a large number of variants of this form of utterance, though he does not attempt any analysis of the differences in their functions (he even implies that there are no such differences). Here we shall follow a tentative classification, based upon an analysis of where in relation to the speaker's behavior the auditor places his attention signals, in which

---

[7] See the work on "operant verbal conditioning." Greenspoon (1962) provides a comprehensive review.

we suggest two main classes of accompaniment signal. These are: the attention signal proper in which *p* appears to do no more than signal to *q* that he is attending, and following what is being said, and what we shall refer to as the "point granting" or "assenting" signal. This most often takes the lexical form of "yes quite" or "surely" or "I see" and it occurs when the speaker is developing an argument by presenting a series of points for which he asks the auditor's agreement. Two examples may help to clarify this distinction:

*Example I*
SJ  It seems a pity that say someone like that and say someone like
    Morrison who is performing the same sort of function
              *mhm*
    um livening the place    up a bit it's a pity they're almost lost
    *mhm*
    to um active politics you know they can air their views and
                                                          *yes*
    that sort of thing but their power is so limited that        it seems a great
    pity somehow.                                                     *mhm*

In this example, taken from a conversation in which the subjects were discussing the functions of the House of Lords, SJ is merely stating his opinions, and his interlocutor's accompaniment signals, which coincide approximately with the ending of each of SJ's points or statements, do no more than indicate that he is still "with" SJ. These accompaniment signals are examples of the attention signal proper, and they are to be contrasted with "point granting" or "agreement" signals, such as occur in the following passage:

*Example II*
JS  Well they're put up as absolute dictators aren't they?
                                              *mm yes*
    I mean in electing a Prime Minister we say: we make you responsible for
    what happens to our country        and therefore indirectly for what
                          *that's true*
    happens to us.

Here JS begins his utterance with a rhetorical question, and he then follows this up with a restatement of the argument, which he structures in such a way that his continuing is dependent upon his interlocutor consenting to, or specifically granting him, the points that he is making.

The distinction in terms of their place in relation to the other's discourse seems clear enough. In Table 8 it will be apparent that the distinc-

Table 8. *Short utterances and gaze direction*

| Type of utterance | Number associated with $q$-gaze | Number associated with $a$-gaze | Sign test (two-tailed) |
|---|---|---|---|
| Accompaniment signals | | | |
| (a) Attention signals | 37 | 16 | |
| (b) Assenting signals | 2 | 25 | $p<.002$ |
| Short questions | 31 | 10 | $p<.0005$ |
| Laughter | 18 | 8 | $p<.04$ |
| Exclamatory utterances | | | |
| Positive exclamations (surprise, delight, joy, increased interest) | 10 | 3 | |
| Negative exclamations (horror, disgust, sadness, disagreement, embarrassment) | 1 | 5 | |

tion in terms of gaze-direction is also quite clear. In almost every case, when $p$ produces an attention signal, he continues to look steadily at $q$. When he produces an "agreement" signal, he looks away. This looking away is typically very brief, usually as short as the utterance itself, and is usually accomplished by merely dropping the eyelids over the eyes, together with a single, or sometimes a double headnod of a rather restricted amplitude.

It should perhaps be noted that within the two main classes of this kind of utterance we have distinguished, there are many further variants which we have not attempted to sort out. For example, in giving the attention signal, $p$ may at the same time hint that he is bored or amused, that he is impatient, that he has not been paying full attention, and so on. These different attitudes may be conveyed by variations in the stress and intonation patterns within the utterance, variations in the relative lengthening or shortening of the syllables, and by variations in the way in which he places his utterances in relation to what the other is saying. What typical kinesic and gaze-direction patterns there are that are associated with such variants is a matter for future investigation. We at present are confident only in the main differences already described.

(b) *Exclamations and laughter.* By exclamations we mean utter-ances, whether requested by the speaker or not, that the auditor pro-duces as a direct emotive response to what the speaker is saying or doing. They may be immediately identified by clear deviations from the speaker's speech baseline. Though many exclamations have a lexical character peculiar to them (e.g. "gosh," "oh golly," "heavens" and so forth) they may also take the lexical character of an attention signal, yet are to be identified as exclamations rather than as attention signals through the overlengthening of syllables, overhigh or overlow pitch levels, and various unusual voicings, such as "squeeze" or whispering.[8] Kinesically, exclamations may readily be distinguished from other accompaniment signals in that they are always associated with relatively marked and prolonged changes in head position, and by a clear change in facial expression.

Associated gaze direction patterns are given in Table 8. It will be seen that during laughter $p$ is more often looking at $q$ than not. Where he is looking during an exclamation depends upon the kind of feeling being expressed. Where this is one of surprise, delight, increased interest, the exclamation is usually accompanied by a $q$-gaze. Where the feelings expressed are of horror, disgust, protestation at something the other has said, $p$ is more likely to turn his gaze away. The difference, thus, would appear to be between feelings involving attention and approach, as compared to those involving rejection and withdrawal. There is one class of exclamations, however, which does not appear to fit this scheme. This is where $p$, the listener, gives expression to a feeling $q$ is also expressing or talking about. For example, NL was describing "lovely old treasures" dug up in the Sutton Hoo Ship Burial, and as he does so, JH emits a prolonged "mmm" thereby showing that she is sharing his fascination with the treasures. These sharing exclamations, of which there are only a few examples in our material, are accompanied by $a$-gaze (usually due to closing of the eyes, rather than a turning away of the gaze). Perhaps here, in expressing his affective unity with $q$, $q$ drops his gaze because at this moment he has no further need to monitor $q$'s behavior: he is sufficiently "in tune" with him to give expression to the prevailing emotion, without having to check that he has it correctly.

(c) *Attempted interruptions.* These were rather rare in the material examined, and no clear pattern can be described for them. However, some distinction can be drawn between interruptions which arise when

---

[8]  See Pittinger, Hockett and Danehy (1960) for a description of these and other paralinguistic features of English.

$p$ misinterprets how $q$ is going to behave, and those interruptions which
arise when $p$ tries to "cut in" on $q$'s talking time. In the latter cases, a
small battle for the time available may arise and here $p$ and $q$ stare fully
at one another as long as the battle lasts.

(d) *Short questions.* These usually are "direct" in the sense that $p$ is
asking $q$ for some quite specific response to his question. Whether $p$
expects his response to be long or short, however, may depend in part
upon the context in which the question is asked, and also upon the way
it is asked, in particular as reflected in the particular stress and intonation patterning adopted. In either case, whether $p$ expects a short
answer to his question (as when he needs some specific information
before he can proceed) or whether he expects a long answer (as where
he uses the question as a means of handing the speaker role over to his
interlocutor), $p$ will look steadily at $q$ while he asks his question, and
where $p$ is asking a series of questions, unless he has to pause in thinking
of the question, or unless he has to pause in formulating it. In Table 8
where the gaze direction associated with questions is given, it will be
seen that there are a number in which $p$ does not look at $q$ as he asks his
question. In a few cases, such questions are asked hesitantly, and as we
have seen, $p$ tends to look away during hesitant speech. In certain other
cases it seems that the $a$-gaze is associated with questions which are
either presumptive, or with questions which broach a subject about
which $p$ has considerable anxiety. In these instances we may be observing cases of $a$-gaze in which $p$, by looking away, is effectively cutting
down his level of emotionality, either by cutting down the intensity of
the direct relationship he has with $q$, or by reducing information intake
from $q$, which would be arousing for him.

## Mutual gaze and emotional arousal

The phenomenon of the mutual gaze has aroused the interest of a number of writers. It has been noted by several authors (Sartre 1956, Heider
1958) that when we observe that another person is looking at us, we are
aware that he is giving us his attention. To be subjected to the continual
gaze of another is a very unnerving experience, for to be the object of
another's attention is to be vulnerable to him. The watcher can anticipate our actions, and this is to be in danger before him. If, however, we
look back at the person who watches us, we thereby indicate to him that
he is as much an object of our attention as we are of his: though the

watcher has the advantage over the watched, if the watched can also watch the watcher, the two become equal to one another. To look into another's line of regard, then, is to meet his intentions "head on," it is to enter a direct relationship with him. In the introduction, we referred to Goffman's (1963) discussion of the role of the mutual gaze in establishing this direct link. We have suggested that when $p$ looks at the end of his utterances, or at the ends of his phrases within an utterance, he is checking on his listener's responses, in particular he may be looking to see if $q$ is still attending to him. By looking at $q$, as we suggested, he also signals to him that he is giving him his attention, and thus if, in looking at $q$, $p$ sees that $q$ is looking at him, he sees that he is being "received." The mutual gaze, momentarily held, at least, would thus appear to be an integral part of the set of signals that people are on the look out for in interaction as indicators that each is still taking account of the other. But the mutual gaze, especially in certain situations, appears to signify more than this. For where it is extended in time, or where one or other participant tries to extend it, he indicates that his attention has shifted away from the common focus which both share in the encounter, and that his attention is specifically directed to the other person. And extended mutual gazes appear to be indicative of an intensifying of the direct relations between the participants. Recent work by Exline has shown how the amount of mutual gaze a person will engage in varies with a number of factors, but principally it appears to increase where $p$ is drawn to the person he is interacting with, either in an affiliative way (Exline 1963, Exline, Gray and Schuette 1965, Exline and Winters 1965) or where he is in competition with the other (Exline 1963). Exline's findings are consistent with the idea that the amount of mutual gaze in an encounter will increase in proportion to the degree to which $p$ and $q$ are directly relating to one another, and that the amount of mutual gaze will decline in direct proportion as the individuals want to avoid or withdraw from this relationship.

In this section we shall offer some observations, derived from only one of the conversations, which suggest that the amount of mutual looking conversants will engage in can serve to regulate the level of shared emotional arousal within it. We have, in this analysis, confined ourselves to the conversation for which sixteen minutes of film were available. In this conversation there was a considerable variation in the level of emotional arousal. Furthermore the two protagonists seemed quite drawn to one another and became well involved in the conversation, in

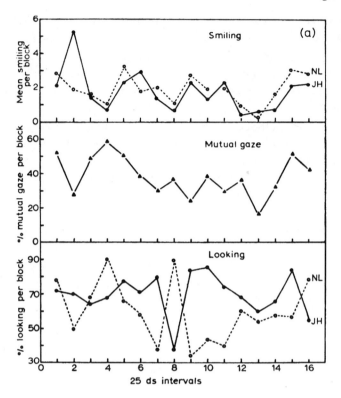

Fig. 4    Mean level of smiling, proportion of time spent in mutual gaze, and proportion of time spent by $p$ in looking at $q$, for successive 25-second intervals. First sample from the first seven minutes of a conversation

a way that did not happen in most of the others. The relationships we shall report were not found to occur with the same clarity in the other samples examined. However, not only were these other samples quite short in comparison, but the range and intensity of emotional involvement was very much less. Thus, while the lack of results from these other samples does not give support to the conclusions we shall suggest, they cannot be said to count against them, either.

As an indicator of level of emotionality, we have taken the intensity of smiling. In the notation developed for the transcription of the films (see Ex and Kendon 1964), the intensity of the smile was scaled on a nine-point scale which, for present purposes, was reduced to a three-point scale of Slight Smile, Definite Smile and Extreme Smile or Laughter. We chose smiling as our index of emotionality because this

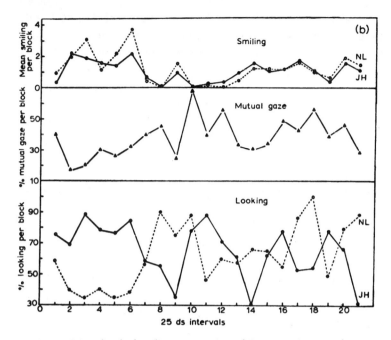

Fig. 5    Mean level of smiling, proportion of time spent in mutual gaze, and proportion of time spent by *p* in looking at *q*, for successive 25-second intervals. Second sample taken twenty minutes later

was the commonest form of emotional expression that occurred, and the variation in emotional expression was, for the most part, in terms of Schlosberg's emotion oval (Woodworth and Schlosberg 1954), from the centre to the periphery, almost wholly within the upper left, or "happy, surprise, delight" quadrant.

The sample was divided into blocks, each approximately fifty half-seconds in length, so arranged that no stretch of mutual gaze was divided. For each block the proportion of time occupied by mutual gaze, the proportion of time in each block that each *p* spent looking at *q*, and the mean intensity of smiling per half-second for each *p* was computed. The results are plotted in Figs. 4 and 5 giving the findings for the first and second samples from the conversation, respectively.

It is to be noted, first of all, that smiling, in each partner, is closely related to smiling in the other. Smiling is a symmetrically reciprocated emotional response, and thus the two participants may be said to be emotionally aroused to roughly the same degree at much the same time.

It will be seen, secondly, that the more smiling there is, the less the amount of time spent in mutual gaze. This relationship appears most strongly in the second sample, but it is present in the first for all except the last 165 half-seconds of the sample. An examination of the inter-relations between the amount of time $p$ and $q$ spend looking at the other and the amount of smiling that each is displaying throws some light on how this inverse relationship comes about. Thus, it will be seen that in both samples, NL's percent looking varies inversely with percent mutual gaze much more closely than does JH's percent looking. In other words, how much mutual gaze there is appears to depend far more upon how much time NL spends looking at JH, than it does upon how much time JH spends looking at NL. Secondly, it will be seen that in both samples, the relationship between the amount $p$ smiles and the amount $p$ looks is much more strongly inverse for NL than it is for JH. Thirdly, whereas JH may or may not be looking at NL when NL is smiling, NL is consistent from the first to the second sample in the inverse relation-ship between looking at JH when JH is smiling. In other words, since NL's looking is affected both by how much JH spends looking and by how much she smiles, it would seem that it is chiefly NL who looks away when the intensity of smiling arises.

In looking away when JH smiles, NL may perhaps be said to be "cut-ting off," that is, he thereby reduces the emotionally arousing input pro-vided by JH, and thereby reduces his own arousal. This interpretation is analogous to the one put forward by Chance (1962) for the gaze-averting postures observed in agonistic encounters between rats and gulls. Chance has pointed out that one of the essential elements in the defensive posture of a fighting rat is that it ensures that it cannot see its opponent. This means that not only is it not receiving input by which its aggressive behavior may be guided, but also the reduced input will lower the rat's general arousal level which, for the rat in this context, has the consequence that its behavior can become more flexible, and it can resume aggressive action. This means that the rat can stay longer in a fight than it otherwise might, which has an obvious biological advan-tage. It is suggested in the present context that for any given encounter there is a definite limit to the level of emotionality that is acceptable (cf. Goffman 1957, 1961), and if this limit is to be observed, there must be some device whereby the excitement can be lowered at those moments where it threatens to rise too high. The aversion of gaze, which results in a breaking of the mutual gaze, may be one device whereby this regulation may be achieved.

In the conversation here analyzed, where there is evidence that the participants, who were of the opposite sex, were attracted to one another, it is likely that anything that indicated an increase in friendliness would be liable to give rise to a good deal of arousal, and it is at these points that we would expect an aversion of the gaze. From the data presented, it would seem that this does indeed happen. It appears to be NL who averts his gaze at an earlier point on the rising curve of emotionality than JH. This aversion of the gaze will have the effect, not only of lowering the arousal of the person who looks away, it may also lead to the lowering of the other person's arousal level. This is because it both reduces the amount of mutual gaze for him, and it may also signal to him that his interlocutor is overaroused, that the conversation is getting onto dangerous ground, and $q$ may, as a result, change his tactics.

## Discussion

In the foregoing, data have been presented which show that direction of gaze changes in a regular fashion associated with other things that people in interaction are doing, notably in association with utterances, certain aspects of their structure, and to some extent with their content.[9] We have offered interpretations of some of these regularities as we have demonstrated them. Here these interpretations will be summarized, and an attempt will be made to set them within the context of other studies.

Broadly speaking, an individual's perceptual activity in social interaction can be regarded as functioning for him in two main ways. On the one hand, in looking or not looking at $q$, $p$ can control the degree to which he monitors $q$'s behavior. We may therefore speak of the *monitoring functions* of gaze direction. On the other hand, in looking or not looking at $q$, $p$ can seek to control the behavior of $q$, insofar as direction of gaze has a *regulatory* and *expressive function*.

These two kinds of function will now be discussed separately, and some remarks will then be added on the functions of the mutual gaze.

---

[9] This aspect of the investigation needs much further development.

*Monitoring functions of gaze-direction*

In looking at $q$, $p$ can gather information about how he is behaving. He can check on where $q$ is looking, how his face looks, and on his bodily posture. He may observe, for example, whether or not the anticipatory changes that presage a "floor take-over" have occurred. We have not, in this study, done more than compare "looking at" with "looking away," and we have not been able to explore what of the other person $p$ sees, or is on the look out for, when he looks at him. The presumption has been that when $p$ "looks" at $q$, he looks at him in such a way that, were $q$ to "look" at him, their eyes would meet. But this is only a presumption, and it might be very informative to investigate exactly where $p$ does look when he "looks at" $q$.

In the data presented we have seen how $p$ appears to "place" his $q$-gazes at those points in his discourse where he may well be expected to be looking for a response from his interlocutor, by which his subsequent behavior may be guided. Thus, towards the ends of long utterances, $q$-gazes are found more often than at the beginning of such utterances (a finding also reported by Nielsen 1964), and it is presumably at the ends of long utterances that $p$ will look for guidance, in $q$'s response to him, for what to do next. Similarly, at the ends of phrases, within a long utterance, $p$ is found to look up, and at these points he may be said to be checking to see that $q$ is still attending. Consonant with this interpretation, that $p$ looks at points of uncertainty in his discourse, is the finding that $p$ looks at $q$ when he asks him a question, and during those interruptions in which he is "battling" for the floor with $q$. Here, in both cases, $p$'s subsequent actions will be highly dependent upon what $q$ does.

It is probable that a number of different monitoring functions should be distinguished for perceptual activity in social interaction. Crossman (1956), analyzing perceptual activity associated with repetitive manual tasks, such as cigar manufacture, distinguished three main perceptual elements: "plan," in which $p$ selects from a number of alternatives a course of action, for example in selecting a tool for the job, estimating the amount of material needed for it. The second element he called "current control." Here $p$ is concerned with error feedback, and it is through this that the action, once begun, is kept in line with its aims. Thirdly, Crossman distinguishes "check," in which $p$ looks to see that his action has achieved the aims set for it. Similarly, it may be that a number of different perceptual elements should be distinguished by which the actions in interaction are regulated. In looking away from $q$ at the outset of an utterance, we have suggested $p$ is planning. The glances that take place during the long utterance, perhaps are in the nature of "current control," and the prolonged gaze with which the utterance ends may be an example of "check."

We also reported that there appeared to be quite large differences between individuals in the amount that they looked at their interlocutor, both when this was measured in terms of proportion of time spent looking, and in terms of the average length of time spent looking, and the rate at which gaze direction changes. Similar marked differences between individuals have been reported by Nielsen (1964) and by Exline, who has also reported an association between amount of "need affiliation" and amount of looking. Such a finding suggests that these individual differences may be stable, although no investigation has definitely established this. If this is so, a number of interesting possibilities are raised. There is the possibility, for instance, that some people are more dependent upon visual information in interaction than others are, and that such people look more as a result. Exline (1963), in discussing the finding that women appear to spend more time looking than do men, refers to Witkin's (1949) finding that women are more "field dependent" than men, and might thus be expected to spend more time scanning their interlocutor.

Another line of inquiry that suggests itself is the possibility that individual differences in looking styles are linked to individual differences in interaction styles, and that these differences may themselves be linked to individual differences in input sampling, such as have been discussed by Broadbent (1958). As Crossman, Cooke and Beishon (1964) point out, the act of perception functions to maintain what they describe as an "internal image, map or model of the environment, from which information can be abstracted to determine future action." In a changing environment, more or less frequent observations or "samples" are required to keep this internal model up to date. In the same paper, these authors go on to discuss some of the factors that determine the frequency of sampling in process control tasks. Among these are included the rate at which the internal image becomes uncertain, as well as a number of other factors having to do with the behavior of the system being controlled. Changes in the internal image may well in part be dependent upon or related to such differences between individuals characterized by "rigidity" or "persistence of set" (cf. Luchins 1959), such that people with highly persistent sets will sample less frequently than people with less persistent sets.[10] In the case of social interaction, $p$ has to act upon a number of assumptions about how $q$ will behave (Garfinkel 1963) which comprise for him his "image" of the situation, sometimes referred to as his definition of it (Goffman 1961). This definition will be set up by $p$ on the basis of information he has gathered about the situation, and in order to keep it in line with those of others present, and to keep his own performance in line, he has to check or sample the situation from time to time. Preliminary data, from a study to be reported at a later date, suggest that individuals who produce long utterances in a version of the Chapple Standard Interview (Chapple 1953) look at their interlocutor less frequently than individuals whose utterances are short. If it is presumed that, in this situation, in which the interviewer permits the subject to talk for as long as he is inclined to, the length of an individual's utterance is governed partly by his "image" of the situation (for instance, his notion of how long it seems to him to be appropriate to talk), then it might be expected that people who, in general, have persistent images and will thus be likely to sample relatively rarely will, in an encounter, tend to look infrequently, and talk at length. Investigation along these lines, linking "sampling styles" with "interaction styles" may throw light on some of the factors which contribute to produce individual differences in interaction styles (such as have been described by Chapple 1940b), and at the same time elucidate the part perception plays in governing the organization of the social performance.

*Regulatory and expressive function of gaze direction*

We have pointed out earlier how, insofar as the changes in gaze direction associated with utterances we have described are regular, they may function for $q$ as signals of $p$'s intentions and expectations, in particular in regard to the use of the available time for talking. Thus, in looking away a moment before $p$ begins a long utterance, $p$ effectively signals to $q$ that he is about to speak, and where $q$ has been looking to him for a response of this kind, it provides $q$ with an indication that his "offer of the floor" has been accepted. And likewise, in the sustained gaze with

[10] I am indebted to Mr. T. R. Watts for this suggestion.

which long utterances are so often ended, $p$ effectively indicates to $q$ that he is coming to an end, and that he expects some response from him. During the course of a long utterance, $p$'s glances at $q$ come at the points at which he receives an accompaniment signal from him, and so may function not only as checks on $q$'s behavior, but as signals to $q$ that $p$ wants confirmation that what he is saying is getting across. It will be seen that, insofar as gaze direction changes do have this signalling function for $q$, they may also be employed by $p$ to regulate the behavior of $q$ by not looking at him, or he can increase his demand for a response from him by looking at him.

Two other investigators have noted the possible regulatory function of gaze direction, besides Goffman (1963) whom we quoted in the introduction to this paper. Nielsen (1964) distinguishes "visual rhetoric" in which $p$ in "looking away during his own speaking [is] a way in which the subject indicated that he was still in the process of explaining himself and thus did not want to be interrupted . . . Looking at the alter towards the end of a remark indicated that the subject was through, as if saying 'That was what I wanted to say. Now what is your answer' " (p. 155). Likewise, Weisbrod (1965), in a study of the distribution of visual attention in a seven-person discussion group, found that the person whom the speaker last looked at before ending was more likely than other members of the group to speak next, and she concludes that looking can serve "to coordinate group action by controlling the succession of speeches" (p. 23).

Besides the "floor-apportionment" function of gaze direction, which may be seen as a specific example of what Scheflen (1963) has distinguished as "regulatory communication," we have also noted other functions of gaze direction, which may more appropriately be termed "expressive." In these cases, rather than directly regulating his relationship with $q$ through changes in gaze direction, $p$ gives expression to his feelings or attitudes. For example, in discussing the observations made on the relationship between mutual gaze and emotionality, we observed how NL tended to look away at points of high emotion. We discussed this in terms of the idea that this aversion of the eyes might function as a "cut-off" act, but it will also function as an indication to $q$ that $p$ is embarrassed, or over-aroused, and the aversion of the eyes may, thus, be incorporated into $p$'s expressive vocabulary. Indeed, that gaze direction changes are given something of the status of gestures, movements having a somewhat context-independent meaning (as shaking the fist is a gesture of anger), has been discussed by several writers (Ortega y Gasset 1957, Ogden 1961, Riemer 1955), though a detailed analysis of the use of the eyes in gesture is a task for the future. Other examples which we have noted include the sustained gaze associated with interruptions, short questions, and the rapidly spoken phrases by which $p$ sometimes prefaces a long utterance, and which appear to function as a "floor-claiming" device. Here $p$ intensifies the level of his attention to $q$, and in this way "bears down upon him." On the other hand, we noted the aversion of the eyes, often accomplished by dropping the lids loosely over the eyes, that occur in association with "point-granting" signals, as if here $p$ is dropping his gaze to indicate that he is not going to challenge further what the other has just said.

Nielsen (1964) has also explicitly recognized the distinction we have drawn between regulation and expression in looking behavior, in that he distinguishes "visual rhetoric," discussed above, from "expressive behavior." Here, he says, "Looking away during listening indicated dissatisfaction with and qualifications of alter's speech. Looking away during speaking indicated uncertainty with statement or a modification of it. Looking at during listening indicated agreement or sheer attention. Looking at during speaking indicated interest in seeing the effect of the remark, and certainty" (p. 155).

## Mutual gaze and the significance of the Look

Our examination of fluctuations in the amount of eye-contact during the course of one conversation showed that it was inversely related to the amount of emotionality displayed by the participants (emotionality measured by the intensity of smiling). Further, it was found that the amount of mutual gaze depended upon how much only one of the participants was looking, and not upon how much the other was looking. We suggested that this participant, who looked away whenever the level of emotionality rose beyond a certain level, could be interpreted as engaging in a "cut off" act, which resulted in a reduction of the arousal of both participants, and that the level of emotionality in an encounter could be regulated by the amount of mutual gaze the participants permitted each other. This idea implies that there is something specifically arousing about the eye-contact itself. This has been recognized by many writers, as we have already noted, and it is closely connected with the phenomenon of the Look, perhaps best described by Sartre (1956), to whose account we have already referred.

There is good reason to believe that to perceive two eyes focused upon one acts as a "release" for specifically social action, though what sort of action this is depends, as we shall see, upon the circumstances in which this perception takes place. The probably instinctive basis for the response to the Look is testified to by three kinds of evidence. First of all, the work of Spitz and Wolf (1946), and of Ahrens (quoted in Ambrose 1961) on the minimal visual stimulus required to elicit a smiling response, arguably the first truly social response a human being makes, suggests that this is two eyes. Secondly, as Tomkins (1963) has pointed out, the belief in the power of the Look appears to be quite universal. Belief in the Evil Eye seems to be quite independent of historical or cultural circumstances, as does the use of large staring eyes in defensive magic. Thirdly, the power of the Look is not confined to human beings. Gibson and Pick (1963) refer to systematic observations on the way the behavior of laboratory Rhesus monkeys changes when they see a human pair of eyes looking at them. Wada (1961) has shown how, when a Rhesus monkey is looked at, a marked change in electrical activity is recorded in the brain-stem. Cott (1957) has noted the widespread use of eyes and conspicuous eye-like markings in threat displays, particularly among birds and insects; Hingston (1933) has described the role of eyes in the intimidation of prey by predatory mammals; and Cott has also described the extremely elaborate camouflage that serves to conceal the eye among many fish, mammals, birds and amphibia. It is as if the eye is "recognized" throughout the vertebrates as a feature which must be specifically taken into account. Argyle and Dean (1965) have argued that to look into the line of regard of another person who is looking at you is to achieve a specific sub-goal of social interaction in which one's "affiliative needs" are gratified, and they imply that this gratification accounts for the fundamental significance of eye-contact. However, although there are experiments which suggest that a person may show his preference for someone by seeking out his gaze more than he seeks out the gaze of another (Exline and Winters 1965), it is hard to see how the weight of evidence that suggests that to perceive another's look is to be threatened in some way, and that to look back at the other's look is to challenge the looker, can be explained by Argyle and Dean. Apart from the descriptive and anthropological evidence for the threatening function of the Look and the combative function of the mutual gaze, Exline has shown experimentally that in competitive interaction people low in "affiliative need" will seek more eye-contact than people high in "affiliative need," but that the reverse is the case in cooperative interaction (Exline 1963).[11] At the very least we must entertain two hypotheses, that on the one hand to engage in eye-contact with someone is to seek to affiliate with him, and on the other it is to challenge him.

However, the present writer agrees with Weisbrod (1965) that it is more economical to suppose that when one perceives that another is looking at one, one perceives that the other intends something by one, or expects something of one. In a word, one perceives that one is being taken account of by another. It seems reasonable to suppose that this will have quite marked arousing consequences, but what line of action it rouses one to take will depend upon the context in which the Look is perceived. This context is determined partly by the expression given the Look (whether the eyes are "staring," or "narrowed," how the eyebrows, mouth and eyelids are disposed, and so on), and partly by the kind of encounter it occurs in (whether in combat or in courtship).

In this view of eye-contact, it is easy to see why it will be sought for in interaction, since we can only be sure that we are being effective in what we do if we know that the other is taking account of it. To receive his gaze is to receive an indication that one is being taken account of. We should thus expect that $p$ will seek eye-contact with whomever he is interacting, regardless of the specific kind of response he seeks from him, and it will be rewarding to him not because through eye-contact any particular "need" is gratified, but because through eye-contact $p$ knows that he is affecting $q$ in some way and that he is, thereby, making progress in whatever he is attempting to do.

## Postscript

The study of gaze direction as a social phenomenon developed very rapidly after 1967. By 1976 Argyle and Cook (1976) were able to review upwards of 400 studies. Since then, many more have been published. Readers wishing to follow the development of this topic should refer to Harper, Wiens and Matarazzo (1978, Ch. 5), Exline and Fehr

---

[11] Moore and Gilliland (1921) and Gilliland (1926) have also used the degree to which a subject can sustain eye-contact with another person as a measure of his aggressiveness, with some success.

(1978, 1982), Rutter (1984), Webbink (1986) and Fehr and Exline (1987). As a perusal of these reviews will show, most of the work on gaze in interaction has concentrated upon measuring the amounts of looking one interactant addresses to another and how this is correlated with various psychological and situational variables. Studies that attempt to examine the patterning of gaze direction in relation to other aspects of behavior in interaction, with a view to giving an account of the role it may play in the interactive process, are much less frequently reported. The single most significant piece of work on gaze in interaction from this point of view, published since the paper reprinted here, is that of Goodwin (1981), although some of the work on the ethology of mother–infant interaction should not be overlooked in this connection (see, for example, Stern 1977, Schaffer, Collis and Parsons 1977, Collis 1977, Fogel 1977, Fraiberg 1979, Field 1982).

# 4

## Movement coordination in social interaction: some examples described

### Introduction

If we are to understand more fully the conditions in which effective and efficient social performance may occur, it will be important to examine in detail the behavior of listeners, and how this is related to the behavior of speakers. As a speaker, we are never indifferent to what the listener is doing. If he drums his fingers, if he frequently shifts in his chair, or looks about the room, or nods his head in an unusual pattern, he may convey the impression that he is bored, improperly attentive or inattentive, or that he is preoccupied. Sometimes this may throw us off balance to the extent that our flow of talk is brought to a stammering halt. More often, perhaps, we leave the encounter with a feeling of discomfort, with a feeling that there was no "rapport." However, we are usually unable to say what it is about our listener's behavior that gave us this feeling. Evidently we may be influenced by quite subtle features of his behavior.

There is a limited amount of work which illuminates some features of the effect of listeners upon speakers. Many studies, for example those reviewed by Greenspoon (1962), have shown that the vocal actions of a listener may "shape" aspects of the speaker's performance. A few studies have demonstrated the influence of such items as nodding, and smiling (Wickes 1956, Gross 1959, Matarazzo et al. 1964), and there is one study that shows that the posture of the listener, and the patterning of his facial displays, have an important influence upon how the speaker will respond to the listener's vocal actions (Reece and Whitman 1962). In all of these cases, however, the investigator has studied only those features of the listener's behavior he has determined on in advance. The

First published in *Acta Psychologica* 32 (1970), 100–25. Reprinted by permission of North-Holland Publishing Co., Amsterdam.

listener is always giving a controlled performance, where what he does and when he does it have been decided upon beforehand, as part of the experimental design. We know remarkably little, in a systematic way, about what it is that listeners ordinarily do, and how what they do is related to what speakers do. It is the aim of this paper to throw some light on this matter.

In this paper some detailed descriptions of the interrelations of the movements of speakers and listeners will be given. These descriptions will provide some further examples of the phenomenon of interactional synchrony, first described by Condon and Ogston (1966, 1967), in which it is found that the flow of movement in the listener may be rhythmically coordinated with the flow of speech in the speaker. We shall also show how the *way* in which individuals may be in synchrony with one another can vary, and that these variations are related to their respective roles in the interaction.

## Interactional synchrony

The findings presented by Condon and Ogston are derived from a very close study of sound film records of people in interaction. The film is examined by means of a time-motion analyzer, a projector in which the film can be moved back and forth by hand at any speed. Small sequences may be examined repeatedly, and then compared with immediate adjacent sequences. In analyzing movement, each body part is focused on separately, and a mark is made on a time chart at the point at which there is a minimally perceptible change in the direction of movement of the body part. Each division on the time chart corresponds to a frame on the film. With a film shot at the rate of twenty-four frames per second (the standard rate for sound film), measurements of time intervals are thus possible to the nearest twenty-fourth of a second. The result of such a plot is a flow chart showing the points at which changes in the direction of movement occur, in each body part examined. A phonetic segmentation of the speech sounds is then undertaken, and this is written in on the time chart so that the relationship between the speech and body motion may be examined.

If this procedure is followed for a stretch of behavior, it is found that the points of change in the movement for the separate body parts coincide. That is to say, the body parts change and sustain direction of movement together. This does not mean that all parts of the body are moving in the same way. As the arms are lowered, the head may turn to the right, the trunk may bow forward, the eyes shift left, the mouth open, the brows lift, the fingers flex, the feet flex from the ankles, and so on. It is further found that some body parts may sustain a given direction of movement over several changes in other body parts. What emerges from this analysis, thus, is a description of the flow of movement as a series of contrasting waves of movement, where within the larger waves, smaller waves may be contained.

Such a description will apply whenever the individual is in motion. When, in a speaker, the body motion co-occurring with his speech is examined, it is found that the points of change in the flow of sound coincide with the points of change in the body movement. But what is found here is that the larger movement waves fit over larger segments of speech, such as words or phrases, the smaller movement waves, contained within the larger, fit over the smaller segments, such as the syllables and the sub-syllabic changes. A fuller account of features of this organization of body motion in its relation to speech may be found in Kendon (1972).

When the behavior of the listener is examined in the same fashion, Condon and Ogston found that while the speaker is speaking and moving, the listener is moving as well. He may be sitting relatively still, not making any specifically gestural movements, but yet moving his hands or head, moving his eyes, or blinking. Where *interactional synchrony* is occurring it is found that the boundaries of the movement waves of the listener coincide with the boundaries of the movement waves in the speaker. For synchrony to occur, in this sense, it is only this coincidence of boundaries that must obtain. The listener may otherwise be moving in quite a different fashion, and he usually is.

Condon finds that, as a rule, speaker and listener are in synchrony up to the word level. That is, we observe changes in the listener's movement configurations that coincide with the boundaries of the speaker's movement changes at the phonic, syllabic and word levels of his speech. The larger waves of the listener's movement, however, do not necessarily coincide with the larger waves of the speaker's behavior, though they may do so on occasion. Thus, if speaker and listener are in synchrony, and the listener lifts a cigarette to his lips, draws on it, and lowers the cigarette again, the boundaries of the major components of this action will coincide with boundaries in the behavior flow of the speaker, but these boundaries will not necessarily also be boundaries of larger waves of behavior in the speaker, for instance the boundaries of his phrases, although they may be, as we will see later.

Condon and Ogston have described examples of interactional synchrony in a number of short examples of filmed interaction. However, they have not as yet dealt with the contexts in which this phenomenon may be observed, nor have they described the nature of the patterning of the listener's movements. In this paper we shall attempt to say something about the context of the examples to be described, and we shall also attempt to describe the patterns of movement in listeners who are directly addressed by a speaker as compared to those who, though yet members of the same encounter, are listening to an interchange they are not directly involved in. In this way we hope to be able to say something about the functions, for the interaction, of the various patterns of behavior that may be observed.

## Materials and method

The material from which most of the examples to be analyzed has been drawn is an eighty-minute 16 mm black-and-white sound film of a gathering in the private lounge of a middle-class London hotel.[1] The chairs were arranged in a rough circle in the room, and the camera, lighting and sound-recording equipment were set up to one side (see Fig. 6). Customers at the bar were encouraged to come in and sit down with their drinks. During some parts of the film, discussion was stimulated by the film maker. For much of the time, however, talk was exchanged in smaller groups around the room. Such an occasion is not, of course, typical of anything that normally occurs in a London pub. However, our interest is not in analyzing the character of the social occasion. Instead, the film has been used as a source for examples of those smaller events, such as the exchange of role of speaker, or the behavior of different listeners in relation to the speaker, which occur in all focused gatherings (Goffman 1963).

The method of analysis employed in this study was as follows: the film was looked at many times on a sound projector, running it at normal speed, and at a slower speed of 16 frames per second. Specific extracts were then selected that were both of good technical quality and that comprised some natural unit of interaction, for instance, a ques-

[1] See Birdwhistell and van Vlack (1961) in Film List on p. 263.

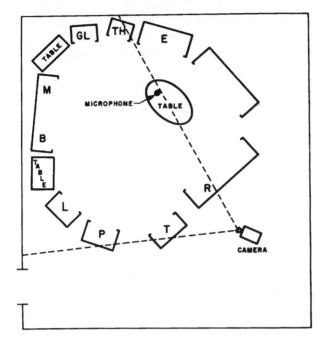

Fig. 6   Arrangement of furniture and positions of the participants (indicated by letters) in the T-extract. Area enclosed by dotted lines indicates the approximate field of view of the camera

tion-answer exchange. These extracts were studied in detail with a Bell and Howell time-motion analyzer. The movements of the body parts were plotted out on a chart on which the intervals represented the successive frames of the film. The movement of any body part was segmented in the same manner that has been described by Condon and Ogston. Divisions within a line representing a body part are made when there is a change in the direction of movement of the body part. The segments of the line thus divided are then labeled, using a set of terms modified from those proposed by the American College of Surgeons for describing the functions of the joints (Boyd and Banks 1965). In this way a kind of flow chart of the movement is laid out. The technique is, thus, to scan the film in small segments, with the aim of picking out those successive groups of frames over which a single direction of movement in a given body part is sustained.

In the present study we concentrated primarily upon the movements of the head, trunk, arms and hands. Facial changes, and details such as eye movements have, for the most part, had to be omitted, since the quality of the film did not permit their accurate transcription.

A magnetic tape recording made from the original soundtrack of the film was used to make the orthographic and phonetic transcript of the speech. The sound was then read from the film, using an optical sound reader, matched with a properly calibrated frame counter, and frame numbers could thus be placed against the phonetic transcript.

## Some examples analyzed

### Introduction

In this section a detailed analysis of a short extract from the pub film will be presented, with briefer references to a number of other extracts. The piece to be most thoroughly analyzed will be referred to as the T-extract. It comprises TRD 009.2.87591–88221.[2] This extract was selected because it comes from a section of the film in which the interactional structure of the gathering is much simpler than it is in other parts, and also the soundtrack is more intelligible here than elsewhere.

Of the persons present, whose locations may be seen in Fig. 6, B is the film maker and L is a psychiatrist, present at B's invitation. All the other men are customers in the hotel. They are middle class in background, and range between thirty and fifty years in age. M is a young woman in her mid-twenties, present because of her acquaintance with the man-ageress.

In the part of the film from which the T-extract was taken, B is acting as a kind of discussion leader, or chairman. By questions and reflections he evoked first from one participant then from another, opinions and feeling about British customs, particularly in respect to the relationship between parents and children and between siblings. In the T-extract itself, B asks T a question, he replies to this with a speech about thirty seconds long; B puts a further question to T, to which he gives a very short reply; B acknowledges this, and then turns to question another participant. A transcript of the words spoken in the extract is given

[2] Each frame of the film is numbered. Sequences from films will be referred to by reference number or title of film, followed by the reel number (where appropriate), followed by the frame numbers. When frame numbers are referred to in the course of a discussion of a specific sequence, only the last three digits are given.

below. Numbers in brackets indicate the lengths of pauses to the nearest twenty-fourth of a second.

B   yeah (20) and then (10) and then what? T: (10) well (12) uh (8)
T   (cont.) ca (6) as the years went by (5) he became more (5)
T   (cont.) shall we say mellowed and matured or possibly (14) less
T   (cont.) (16) to some extent less interested in children (9)
T   (cont.) ten years later (11) twelve years later (3) other children
T   (cont.) arrived (9) then (16) possibly he couldn't be bothered (6)
T   (cont.) but (7) at (3) the same time (12) he was (30) more used
T   (cont.) to children and prepared to give and take B: well now did
B   (cont.) you become the did you become then the part of the
B   (cont.) disciplinarian in the family? T: (15) well I tried to

In the account to follow, we shall first concentrate on the relationship between the behavior of T and B, and then we shall look at the behavior of some of the other participants, during the same exchange. Some of the descriptions are accompanied by diagrams which show some of the components of movement, and how this is related in time to the accompanying speech and movement of each interactant. The movement components in these diagrams are labeled by letter, and they will be referred to in the text by a letter in parentheses, following a description of the movement.

*T and B description*

When B puts his first question to T, he faces him and points at him with an extended arm. As will be seen from the diagram (Fig. 7), B turns his head to look at T, and swings his arm round to point at him (B), before his question is uttered in its complete form. That is, he first turns to face T, and to point at him, and then he puts his question. T is sitting forward in his chair (see Fig. 8). Just at the beginning of the second to last syllable of B's question, at 643, T begins to lean back in his chair (b) and it is only after his back is fully in contact with the back of his chair that he begins his utterance, though during this shift in posture he emits three short vocalizations. These are high pitched, cut off short, almost glottalized. The first two, [wɛl] and [ɜ:], are best described as "ready" signals, but the third, [kʌ], is probably the first part of an unfinished word. The posture that T moves into here (the movement lasts from 643 to 688) is the one that he maintains for the rest of his utterance. His shift in posture, initiated before any vocalization, is his first response to B's question,

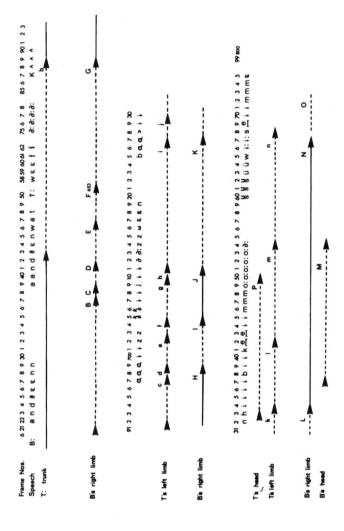

Fig. 7  Diagram to show speech and movement components between 87622 and 87777 in the T-extract from TRD 009. Movement components are labeled by letter and are described in the text. Errors in diagram as originally published have been corrected.

98

Fig. 8    Tracing from frame no. 87640 in the T-extract showing T in "forward position," B pointing at T, and M and Gl. R, P, L, and Th who are all partly visible in this frame have been omitted from the tracing for the sake of clarity

and it may be said to mark the change in his position in the interaction from that of a listener to that of a discourser.

Scheflen (1964) was the first to point out that when an interactant changes his mode of participation in an interaction, he generally alters his posture in a fairly substantial fashion at the boundary of this change. In T's case, there are other examples in TRD 009 in which he changes from "sitting forward" to "sitting back," in both cases prior to taking the floor as a "discourser."

Concurrently with T's change in posture, B also moves. He leans back slightly and lifts his head, and at the same time he lowers his forearm and rotates it inwards, while flexing his elbow and wrist slightly, so that he is no longer pointing directly at T, though his arm is still extended (D-G). At 688, however, B becomes quite still, and he remains still until 698 (H), which is the point at which T completes the preparatory phase of his left arm which co-occurs with his speech. It is to be noted that the point where B ceases to move is also the point where T releases the vowel of [kʌ]. It may be that B here ceases to move because he holds himself ready for the onset of T's utterance, the imminence of which is announced by [kʌ] and by the virtual completion of his posture shift.

From 699–794 B moves his hand slightly to the left, then holds it still (I, J) and then, at 711, he begins to move his hand and arm to the right, coming to point directly at T again at 726 (K). His hand is then moved slightly to the left again (L) and then, after a brief period of immobility, he cocks his head to the right (M). T's movements during the same period are as follows: over the first phrase of his utterance, he moves his left arm first out to the left (c), then following some small movements in the hand, it is moved right and lowered to his lap (g). Then it is raised again, and again moved out to his left (i). Then, over the first part of the second phrase of his speech he cocks his head to the right (p). B, as we saw, begins to move his right arm to the right at 711. This is at just the same moment as T begins the second of his leftward movements of his left arm. And then, B's headcock, though it begins after the beginning of T's head movement, it begins at a boundary in T's speech, and it ends precisely as T ends the syllable "more," at 753. After this, B changes to a new posture (O), and he remains relatively still for most of the rest of T's discourse.

During the section we have just described it will be seen that, when B is moving, his movements are coordinated with T's movements and speech, and that in their form these movements amount in part to a "mirror image" of T's movements: as T leans back in his chair, B leans back and lifts his head; then B moves his right arm to the right, just as T moves his left arm to the left, and he follows this with a headcock to the right, just as T cocks his head to the left. We might say that here B dances T's dance.

This period during which B partly mirrors T's movements lasts for about five seconds. At 768 he begins to move into a new posture, as already mentioned. Here he sits still with his pipe in his mouth, which he holds with his right hand, and he remains still, except for movements in the eyes, mouth, and fingers of the right hand. This position B maintains until 068 and, apart from the minor movements mentioned, he produces one complex headnod, which comes at the end of T's sixth phrase. There are two observations to be made here. First, it is to be noted that compared to the first phrase we have described, there is now a relative absence of movement in B, in spite of the fact that T continues to engage in considerable movement and B continues to look at him. However, such movements as he does make, the eye blinks, eye-shifts, and mouth movements, so far as we were able to establish their boundaries, appeared to be coordinated with the patterning of T's speech. For instance, from 810 to 815 B lowers his fingers over the bowl of his pipe. This movement coincides exactly with the middle syllable of "possibly" in T's speech. Again, B moves his eyes off T to his right from 867–875. At the moment T utters the stressed syllable of "interested" however, B moves his eyes to look back at T. This is in contrast to what happens during the multiple headnod. Here the individual up-and-down components of the headnod do not appear to be in synchrony with T's speech. This is of interest in that it perhaps suggests that where the listener ceases to receive what the speaker is saying, but initiates a response to it, he then organizes his behavior in his own time, not that of the speaker.

B remains in this relatively quiescent "listening" position for most of the rest of T's discourse. Then, at 068, and for the remaining part of T's discourse, he behaves in a markedly different fashion. This last part of T's discourse consists in the two final phrases of T's speech. They are introduced by the connective "but" which, in the stress it receives, and in its position between two pauses, and in the way it contrasts in pitch the exaggerated fall in pitch over the word which terminates the preceding phrase, appears to signal that the speech that is to follow is to bring the discourse to an end. T also marks this connective kinesically, for associated with it there is a marked change in the position of his head (see Fig. 9). He tilts his head back (b) and then, as he enunciates the "but," he tilts his head markedly left (c), and this is then followed by a forward head tilt, combined with a movement to the right, this movement being associated with the first part of the following phrase (f). At 068, which is the point at which T begins the head movement to the left that is associated with "but," B drops his eyelids over his eyes, and tilts his head markedly forward and to the left (B). He follows this at 084 with a further tilt forward of the head. This is the point at which T begins his penultimate phrase, "at the same time ... ," and this, it is to be noted, is accompanied by a forward and rightward movement of the head. This movement brings T's head into a position that mirrors that of B.

What we see here appears to be the reverse of what we saw at the outset of T's discourse. There B appeared to first pause in his movements, and then mirror the movements T was already making. Here he initiates

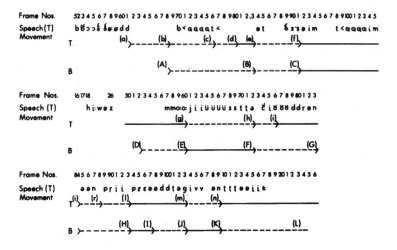

Fig. 9 Diagram to show speech and movement components between 88052 and 88224 in the T-extract of TRD 009. Explanation in text

a movement, a left and forward tilt of the head, in time with a change in movement in T, and this movement T then comes to mirror. At the outset, B picked up T's dance. Here, T picks up B's dance.

For the rest of the discourse B now moves his head and though, as may be seen clearly from the chart, his movement components are quite synchronous with components of T's behavior, we do not now see mirroring. Instead, it is as if B is acting out a kinetic representation of certain features of T's speech. Thus, he holds still over the pauses and over T's "he was," but then lowers his head in association with "more" (E), holds still over "used to" (F), and then tilts his head forward very markedly over "children," where T lowers the pitch of his voice (G). He then lifts his head up high over "an pre-" (H) – as if to meet the high pitch level in T's voice here – he then holds (I), then lowers his head (J), as T produces the last part of this phrase and then, at the boundary between "and" and "take" he initiates a wholly new movement pattern – head goes up, back and to the right, left hand moves out left – which is associated with the question he now puts to T (L). Note how the movements associated with asking the question begin before any vocalization, and it begins just at the point at which it becomes clear how T is going to finish.

Shortly following this question of B, T replies with a short phrase: "well I tried to," with the primary stress brought out strongly on "tried." As T gives this reply, B lowers his head and then turns it to face another participant with whom he will shortly engage. This head movement is timed to take exactly as long as T's reply. It is lowered slowly over "well I," more rapidly over "tried," and the turn to the right begins immediately afterward, and ends as T's utterance ends. Here, evidently in one movement, B signals his disengagement with T but, as he does so, because of the way his movement is timed and shaped, he also acknowledges his receipt of T's reply.

## T and B: discussion

To begin with, we have seen that the listener, B, is in synchrony, in Condon's sense, with T. Our initial aim, to describe another instance of interactional synchrony, has thus been accomplished. Secondly, however, different phases in B's movements could be observed. First B "mirrored" the movements of T, then he became quiescent, and then, over the last two phrases of T's speech B again moved conspicuously. Here, however, he did not pick up the movements of T. It appeared that he raised and lowered his head in relation to the rise and fall of the pitch of T's voice, and it was T who brought his head into alignment with B's head, rather than the other way round

The phenomenon of movement mirroring, which has been observed in a number of instances in TRD 009,[3] appears to occur only between the speaker and the person he directly addresses. As in the T extract, so in the other instances examined, it occurs most conspicuously at the very beginning of an interchange. Other participants may move concurrently with the movements of speaker and listener, as the axis of interaction between them is set up, but their movements are either of quite a different form from those of the direct addressee, or else they have a different timing. By mirroring the movement of the speaker, the person directly addressed thus at once differentiates himself from the others present, and at the same time he heightens the bond that is being established between him and the speaker. For the speaker it can serve as visual confirmation that his speech is properly directed, and for the others present it can serve to clarify the way in which participant activities are being patterned.

---

[3] Instances of movement mirroring associated with the establishment of an axis of interaction have been observed, for example, in TRD 009. 2.23507 et seq., TRD 009. 1.24577 et seq., and GB-SU-008 (the Doris-therapist film).

Mirroring of movement is not continuous in conversational inter-action. As we saw, B soon moved into a new position in which his move-ments were much reduced, though there was no change in the amplitude of T's movements. Similarly, in other examples we have looked at, the listener will shift synchronously with the speaker into a position which mirrors his initial head position, but he thereafter remains relatively still. Nonetheless we may see movement mirroring intermittently within an ongoing interchange. Thus when, in an interchange, speaker and listener mirror one another's postures, if there is a change in posture which does not reflect a change in the relationship, such posture shifts often occur synchronously, and in these instances we may again get movement mirroring.[4] This is in contrast to those occasions when there is a change in the relationship between the participants in the inter-change, for instance where one starts to ask the other questions. We may then see synchronous posture shifts, or head position shifts, but the movements are differentiated, not mirrored. An example of this occurs in TRD 009.1.24849–24941, which is described later (see below, p. 109).

In the third phase of B's behavior that we distinguished, we observed that here B initiated movement, which T then came to follow. We also observed that these movements appeared to be related to the vari-ations in pitch level of T's speech. It seems probable that these move-ments serve to give advanced warning that B wants to speak when T is finished and, further, it may be that in overtly "beating time" to T's speech, he may thereby facilitate the precise timing of his own entry as a speaker, much as a musician may begin to move conspicuously with the music, as he readies himself to enter with his part at the right moment.

## The other participants

We have described T and B together as forming an axis of interaction within an ongoing encounter. The others present are not direct partici-pants in this axis, though they all of them are in a position to become

---

[4]  A good example can be observed in TRD 009.2.71810–71970, where G and Th, who have constituted an axis for some time and who maintain postural congruence through-out, readjust their postures simultaneously, still keeping congruence. This occurs at what is certainly a point of change in the axis, but it occurs within the axis, not at its boundaries.

actively involved at any time, as indeed they do. Relative to the interactional axis between T and B, these others may be referred to as the non-axial participants. It is of some interest to look at their behavior during the interchange between T and B. As we shall see, in several cases this is related to the behavior of these two, though in form it is sharply differentiated from it.

M can be dealt with quite briefly. Her posture (which may be seen in Figs. 8 and 10) is maintained throughout T's discourse. She does not move, and she does not nod her head or show any of the kinds of reaction we noted in B, but she looks continuously at T. This is a very typical configuration for those who are attending closely to an interchange. Examples can very easily be found, for instance in TRD 009, 1.23507–23728, where E and Gl are oriented to the axis between Th and H, they both display behavior very similar to that of M here. They sustain a particular posture with the minimum of movement, and they maintain an almost constant line of visual orientation.

Gl, however, in the T-extract, does show considerable movement and this may now be compared to the behavior of T and B. When the extract begins, Gl's head is sunk on his chest, with no rotation, and his right forearm lies along the arm of his chair, the hand hanging free from the wrist. The left hand is placed deep in his left jacket pocket (see Fig. 8). A minor movement of the fingers of the right hand is observed concurrent with B's "yeah" and then, at 629, he turns his head right, to look at B. This head turn begins one frame after B's first "and then" has ended. Gl's head remains oriented to B until 678, when he turns to look at T, and this turn begins immediately after T's third brief vocalization [kʌ]. He then begins the first of two major shifts at 704. Here he lifts his left hand from his jacket pocket and moves it to the right, close to his body. He then moves it to the left again, to place it in his trouser pocket. At the same time, he bends his right arm at the elbow to bring his right hand, held as a loose fist, into contact with his right ear. He reaches this position at 730, coincidentally with a boundary in the behavior of both T and B. This shift, thus, fits over T's opening phrase in somewhat the same way as B's movements do but in form it is quite different from B's movements and, further, its segments do not have quite the same precise relation to T's speech as do the components of B's movements. Gl remains virtually still until 739, when his head begins to move preparatory to his second major shift. This has two segments: in the first, ending at 759, he moves his right hand down from his ear to his chin. This

Fig. 10    Tracing from frame no. 87977 of the T-extract showing T in
"back position" and talking, B in "listening position" and M and Gl.
Other participants have been omitted for the sake of clarity

movement co-occurs with T and B's movement over "more" and the
subsequent pause. This is maintained with some minor movements,
until 766 and at 767, coincident with B's shift to his "listening"
position, Gl shifts his head slightly and moves his arm away from his
chin, by extension from his elbow (which rests on the arm of the chair)
to a point where it is held at approximately 80° to the arm of the chair,
the fingers held in a loose fist. He reaches this position at 793, close to
the same point at which B reaches his listening posture. Apart from
some minor movements, Gl now holds this position for the rest of T's
discourse (Fig. 10). Perhaps it is worth remarking that this position is
somewhat analogous to B's position. One could imagine how Gl is holding onto the bowl of a pipe with a very long stem. It is possible that in
adopting an analogous posture Gl thus shows that he is sharing B's role
as listener.[5]

Sometimes a non-axial participant will be smoking or drinking. It is

[5] Compare Scheflen's (1964) observations on the significance of postural parallelism.

of interest to observe how the movements involved may be closely coordinated with the behavior of the speaker. An example which illustrates this clearly can be found in TRD 009.1.32427, et seq. The participants are X, a donnish Lancashireman who talks at length on regional variations in the British ethos. He has an argument with N, a stocky traveling salesman with a sharp tongue and a London accent. Between these two sits an elegant and attractive young woman, G, who works as a lingerie model for a London firm. G and X spend a good deal of time in close tête-à-tête, much to the apparent disgust of N, who is drawn to G. The argument between X and N is quite bitter and it is concerned with whether the British are "self-conscious" or not. It perhaps derives much of its animus from the rivalry between X and N for the attentions of G. Needless to say, it is X, with his superior airs and sophisticated Oxford talk, who wins out, and later on in the evening he and G withdraw together.

The piece dealt with here comes at the very beginning of this argument. It covers N's first entrance into discussion with X, and X's immediate reply. X has just been asked to repeat a large part of his argument for the benefit of someone on the other side of the room who has been drawn into the discussion by B. He says: "In fact we've got to go way back to the conversation in the bar, because this is what it was built up on." A slight pause follows and then he says "um" but N enters with "self-consciousness wasn't it?" X replies: "Not entirely, it goes way back to the type of investigation our friend here is carrying out." The relations between X's speech and G's movements here are given in Fig. 11. Three movement lines are used here: line 1 for the left index finger, line 2 for the left limb, and line 3 for the trunk. Segments of the diagram referred to in the following description will be specified by the line number and letter.

During the early part of X's first sentence from this stretch, G is drinking, she leans forward and places her glass on the table, just at the point where N begins "self-consciousness . . . " She remains still, hand on her glass, during this utterance (2a) but just as it finishes she withdraws her hand and moves it over to her right hand which is holding her cigarette (2b). She takes her cigarette between her first and second fingers of her left hand (2c), and lifts it away from her right hand just as X begins "it goes . . . " (2d). She extends her left hand, and leans forward to position her cigarette over an ashtray which is on the table in front of her (2e, 3a). She lifts her index finger (1a), holds it momentarily (1b),

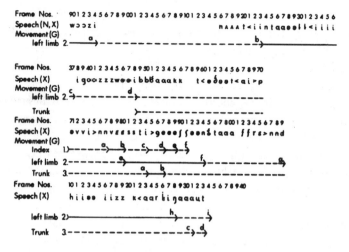

Fig. 11    Diagram to show speech of N and X and movement components
of G between 32590 and 32740 from reel 1 of TRD 009. Explanation in
text

raises it further (1c), brings it down sharply on the cigarette to knock off
the ash (1d), holds it down on the cigarette (1e), raises it again (1f) and
then leans back in her chair again (3c, 3d). It is to be noted how the index
finger is raised at the boundary between "type" and "of," how it is lowered onto the cigarette precisely as X utters the stressed syllable of
"investigation," and how she reaches her chair again at precisely the
moment he concludes with the word "out." The whole action, leaning
over to tap ash off the cigarette and leaning back again, in itself an action
that has no direct social pertinence,[6] is yet done in time to the rhythm
of X's speech. Subsequently, she sits, left finger touching the back of
her right hand, looking at N, who now demands a definition of "self-
consciousness." X then tries to answer him, in a series of measured
phrases, and it is noteworthy how, at the end of each of these phrases G
changes her pose somewhat. Earlier, during the first part of X's dis-

---

[6]  It is sometimes argued that all behavior of others is "socially pertinent" to the extent
that it provides information to others. This is, of course, true. Nevertheless one must
distinguish between behavior which is specialized for social interaction, such as talking,
gesticulating, and certain kinds of postural adjustment, and behavior which is non-
specialized for interaction, of which smoking is an example. Such interactively non-
specialized behavior may, of course, be coordinated into the interaction, as in the
example described here, and in this way it may come to have some interactional *function*. This should, however, he kept distinct from whether the behavior is also specialized for that function.

course we can observe her doing the same thing. She shifts her position slightly from time to time, as she sits quietly and listens to X. But these shifts in position occur at boundaries in X's speech-flow, not at random, or according to some rhythm of her own. Thus G, though not directly addressed, moves in time with the rhythm of X's behavior. These movements have no clear signal-quality, and they are quite different from the kind of movements she makes when she is turned toward S, listening to him appreciatively as he talks to her.[7]

In contrast to these instances, where the movements of the non-axial participants are clearly differentiated from those of the speaker, as well as from those of the active recipients, we may observe how, in his movement, the non-axial participant appears to be taking the part of the speaker. Thus, in TRD 009.1.24849–24941 Gl and M are talking together. P is sitting next to M in a forward posture, closely attentive to their discussion. They are discussing the place of women in bars and M has been saying that she would never go into a bar on her own. Gl says: "Why is this?" cocking his head sharply to his left as he does so. Concurrently, M rotates her head to her right, and down, away from Gl, turning away as she formulates her answer. P, however, moves his trunk slightly to the right and forward, a trunk movement which is analogous to Gl's head movement. Other examples have been noted in RFP 001.61. This is a psychotherapy film in which there are three participants, the patient (a male), the therapist and the patient's (male) nurse. On several occasions when the therapist questions the patient, concurrent movement may be seen in the nurse. For example at 01120 et seq., E (the therapist) is trying to get the patient to remember how many times they have met, and he counts out the occasions on his fingers. Concurrently the nurse moves his fingers in a way which looks very like a highly abbreviated version of the therapist's movements.

In both of these instances, there is a sharp differentiation in the roles of the speaker and active recipient. The relationship is interrogatory. In many situations, of course, the identity of the non-axial participant with the speaker's role is much more conspicuous, indeed it may be formulated in seating positions, clothing, and in the explicit ritual of the occasion as in interviewing committees or committees of inquiry where there is one witness and many questioners. Here we often find one individual who is said to speak for all of the others, while the others sit beside the

[7] This may be observed through much of reel 2 of TRD 009.

speaker sharing, sometimes in a more restrained fashion, his postures and demeanor.

To return, once again, to the T-extract, it is worth looking, briefly, at the behavior of P and L. These two differ from the others present, in that for much of the T-extract they are not attending to the prevailing interactional axis, but are engaged in a little interchange of their own. In this interchange, L offers a cigar to P, which P takes, and L then lights P's cigar, then his own, and then they both turn their attention to T. Of interest here is the way P and L's behavior is coordinated first with one another in a reciprocal fashion and then with T.

We do not see the beginning of this interchange between P and L. At 591, when the T-extract opens, L is already fumbling in his jacket pocket for his cigars, and P is fully turned to L. P follows with his eyes the progress of the cigar box as L opens it and moves it over to P to offer him one. P takes a cigar, and as he does so, L withdraws the cigar box to take one himself. P then holds his cigar, eyes still on L, and does not move to put it in his mouth until L does so – an interesting instance of how two people in interaction will keep their actions in pace with one another, even where such a temporal coordination is not essential for the maintenance of the interchange. L then moves over with a flame to light P's cigar, and P's movement is nicely coordinated here with L's movement as he brings the flame. P then draws on his cigar as L is lighting his own, and blows smoke from his mouth. He then turns to L who, having got his cigar going, now turns his attention to T. P then also turns to T, and it is noteworthy that as he does so he changes his posture somewhat, coming to rest his head on his fist. What is of particular interest here, however, is that the movements of P and L, though now not reciprocal and quite different in form, nonetheless are synchronous – boundaries of their components coincide, that is. It is as if they are both dancing to the same beat, though the movements they make are quite different. This analogy is not too far fetched. They are now both attending to T and, in doing so they both move synchronously with him and hence synchronously with each other.

In the behavior of P and L, thus, we can observe a variety of the ways in which two people may interrelate their activities, which are different from those we have already considered. Thus P's movements are synchronous with those of L as he follows or tracks L's movements. P and L move in a reciprocal coordination, as when L moves the cigar box over to P, and P moves over to take a cigar; or when L moves over with a lighter, and P leans forward to meet the flame. P waits for L to begin carrying his cigar to his mouth, before putting his own in, so keeping pace with L. Finally, at the end, P and L's movements are synchronized not through their attention to each other, but through their common attention to a single focus.

It may be worth noting that the interchange between P and L is initiated in association with the beginning of a unit of interaction, the T-B axis. This is but one instance of a phenomenon that is recurrent in this film, and which is probably characteristic of the behavior of non-axial participants generally. That is, gross posture shifts, and actions pertaining to sub-involvements such as drinking or smoking, tend to occur in association with points of change in the interactional structure of the gathering. Typically, when someone stops speaking and another begins, if this is in the same axis, we see orientation changes in several of the others. In addition, sips of drinks are taken, if glasses are already in hand, and puffs of cigarettes are taken, if these have already been lit. Where there is a change in who is talking with whom, a change in the interchange or interactional axis, that is, or where the whole direction of the interaction changes, we see larger changes in the participants. Gross shifts of posture occur, cigarettes or pipes are lighted, or glasses are drained or put down, or glasses are picked up. Often such actions by non-axial participants are not simultaneous, but they occur in sequence, as if each triggers the next. This seems to occur in particular where only some of the non-axial participants are attending to an axis which changes, while others are attending elsewhere. In this case, the gross posture shift, or drink or smoke of one, will be picked up by another, and then another, and we see a series of such actions going round the circle.

A number of examples of this phenomenon have been collected, but a more thorough analysis will be reserved for another report. Gatherings vary in the degree to which the attentional foci of those present are coordinated and it may be that the level of joint involvement in a gathering may be gauged by the tightness of clustering of posture shifts, and actions related to sub-involvements like drinking or smoking. Where there is tight clustering, the attentional involvements of the participants are probably more closely coordinated than where it is loose. In this case the occasion would be said to be more diffuse. Furthermore, for any given individual his degree of "presence" in the gathering may perhaps be gauged by the degree to which his posture shifts, and other actions are coordinated with those that occur in others present.

## Conclusions

In this chapter an attempt has been made to give detailed descriptions of the way in which the behavior of speakers and listeners are inter-related. We have had three aims. First we wanted to describe some further instances of the phenomenon of interactional synchrony, as this has been described by Condon. Secondly, we wanted to see if there was any patterning in the listener's flow of movements that could be described in terms of the way it is related to the speaker's movements. Thirdly, we have attempted to contrast the behavior of the listener who is directly addressed by a speaker, with the behavior of those who are participants, but who are not directly involved in the interchange.

In the examples described we have illustrated interactional synchrony, and we have seen that it may occur even when the individuals who are "synchronous" with one another are not looking at each other. This suggests that the coordination of the listener's movements with the behavior of the speaker is brought about through the listener's response to the stream of speech. Where, as we saw in the behavior of B, the listener imposes an organization on his movements which "fit" with those of the speaker, visual input is clearly being used, but for interactional synchrony to arise it is evidently sufficient for the listener to hear the speech of the speaker.

The precision with which the listener's movements are synchronized with the speaker's speech means that the listener is in some way able to anticipate what the speaker is going to say, as indeed current work on speech perception leads us to expect. This work tends to support the analysis-by-synthesis theory of speech perception. On this theory, it is supposed that the listener samples input from the speaker intermittently and then, on the basis of these samples, constructs a version of the message which he then checks against later inputs. He can be said to construct a running hypothesis about what the speaker will be saying a moment hence (Neisser 1967). In this way, if his construction of what the speaker is saying is correct, his present understanding of the speaker can coincide precisely with what the speaker is saying, as in a tracking task, where precise tracking is possible only if the tracker is able to make predictions about the course the target will take (Poulton 1957). If we allow that cognitive processes and bodily movement are interrelated, we may expect that the processes involved in the processing of speech by a listener may affect his movements or even be marked in movement. This seems especially likely here where there is such a close relationship between movement and speech production, and where, in listening so many of the same mechanisms are probably involved.

It is to be noted that the analysis-by-synthesis theory of speech perception allows for flexibility in the size of the speech unit that is processed. The listener can synthesize expected units of speech in terms of syllables, phrases, or larger semantic units. It seems probable, indeed, that this process of synthesis goes on at several of these levels at once. It would be interesting to know if the listener marks in movement differentially the size of the unit of speech he is processing. If this were so it might be possible to gather from his patterning of movements his level of comprehension of the speech.

There is much more about interactional synchrony we would like to know, as need hardly be said. For example, we know nothing about the conditions in which it does not arise. Clearly, for it to arise the listener must pay some degree of attention to speech, but it would be important to know what degree this must be. We may presume that it will be that level that is required for comprehension of the speech, perhaps as much as is needed for someone to be able to "shadow" the speech. This will also mean that we may not find interactional synchrony where the rhythmical features of the speech are unfamiliar to the listener, or where he cannot understand the words, either because of their unfamiliarity, or because of a high noise level. Questions of this sort are clearly open to experimental exploration.

The other main question of interest, of course, and the one that has chiefly informed the present inquiry, is the possible function of interactional synchrony in the process of interaction itself. Much of the listener's movement may be perceived by the speaker and it may, just insofar as it is a symptom of the listener's comprehension, form an important source of feedback for him. There are additional possibilities, however. In an experiment by Argyle et al. (1968) it was found, among other things, that an interactant A would feel more uncomfortable in an interaction the less easily he could see his partner, only in the condition where his partner at all times could easily see him. If he could not be seen by his partner, the ease with which he could see his partner made no difference to his comfort. A possible interpretation of this finding is that a speaker needs information about his listener to enable him to regulate those aspects of his behavior that are visible to his partner. In other words, where vision can be used in interaction it becomes important to the interactants that there is a mutual regulation of movement, as well as a pacing of utterances. It seems probable that the synchronization of movements in interaction is important because this is one of the means by which is achieved that delicate coordination of expectancies among participants, so essential to the smooth running of an encounter (Goffman 1957, 1961). This becomes particularly important at those points where an interchange is being established, and where it is to be disbanded, and it is perhaps for this reason that we found that shared rhythmicity in movement was most conspicuous at the beginning and at the end of the interchange. To *move* with another is to show that one is "with" him in one's attentions and expectancies. Coordination of movement in interaction may thus be of great importance since it provides one of the ways in which two people signal that they are "open" to one another, and not to others.

## Postscript

In a series of publications Condon (Condon 1976, 1977, 1979, 1982; see Kempton 1980 and Gatewood and Rosenwein 1981 for reviews of his work) has proposed that the microsynchronization of speech and movement between interactants described in this chapter occurs always and continuously. He has even claimed to show that it occurs between adults and very young infants (Condon and Sander 1974a, 1974b). He proposes to account for this in terms of a process of "entrainment" whereby each participant in the interaction is "driven" by the rhythmicities in the other's vocalizations. He appears to believe that the synchronization that he observes is an inevitable product of the reception of auditory stimuli. Rosenfeld (1981) has termed this "deterministic microsynchrony" and has offered an incisive critique of the theoretical and methodological difficulties involved in substantiating this phenomenon.

It will be seen that my observations on interactional synchrony and the interpretation I give of it differ from those of Condon. I have not found sustained synchrony between participants in interaction at all times, but, as the work reported in this chapter shows, I do find it to occur from time to time in interaction in ways that suggest that it is a manifestation of attentional and affective attunement. In my view, interactional synchrony is best regarded as an achievement of the interactants that is attained when the participants come to govern their behavior in relation to one another in respect to a commonly shared frame or joint plan of action. Interactants come to be able to behave together as if they share a common musical score and this can make possible a very high degree of temporal coordination between them. The high degrees of synchronization that can be observed from time to time in interaction, thus, arise when people's expectations about each other's behavior are exceptionally well attuned.

Other work on the way in which the behavior of interactants may be temporally coordinated includes work on the temporal relations of utterances in conversation (Pelose 1987 provides a useful bibliography for much of this work), the rhythmic coordination of behavior in interviews (Erickson and Schultz 1982) and in other kinds of conversations (Bennet 1980). Some of this work has been done using techniques of film analysis very similar to those employed for the work reported in this chapter. Particularly notable has been the extensive amount of microanalytic work done on mother–infant interactions by Colwyn Trevarthen (Trevarthen 1977, 1979; Trevarthen and Hubley 1978) and Daniel Stern. Stern, in particular, has emphasized the extreme closeness of timing that may be observed in the way in which mothers and infants interact together and has proposed that, from an early age, people are able to build schemata in terms of which they interpret the structure of each other's patterns of action. Acting in terms of such schemata, participants become able to coordinate their behavior with one another to a very high degree (see, especially, Stern 1977; Stern and Gibbon 1978; Beebe, Stern and Jaffe 1979; Stern 1985).

# 5

## Some functions of the face in a kissing round

### Introduction

In this paper we undertake a detailed analysis of a film specimen of a couple who are engaged in kissing one another. In undertaking this analysis we shall contribute to the study of kissing, but we shall also be able to show something of the subtlety and complexity of the role of the face in social interaction. Most studies of the face have considered it solely from the point of view of its role in emotional expression, and the focus of interest of these studies has been, accordingly, upon facial patterns as symptoms of affective states. In consequence, we have almost no systematic knowledge of how the face functions in social interaction. An important aim of this paper is to demonstrate how the behavior of the face may be studied within social interaction and how we may examine its integration with the other aspects of behavior that may there be observed. In this way we shall be able to see what part the face plays in the interrelating of the behavior of the participants. The findings of the analysis will be discussed in relation to more traditional studies of the face, and also in the light of some more general theoretical considerations regarding the organization of behavior in face-to-face interaction. We may also note that, in using a kissing round for analysis, we shall be making a contribution to the as yet hardly existent literature on the behavior of human courtship. Although we deal with but a single couple and with but a very small fragment of their interaction, the close analysis we here present will enable us to raise questions appropriate for any further study of the behavior of human courtship.

The principal question that has been pursued in most studies of the

First published in *Semiotica* 15: 4 (1976). Reprinted by permission of Mouton Publishers.

human face has been whether or not observers can distinguish facial expressions reliably in terms of the different emotions different facial expressions are presumed to be expressing. This line of inquiry is usually traced back to Darwin (1872) for he claimed that there are distinct patterns of behavior by which different emotions find expression. A very large proportion of the work done, mainly by psychologists, can be seen to have arisen in response to this claim. The main method that has been followed has been to present subjects with faces in various poses, portrayed either in diagrams, still photographs or, occasionally, moving pictures or live performers, and ask them to label the presentation in terms of an expressed emotion. In this work, which has been extensively reviewed several times (e.g. Bruner and Tagiuri 1954, Woodworth and Schlosberg 1954, Davitz 1964, Izard 1969, Vine 1970, Ekman 1973), it is always assumed that a facial expression is an expression of emotion. Many of these studies also assume that there are a limited number of discrete, primary emotions which can be defined in terms of behavioral, psychological, and, occasionally, experimental features, quite apart from the way the behaving individual may be interrelated with the behavior of others. These studies are addressed, thus, to the significance of facial behavior for the state of the individual and they are not concerned with how the facial behavior of one individual affects, or is related to the behavior of others in the situation of a social encounter. As Vine concludes, from his review of the field: "Undoubtedly there is much that can be discovered from the results of the recognition studies, but they tell us little about the functioning of facial-visual communication in day-to-day social behavior "(Vine 1970, p. 304).

This investigation will begin, therefore, not with emotions, but with behavior. It will start by looking at behavior from the point of view of how it functions in sustaining the patterns of behavioral interrelatedness that obtain between individuals when they are in each other's presence and which constitute occasions of interaction. With regard to the face one asks, thus, not what feelings does the face express or how it does so, but what does the face do? One then proceeds to determine, within the context of an ongoing interaction where, in relation to the rest of the behavior, the various patterns of behavior observed in the face can be seen to occur. The question at issue is, what functions *for the interaction*, do these differentiable units of facial behavior have? From this point of view, in other words, the question of what organismic or affective state is supposedly made manifest in the face is not relevant.

What is relevant is what difference different facial patterns make to the organization of the behavior in the occasions of interaction in which they occur.

Remarkably little research on human facial behavior has been carried out from this point of view. Some of the work on the infant smile, summarized, for example, by Bowlby (1969) and Vine (1973b), has examined the role of the smile in mother–infant interaction. Blurton-Jones (1967), Grant (1969), Brannigan and Humphries (1972), and McGrew (1972) have reported observational studies of facial (and other) behavior, mainly in small children, and here a major interest has been in its signalling function. Eibl-Eibesfeldt (1970, 1972) has also reported extensive observations on several different patterns of facial behavior, collected from a wide range of cultural contexts, and here again the focus is upon its signal or communicational function. Reece and Whitman (1962) and Rosenfeld (1966a, b; 1967) have reported experimental studies in which the influence of smiling on other aspects of the interaction has been studied. The study of gaze direction functions in interaction, reprinted as Chapter 3, also included some observations on the interactional functions of smiling. Birdwhistell (1970) has discussed the face from this point of view in several of his essays. Thus in his essay on smiles he points out how they have a wide variety of social functions, and that to consider them merely, in his phrase, as "visible transforms of an underlying physiological state" (Birdwhistell 1970, p. 32) would be to miss this aspect of their functioning entirely. In other essays he describes how the movements of the face may be brought into play in association with speech, and how these movements, along with movements of the head and limbs, have a complex relationship to the structuring of speech, both as an activity and in respect to its content. Facial displays can serve to mark out points of emphasis in speech, they can serve to mark off whole segments of speech as distinct units or as contained or embedded units, and they can also provide a commentary and supplement to what is being said. If we watch the faces of listeners, too, we can see that nods, smiles, frowns, raised eyebrows, appear frequently in some circumstances. Such facial behavior probably plays an important part in the regulation of the behavior of the speaker. Similar observations have been made on the regulating function of facial behavior by Ekman and Friesen (1969).

It will be seen, thus, that when one takes as one's starting point the behavior of the face itself, and when one then considers what the relationship is between the behavior of the face and other aspects of behavior that may be going forward in interaction, it becomes apparent that the face is involved in a wide range of functions. The preoccupation with the face as it expresses, or in some other way manifests emotion, has left these other functions of the face unexplored. From the point of view of the development of a theory of the communicative functions of human behavior, however, it is of great importance to consider the face in all its various functions. It is hoped that the present study will contribute to such a broader, communicative approach to the face.

## Material for this study

If we are to study the behavior of the face in its natural context, it will be necessary to acquire some good specimens of facial behavior which can be examined in detail and at leisure. This is best done by the use of 16 mm film, which allows for the repeated study of the specimens and which allows one to see the behavior of the face as it develops in time. For our present interest, it is of great importance, in acquiring these specimens, that one should film in such a way that the faces of the several individuals who are in interaction are always visible. If this is not done, one cannot hope to analyze the way in which the behavior of the face is integrated into the interaction. Other workers who have used film in the study of the face, including Landis and Hunt (1936), Thompson (1941), Frijda (1953), Lynn (1940), Coleman (1949), Haggard and Isaacs (1966), Eibl-Eibesfeldt (1970), and Ekman (1973) have not been concerned with interaction and in filming they have filmed individuals separately.

The analysis undertaken in this paper is of a four minute 16 mm film record, here to be known as C14.1.[1] The couple filmed in C14.1 were observed sitting on a park bench and as they were seen to be actively engaged in a kissing round, the camera was set up. The camera was

---

[1] I am indebted to Peter Jones and BBC Television for this film specimen. The specimen was originally part of some footage that was made for the film *What's in a Face*, directed by Peter Jones and first shown on BBC Television in 1973. See Liggett (1974, p. 262) for a still from the portion of this film that was analyzed.

The film was analyzed using a Bell & Howell 16 mm sound projector modified for operation by a handcrank and an L-W Athena. The film was not frame numbered and a frame counter was used. The frame counter was set at zero for the first frame of the film in which the couple appeared in a close "two-shot." The film was shot at twenty-four frames per second.

started as soon as possible thereafter and kept running continuously until the kissing round ended. The camera was restarted when the couple started a new round of kissing. C14.1 thus contains two segments, each approximately two minutes in length and each of which shows a kissing round from very shortly after its beginning until its end. The first segment of this specimen was analyzed first. The second segment was examined in detail later as a way of checking some of the relationships we were able to observe in the first. Here we will present the details of the first segment only, although the second segment will be referred to for additional examples.

In filming the present specimen a 500 mm lens was used and the camera was placed about 100 yards away from the couple. No attempt was made to hide the camera. As far as can be told, the couple remained unaware that they were being filmed. The lens was focused in such a way that only the head and shoulders of the two were in frame and, since the camera was behind the bench on which they were sitting, their faces could be seen in profile whenever either of them turns to face the other. In the period during which they were filmed, the couple repeatedly turned to face one another, and they moved their faces close together for kissing, nose rubbing, forehead touching and neck nuzzling.

There are several limitations to the specimen used in the present analysis which should be noted. First, as we have just said we see the faces of M and F only when either turns to face the other. That is, we see their faces only during certain phases of the interaction and not all of the time. Second, we are limited in that we can only see the heads and shoulders of F and M. A wider angle could have been used, perhaps, but had this been done we would have lost the extreme detail of facial behavior that we were able to acquire with this film. Ideally, a second camera should have been used at the same time. Given the circumstances under which the film was made, this was not possible. Third, we know nothing of the wider context of the behavior recorded. We do not know the place of this particular fragment of interaction within the larger period of time during which M and F were together, and of course we know nothing of their relationship. Finally, owing to the way the cameraman started and stopped the film, we see the ends of two kissing rounds, but not their beginning and we see nothing of the behavior between kissing rounds. Furthermore, no sound recording was attempted. At certain times in the specimen we can tell where utterances occur from lip movements, however these have been ignored in the present analysis.

Despite these limitations, we believe that the present analysis and discussion will prove useful, both because it will serve to show how the face may function in interaction with a degree of detail that has not been achieved elsewhere. Also, the interaction recorded in this specimen is highly characteristic of one sort of human courting behavior. A detailed description is worthwhile, therefore, insofar as there are virtually no other accounts of the details of courting behavior available.

## Analysis

In the account to follow we shall consider first, the *repertoire of facial patterns* observable in F and M. Second, we shall describe the action-sequence they together engage in. That is, we shall distinguish a number of "action elements" and describe how they are patterned in time. We shall see that in terms of these actions the kissing round can be divided into a number of phases according to differences in the way these actions are interrelated. Finally, we shall examine the *relationship between the different facial patterns and the action-sequence*. We shall see that whereas M's face shows very little change, F's face is highly variable, and we shall see that M's actions are highly interdependent with F's actions and with the behavior of her face. F's face, it will appear, functions to regulate M's behavior. We shall also be able to suggest what the different functions may be for the different kinds of facial patterns F displays.

### The repertoire of facial patterns

Since the original publication of this study, Ekman and Friesen have described their Facial Action Coding System. This is described briefly in Ekman and Friesen (1976) and fully presented in Ekman and Friesen (1978). In this system, the appearance of the face is scored in terms of Action Units. These are minimally discriminable appearances in each of several regions of the face, defined in terms of the facial muscle groups that operate to produce differences in facial appearance. The system makes possible detailed analytic descriptions of facial behavior. It has been applied in a number of areas of research, most notably in the study of the development of facial expressions and in the study of the use of the face in American Sign Language. Fridlund, Ekman and Oster (1987) review some of this work. Ekman (1982) gives an account of the system in the context of an historical review of the whole question of the measurement of facial behavior.

The FACS method of analyzing facial behavior probably could have been used in the material studied in this paper and it would have been appropriate to do so, for we were interested in a purely descriptive analysis of the face and not one that pre-judged the configurations in terms of supposed "displays" or "emotional expressions." However, at the time, no suitable system was available. What is used here is a modified version of a notation system developed by Jacques Ex and myself in 1964 (Ex and Kendon 1964). The notation was developed in reference to the film specimens of people in conversation that were used in our study of gaze direction in interaction (see Chapter 3) and the glyphs of the notation were designed to accommodate the full range of behavior observed in each of three regions of the face: the brows, the eyes and the mouth. The notations used are presented in Fig. 12. It was developed as a means of writing down the pose of the face as this could be observed in each frame of the film. From such a transcription, phrases of facial behavior could then be reconstructed.

An examination of the film specimen used in the present study shows that the faces of the two individuals show periods of quite rapid change alternating with periods in which the pattern of the face is more sustained. The Ex and Kendon notation system was found to be adequate for characterizing these more stable periods of facial patterning. A list of the patterns that were recorded in this way in the order in which they appeared and the length of time for which they were observed is provided in Fig. 13.

It will be noted from Fig. 13 that M's face is almost the same each time it is observed. In contrast, F shows considerable variation in pattern. For F, twenty-three periods of relative stability of pattern were observed in the segment analyzed. Many of these periods are rather similar to one another, however, suggesting certain repetitions in the facial patterns of F. The twenty-three periods of relative stability have been grouped into nine classes of facial pattern. The groupings that we arrived at were as follows:

A    "Base face": Brows and eyes open, lips closed, at rest. Occurs once in 14.

B    "Closed smile": Brows and eyes at rest; lips closed, with upper lip retracting to form smile. Occurs in 11, 13 and 17.

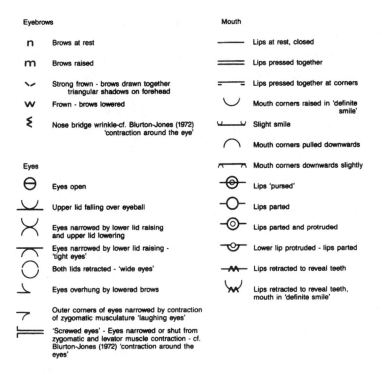

Fig.12    Explanation of facial notation (modified from Ex and Kendon 1964)

C    "Teeth smile": Brows at rest to wrinkled; eyes open to "laughing" or "screwed"; lips retracted to expose teeth and drawn laterally in smile. Occurs in 3, 5, 7, 10, 18 and 23, and in an extreme form in 6.

D    "Kiss face I": Brows at rest; eyes closing by falling upper lid; lips parted and protruding slightly. Occurs in 4 and 8, both occasions when F is approaching to kiss M.

E    "Kiss face II": Brows drawn together somewhat; eyes "tight"; lips parted and slightly protruded tight at corners with some slight smile. Occurs in 21, just prior to lips to lips kiss.

F    "Dreamy face": Brows raised; eyes "tight"; lips parted with some downward tension at the corners. Occurs in 14.

G    "Lip forward": Brows at rest, eyes closed by upper lid fully lowered over eye; lips parted with lower lip pushed forward slightly. Occurs in 1, 9 and 15 as F is turning away from M after being kissed.

## F's FACE

| # | BROWS | EYES | MOUTH | GROUP | DURATION |
|---|---|---|---|---|---|
| 1. | n | (symbol) | (symbol) | G | 151-161 |
| 2. | (symbol) | (symbol) | (symbol) | I | 179-196 |
| 3. | n | (symbol) | (symbol) | C | 197-261 |
| 4. | n | (symbol) | (symbol) | D | 266-278 |
| 5. | n | (symbol) | (symbol) | C | 304-380 |
| 6. | (symbol) | (symbol) | (symbol) | C | 470-506 |
| 7. | n | (symbol) | (symbol) | C | 591-666 |
| 8. | n | (symbol) | (symbol) | D | 667-692 |
| 9. | n | (symbol) | (symbol) | G | 736-742 |
| 10. | n | (symbol) | (symbol) | C | 790-850 |
| 11. | n | (symbol) | (symbol) | B | 961-1026 |
| 12. | n | (symbol) | (symbol) | A | 1070-1074 |
| 13. | n | (symbol) | (symbol) | B | 1079-1090 |
| 14. | m | (symbol) | (symbol) | F | 1132-1235 |
| 15. | m | (symbol) | (symbol) | G | 1551-1574 |
| 16. | n | (symbol) | (symbol) | A | 1584-1586 |
| 17. | n | (symbol) | (symbol) | B | 1587-1617 |
| 18. | w | (symbol) | (symbol) | C | 1862-1918 |
| 19. | w | (symbol) | (symbol) | C | 1931-2020 |
| 20. | V | (symbol) | (symbol) | I | 2130-2254 |
| 21. | n | (symbol) | (symbol) | E | 2259-2282 |
| 22. | m | (symbol) | (symbol) | H | 2307-2338 |
| 23. | m | (symbol) | (symbol) | C | 2715-2809 |

## M's FACE

| # | BROWS | EYES | MOUTH | DURATION |
|---|---|---|---|---|
| 1. | (symbol) | (symbol) | (symbol) | 188-235 |
| 2. | (symbol) | (symbol) | (symbol) | 313-360 |
| 3. | (symbol) | (symbol) | (symbol) | 553-569 |
| 4. | n | (symbol) | (symbol) | 1056-1103 |
| 5. | n | (symbol) | (symbol) | 1120-1246 |
| 6. | (symbol) | (symbol) | (symbol) | 2147-2325 |
| 7. | (symbol) | (symbol) | (symbol) | 2694-2712 |

Fig. 13   Periods of sustained facial pattern. Notations for each of the periods of sustained facial patterns for M and F in the First Segment of C.14.1. The duration of each pattern, as it could be seen in the film, is given in terms of numbers of frames, counted from the zero frame. Zero frame is explained in the text

H   "Wide face": Brows raised; eyes open wide; lips parted smiling; mouth open. Occurs in 22.

I   "Frown face": Brows drawn together; eyes "frowning"; lips straight, tight at corners, upper lip retracted to reveal teeth. Occurs in 2 and 20.

If we may thus identify nine distinct facial arrangements, it may be remarked that F displays a considerable repertoire, even within such a short stretch of time and despite the repetitions already noted. If the face is to be regarded solely in terms of its affective functions we would be led to remark on the range of feeling or emotion F has in this short period of time. Perhaps she does have such a range of affective experience here. However, to say this directs our interest to F and her inner states and away from the question as to whether these different facial patterns serve any functions within the interaction. We turn, therefore, to look at the relationship between the appearance of these facial patterns and the other behavior that can be observed. To do this we must first consider the sequence of action.

## The action-sequence

The specimen we are here concerned with is a specimen of what we have called a "kissing round" which is a fairly common kind of interaction that can be observed in courting couples. This kissing round occurred while the couple was stationary, seated in a very close side-by-side on a park bench. M and F were so close to one another that their bodies were in contact from the shoulder downwards. M had extended his left arm along the back of the seat and thus had his arm around F's shoulders. Such "sitting together" within which kissing rounds often occur is, of course, a common pattern of behavior in couples in Western urban settings.

In a kissing round what we commonly observe is that the male or female, or both together, repeatedly orient their faces toward each other and move closer to make physical contact, either with the lips, the tip of the nose, the forehead or the cheek. The point of physical contact is variable. In the present specimen, M and F contact each other's necks, earlobes, noses, foreheads, cheeks and lips. Associated with such facial contacts, various huggings, strokings and other kinds of contacts may be made with the limbs. In the present case we shall not be concerned with these, for nothing of this could be seen, owing to the way in which the film had been made.

For the purposes of the present analysis, five different head orientations were distinguished in terms of the different directions $p$ was observed to point his face, relative to $q$'s head. If $p$ oriented his face fully toward $q$'s head he was said to be *facing q*; in this case, $p$'s face could be seen in full profile in the film. If $p$'s face could be seen in partial profile, $p$ was said to be *quarter-facing forward*. If only $p$'s cheek and tip of his nose could be seen, p was said to be *half-facing forward*. If none of the face could be seen and only the back of the head, p was said to be *facing forward*. Here, presumably, his face was oriented to the front of him and he was facing neither toward nor away from, the head of the other. If p rotated his head any further in the direction that would point his face away from q, he was said to be *facing away*. p was said to *approach* if he moved his face closer to q. This would include approaches to physical contact. p was said to *back-off* if he moved his face away from q, at the same time maintaining his face in *facing* orientation. *Lean forward/Lean away* was used to refer to forward and backward movements of the whole trunk. It occurs only in F who was observed to lean forward and towards M thus leaning in front of him.

In terms of these phrases of action a diagram of the specimen has been constructed (see Fig. 14). This shows the relative temporal extent of the head orientations of *facing* and *quarter-facing* for M and F, periods of *approach* and *back-off* and *leaning* and periods of physical contact. It also shows, for F, the facial patterns that were observed. *Half-facing*, *facing forward* and *facing away* have not been marked in the diagram but their occurrence is given in Table 9, which gives a detailed account of the action-sequence of the specimen.

*Analysis of the action-sequence*

We may begin by noting that there are periods of time within the segment being analyzed, during which F and M do not have their faces turned toward one another. They are either turned away from one another or both are facing forward. We shall refer to such periods as periods of Disengagement. Such periods of Disengagement separate periods of Involvement, in which either or both is facing or quarter-facing the other, approaching, leaning or touching. These periods of Involvement may be seen as being grouped into Phases, which are distinguished from one another in terms of how M and F relate their actions one to another:

*Phase I* In each period of Involvement in this phase, F faces M and then approaches him to kiss his neck, to touch noses with him or to touch foreheads with him. Each period of Involvement is begun by F – that is, she is the first to begin facing or approaching M in each case.

*Phase II* M is the first to turn to F. F part-turns to M. There is no approach and no physical contact.

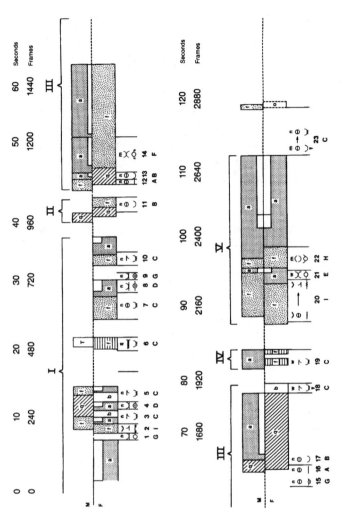

Fig. 14   This presents a map of the action-sequence of the first segment of C.14.1, together with the locations of all of F's facial patterns. The map has been plotted to the nearest eight frames ($1/3$ of a second). In the interests of clarity of presentation only facing (f), quarter-facing (q) and approach (a) head orientation units have been plotted. l = lean-forward; b = back-off; o = turnaway; white blocks on center line represent periods of physical contact. Exact time relations between M and F's actions are given in Table 9.

128

*Phase III* Periods of Involvement in this Phase are begun by M, and he approaches F to kiss her neck or her cheek or to touch noses with her. In this Phase F faces or part-faces M but she does not approach him. Phase III, thus, is in some ways a reversal of Phase I.

*Phase IV* M initiates and approaches F as he does in Phase III. F, however, leans toward M, and in front of him. There is no physical contact.

*Phase V* F begins the single period of Involvement in this Phase; M and F, facing each other, each approach and kiss lips to lips; each then kisses the other's neck. Except for the initial stage of F's approach to M, M and F show much greater symmetry in their behavior than they do in the other phases.

Following Phase V each turns 180 degrees away from the other and then remains facing forward. Shortly after this the cameraman stopped the film, for the kissing bout was over.

It will be seen thus that in Phases II, III, and V we have approaches and physical contact which in Phase I are initiated by F, in Phase III by M and in Phase V, it becomes mutual. Phases II and IV, it will be noted, are very brief compared with the other phases. They are distinguished here because, though in both cases M initiates them, there is either no approach (as in Phase II) or the approach is not reciprocated by F in the way it was in the preceding Phase (Phase V). As we shall see later, there are other features of behavior in these Phases which set them apart. We shall see first they are a special kind of Phase. They appear to bring about changes in established routines, rather than themselves being routines.

A more detailed account of the action-sequence of this kissing round is given in Table 9 in which all the periods of Involvement and Disengagement that occur within the sub-phases are given. This detailed account will be referred to throughout the discussion to follow. Accordingly, we have numbered the various sub-phases and other points of change within the action-sequence for ease of reference. This table should be read in conjunction with Fig. 14.

*The relationship between the action-sequence and facial patterns*

We shall now examine how F's face varies in relation to the Phase of the kissing round and the action within the Phase. We shall see how the role

Table 9. *Action-sequence of C.14.1, first segment*

*Phase I*
  1. F kisses M's neck (0149)
  DISENGAGE:  F faces forward from M (0177)
                 M faces forward from F (0181)
  2. a. F faces M (0200); M faces F (0214)
        F, still facing M, approaches M and they touch noses (0228)
     b. F backs off M (0258); M half-faces F (0304)
        F approaches, kisses M's neck (0295)
     c. F backs off M (0321); M faces F (0323)
        F and M, facing each other, approach, touch foreheads (0356)
  DISENGAGE:  F faces forward from M (0416)
                 M faces forward from F (0445)
  3. F quarter faces M (0477); M faces away from F (0477)
     F Faces M (0501)
     F leans forward and toward M (0533); M lowers head in forward (0533)
  DISENGAGE:  F faces forward from M (0591)
                 M half-faces F (0601)
  4. F faces M (0653); M faces forward (0643); M faces away (0760)
     F approaches and kisses M's neck (0729)
  DISENGAGE:  F half-faces M (0787)
                 M faces away (0795)
  5. F faces M (0810); M faces forward (0931)
     F leans cheek against M's cheek (0876)
  DISENGAGE:  F faces forward (0937)
                 M faces forward (0931)

*Phase II*
     M half-faces F (0958)
     F quarter-faces M (0993); M faces forward (0989); M faces away (1047)
     F faces M with head tilted back (1020)
  DISENGAGE:  F faces forward (1062)
                 M faces away from F (1047)

*Phase III*
  1. M faces F (1077); F quarter-faces M (1132)
     M kisses F's ear (1111)
     F faces M (1250); M touches noses with F (1229)
     M kisses F's ear (1505); F quarter-faces M (1514)
  DISENGAGE:  M faces away (1566)                              *
                 F tilts head back and rotates rapidly ("shake"), and quarter-
                 faces M (1571)
  2. M quarter-faces F (1606); F faces M (1858)
     M approaches and kisses F's cheek, neck (1850)
     F backs off (1889)
  DISENGAGE:  M faces forward from F (1902)
                 F half-faces M (1934)

Table 9 (*cont.*)

---

*Phase IV*
   M faces F and approaches (2009); F faces M (1027) and, while facing him, leans toward M (1967); leans away (1991); leans toward M (2011)
      DISENGAGE: M leans away from F, faces forward (2111)
                       F leans back from M, faces fully away (2106)
*Phase V*
   F faces M (2239); M faces F (2244)
   F approaches M, M approaches F (both facing, M and F kiss lips to lips) (2283)
   M and F kiss each other's necks (2686)
      DISENGAGE: F backs off M, looks behind (2722), half-faces M (2870)
                       M backs off, F faces away (2855)
   M faces F (2874); F faces away (2887), then turns to half-face M

            KISSING ROUND ENDS: CAMERA STOPS

---

of F's face in the kissing round may be inferred from the contexts of occurrence of her various facial patterns.

*(i)     Fa C ("Teeth smile") and Fa B ("Closed-lips smile"): An examination of their contexts of occurrence.* We may begin by noting the contrast, in terms of F's facial displays, between Phase I and Phase II. In Phase I F initiates each period of Involvement and in each instance that she turns to M she has some version of Fa C: smile with teeth showing, sometimes with open mouth as well. If M then faces F, as he does in I.2(a) and I.2(c), M and F approach each other and touch foreheads or noses, but they do not kiss. If M does not turn to F, but faces away from her as she turns to him (which he does in all the other periods of Involvement in this Phase), then F approaches and kisses M's neck, leans in front of him, or leans her cheek against his.

In contrast, in Phase III, M begins each period of Involvement by first turning to F and when he does so, F does not move towards him but remains still. Here she shows Fa B ("closed-lips smile"), and M then approaches her and kisses her. Fa B is thus associated with M kissing F, while when F shows Fa C ("teeth smile") she is active in approaching M and if M approaches her he does not kiss her.

These observations suggest that Fa B functions as a signal to M that F is receptive to approaches and kisses from him, whereas Fa C is part of a configuration that serves to divert him from approaching and kissing. A closer examination of the relationship between the patterning of action and these facial arrangements of F serves to confirm this interpretation.

First, it will be seen that each time M kisses F, M waits before finally approaching her until she shows Fa B, as if the appearance of Fa B is the signal that gives M clearance for this final approach. Whenever M kisses F he always proceeds in two steps: he turns to face F, then he approaches her. On each occasion we may note that M does not begin his approach until *after* F has shown Fa B. In the first period of Involvement of Phase III M turns to F and remains still, F part-turns to M with parted lips, her lips then close to produce Fa B and only when she has completed this does M begin his approach. In the second period of Involvement in Phase III this sequence is repeated, though here F changes to Fa B from Fa A ("neutral face"). Once again, however, M does not begin his approach until she has done so.

If we now look at the second segment of C.14.1, we see exactly the same sequence again. That is, here, beginning at frame 4198, M turns his head toward F, F turns to M and changes from Fa A to Fa B, whereupon M approaches and kisses her. These three sequences are diagrammed in Fig. 15, so that the exact time relations of these phrases of behavior may be seen.

Let us now examine the contexts of occurrence of Fa C, "teeth smile." We have already observed how Fa C appears consistently throughout Phase I, where F is active in approaching M. Here, also as we have seen, if M approaches F, he does not kiss her. We may now note that Fa C also appears at points which come just prior to changes in the relations of M and F's actions, where the change is either to a relationship in which F again takes the initiative in beginning new periods of Involvement, or to one in which she turns away when M approaches her. Thus whereas at the end of III.1 F shows Fa G, and when M again turns to her F responds with a part-turn and Fa B, as she did before, at the end of III.2 she shows Fa C. This is also the end of Phase III, and in the next Phase, though M approaches F again, he does not kiss her, and F now actively approaches M, showing Fa C throughout. Similarly, we may note how Fa C re-appears as M and F disengage from mutual kissing at the end of Phase V. When M turns to F yet again, as he does beginning at 2856, F turns rapidly away from him and a prolonged period of Disengagement follows. It will be seen from these observations that the facial pattern F shows at the *end* of a period of Involvement gives an indication of how she will behave in the next period. When she shows Fa C in such a context, this indicates that she will next take the initiative in relation to M.

Finally, further confirmation of our hypothesis about the functions of Fa C is derived from the second segment of the film. After a period in which M kisses F (already referred to above), and after a brief Disengagement, M again turns to F, but this time F turns to him with parted lips and exposed teeth. Here again, M does not commence any approach to F and they do not kiss.

We may conclude, thus, that these observations, when taken together, suggest that when F shows "teeth smile" she will be behaving in relation to M in a way quite different from the way she behaves when she shows "closed lips smile" or Fa B. Fa C signals that F is active in relation to M, and that M is not to kiss her. Fa B signals that F is receptive to kissing approaches from M.

*(ii)* *An examination of Phases II and IV.* Further support for the functional role we have proposed for Fa C and Fa B in this kissing round may be derived from an analysis of Phases II and IV. This analysis will also suggest how these phases serve to bring about change in the relationship of M and F's behavior. These Phases are both much shorter than the others and they intervene between Phases in which a repetitive pattern of interaction has been going on. Whereas Phases I and III have the character of routines, Phases II and IV appear to be negotiations.

In Phase II, for the first time in the sequence, M takes the initiative in starting a period of Involvement. He turns to F and F follows with a part-turn to M. Her lips are parted as she turns to M, but then she closes them to produce Fa B. As F closes her lips here, M turns away. F then turns somewhat more fully to M, still with Fa B, but now with her face tilted up slightly; then she also turns away. The next period of Involvement begins twenty-eight frames later (one and one sixth seconds) at frame 1049. Here Phase III begins.

It will be seen that the pattern in Phase II is a partial version of the pattern in Phase III. Such a pre-enactment, we suggest, enables F and M to come to an agreement as to what the next routine of interaction shall be. There are two possible ways by which it may do this. When M takes the initiative in turning to F at the beginning of Phase II he is doing something new in relation to what has preceded this. In doing this he could be regarded as proposing that a new routine be established. F's part-turn and Fa B is then a reply to this proposal, a reply which serves to suggest

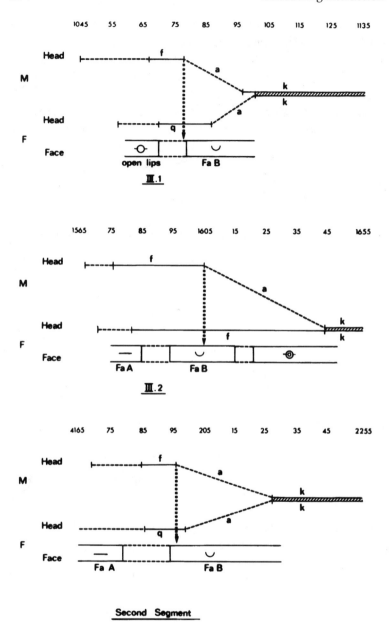

Second Segment

what this new routine might be. Alternatively, M's initiative may be more specific. It may be that it constituted a proposal that he should now do the kissing; F's part-turn and Fa B would in this case constitute her acceptance of this proposal. In either case, we may observe here how F's Fa B appears to serve as a signal to indicate what she is prepared to do next in relation to what M will do.

Turning to Phase IV, we may observe again how it partly foreshadows the pattern of interaction of Phase V. Here, however, it is not the specific routine of Phase V that is foreshadowed. It is, rather, that it will be F's turn to initiate periods of Involvement.

Phase IV is begun by M who turns to F in just the same way as he has been turning to her throughout Phase III. F responds, not by a part-turn and Fa B, but by leaning forward in front of M, with Fa C. Thus whereas in Phase II we had what in effect appeared to be a tryout for the pattern that was to follow, here one participant persists in the already established pattern while the other one now reciprocates differently. However, it will be seen that F, in reciprocating M's approach by leaning forward and with Fa C, is adopting a pattern of behavior which she has used in Phase I. Thus she refers back to an earlier behavioral interrelation, in which she is the initiator of Involvements, and in this way she sets the stage for reestablishing that relationship. And indeed, as may be seen, Phase V is initiated by F.

Fig. 15   These diagrams show the relationship in time between M's orientation and approach components and F's orientation and approach components and changes in F's face, for the beginning of kissing involvements at III.1, III.2 and the Second Segment.

For both F and M the lines represent orientation components and their convergence represents approach. Broken lines represent movement. Line segment labeled f = face; q = quarter-face; a = approach; k = physical contact. The boxes below F's head components indicate stable facial patterns when enclosed by continuous lines. Periods of change are represented by broken lines.

The perpendicular line beginning at the start of M's approach component indicates the relationship between the beginning of this and the state of F's face. Note that in each case M does not begin his approach until F has completed the formation of the facial pattern Fa B or "closed lips smile."

The diagram is begun in each case at the point where either F or M begins to change from Disengagement (facing forward) to Involvement (quarter-facing or facing).

We may now observe that just as Phase II and IV appear to fore-shadow the new routines that are to follow and so serve, as we suggest, to bring about the consensus upon which those new routines are based, so the occurrence of these Phases is itself foreshadowed. There are features of F's behavior that immediately precede these Phases that appear to hint at the new relationship that is to be established. Thus it will be seen how, in Phase I, in which F takes the initiative and is active in approaching M, in F's last approach to M in this Phase (at I.1), she leans her cheek against M instead of kissing his neck or touching fore-heads with him. In so doing, though she is active in her approach, she here ceases to act *on* M, but leans on him, and so becomes passive in relation to him. Thus she hints at a new mode of relating to M and so creates for him the opportunity of trying out, or proposing, a new routine.

Similarly, F does not switch to the mode of response she adopts in Phase IV without warning. We have already described how, at the end of III.2, as she moves away from M after his kiss, she displays Fa C. Fa C, as we have seen, occurs when F is the initiator of Involvements. Thus, in ending the second period of Involvement of Phase III with Fa C, in the facial pattern she adopts she hints at the change in the relationship of her behavior to that of M that will be brought about through the enactment of Phase IV.

*(iii)    Other facial patterns and their place in the interaction.* We have noted so far that when F takes the initiative in facing M, and when M approaches F and kissing does not take place, F displays Fa C ("teeth smile"), whereas when M turns first to F and F then shows Fa B ("closed-lip smile"), M approaches her and kisses her, while F remains relatively still. We adduced several observations to suggest that M's approach to F to kiss her was contingent upon F showing Fa B, whereas when F used Fa C this served to signal that she was not receptive to kiss-ing approaches by M. We turn now to consider some of the other facial patterns F shows.

Phase III includes three approaches by M. In the first M turns to F, F part-turns to M and displays Fa B. Thereupon M approaches and kisses her. He then pulls back a little and M and F each face each other, M intermittently touching F's nose with his in a light brushing fashion. Here we observe Fa F, or "dreamy" face. Following this, M reapproaches F for a further and this time very lengthy period of kissing.

Fa F may here serve to provide M with information about how F is responding to his kissing, and so how she will behave in response to his continued advances. Notice that the first of M's three kissing contacts with F is very short. During the period of nose touching which follows, M would be able to perceive F's face and so, perhaps, check on how she is responding to his kissing. Here F's face serves as a source of information both on what she will do next and also on what she will let M do.

Phase V, in which lips-to-lips kissing and a mutual embrace occur, is very interesting from the point of view of F's facial behavior. She shows here a whole series of different patterns, each developing in a continuous fashion from the preceding one. The notation system employed in this paper was not adequate to describe all these changes, and here only four patterns have been marked: two variants, both labeled I ("frown face"), E ("kiss face II") and H ("wide face").

F initiates Phase V with a turn from turned-away to facing M. This turn is begun very abruptly and the movement is rapid. In this it is different from the other turns she makes. Once facing M she moves slowly closer and closer to him. As she moves closer she speaks and at the same time her brows are drawn together in a strong frown, her eyes are actively narrowed and her lips are drawn back at the corners tightly. As she moves yet closer she begins to retract her lips to show her teeth. Then, the extreme tension goes out of the eyebrows, the lips are momentarily inrolled, but then they are parted and protruded forward slightly, the eyelids are partially lowered and for a moment, just prior to the actual contact of her lips with M's, F's face shows a distinctive and recognizable pattern, Fa E, which we have here nicknamed "active kiss face II" but which could be called "passionate kiss face" since it is the kind of face that is seen in females in kissing that is serious and erotically arousing. At the moment of osculation, however, F's face suddenly changes to Fa A, "neutral face," and immediately after the kiss her eyes are opened "overwide," the brows are raised, and the lips parted relaxedly. This is Fa H, which has a look of child-like wide-eyed innocence about it. Thereupon, M and F fall with vigor on each other's necks, in what appears to be a rather intense mutual embrace.

The facial patterns F here shows in this sequence are far different from what one expects to see in seriously erotic or passionate kissing. It is as if F is here regulating the amount of arousal M can achieve by herself offering displays that do not otherwise fit the immediate context.

Thus she turns to M with vigor and approaches him with "fierce" faces. Yet, for but $9/24$ of a second, just before their lips touch, F's face is posed for passionate, not for playful kissing. Here, perhaps, she hints at passions someday (or sometime) to be aroused. Perhaps we see here an instance of what appears to be a common principle of courtship: the continued interest of the other partner is maintained, and even heightened, by fleeting displays of behavior that belong to later stages of the courtship program.[2] If F can hint to M what possibilities the future holds in store for him, she can hold his interest.

Two other facial patterns may now receive brief comment. Fa D ("kiss face I") occurs twice, both times when F is approaching to kiss M. It is a facial pattern that arises as F prepares to perform an action that is carried out by the lips and we see the lips preparing for the contact that they will make as she approaches. Fa G ("lower lip forward") occurs twice as F is turning away from M after being kissed by him. As we shall note in a later section of this paper, this facial pattern is seen in precisely the same context in other kissing couples.

*(iv)    A note on tongue protrusion.* It is noteworthy that when F backs off from M at the end of Phase III, and when she turns sharply away from M at the end of Phase V, she protrudes her tongue from her mouth. The phenomenon of tongue showing has received extensive discussion by Smith, Chase and Lieblich (1974). They conclude that the common feature of all the contexts they observed in which the tongue is shown is that $p$ is reducing, cutting off or forestalling involvement with another or others. In the present specimen F shows her tongue when she is backing off or withdrawing from M, on both occasions following upon a prolonged period of intensive kissing. What then follows is a period in which, despite M's approaches, F turns away from him (after Phase V) or does not permit kissing (as in Phase IV). The appearance of her tongue at these points is thus in accord with what might be expected in the light of Smith et al.'s observations.

Another observer of tongue showing is Eibl-Eibesfeldt. His interpretation is quite different from Smith's. He refers to "tongue flicking" in which the "tongue is put out fleetingly . . . " and observes that this serves as an invitation to flirtation. He states that girls of easy virtue in Central Europe signal their sexual availability by showing their tongues, and

---

[2] I am indebted to a conversation with Desmond Morris for this suggestion.

that among the Waika Indians it is used by both sexes as an indication of sexual interest. Eibl-Eibesfeldt suggests that this is a ritualized form of licking (Eibl-Eibesfeldt 1972, pp. 141–2). Insofar as licking another entails great physical intimacy, to show the tongue in this way could come to function as a sexual signal insofar as it suggests a readiness for closeness.

The observed instances of tongue protrusion in the present specimen and the contexts in which they occur are, as we have seen, associated with F's withdrawal from periods of intense Involvement. As we have said, this fits more closely to what might be expected in the light of Smith's observations. Although on the basis of this alone, we are in no position to draw any conclusions about the validity or otherwise of Eibl-Eibesfeldt's or of Smith's suggestion, we do suggest that very detailed analysis will be required even of such an apparently simple gesture as tongue showing, before speculation about its possible derivation becomes worthwhile. Since Eibl-Eibesfeldt supplies no details as to when, within the interaction sequences he has observed, tongue showing occurs, we cannot comment further. We would merely like to point out that the present specimen provides an example of tongue showing in a flirtatious or courting interaction which, although superficially it might seem to fit with the examples Eibl-Eibesfeldt has provided, and so support his interpretation, yet an analysis of the context of occurrence of the tongue showing within the interaction shows that it could as well be seen to support the interpretations of Smith et al.

## Discussion

We shall now consider the foregoing analysis in relation to three different questions. First, we shall examine it from the point of view of its relationship to more general considerations about the organization of face-to-face interaction. Second, we shall discuss the implications of our approach for the study of the face. Third, we shall touch briefly upon the implications for the study of human courting behavior.

### The kissing round and the organization of interaction

When individuals engage in face-to-face interaction their behavior tends to become systemically interrelated. That is, each continuously adjusts his behavior in relation to that of the other, and they tend to establish stable systems of relationship so that we may speak as if their behavior is governed by shared sets of rules. Goffman has dealt with this in his analysis of what he has called *focused* interaction (Goffman 1957, 1961, 1963) where he has suggested that on such occasions participants come to govern their conduct in accordance with a jointly established "working consensus." Occasions of focused interaction are highly complex in their organization and in attempting to analyze the way in which the behavior of participants in them functions, it is useful to regard an occasion of focused interaction as comprised of a system of systems of behavioral interrelations with many different levels of organization.

In reference to the specimen analyzed in this study, we may see that the "kissing round" here dealt with is but one small system of behavioral relationship that exists within the framework of other relationships which extend over much longer periods of time and which integrate such small sub-systems into more inclusive organizations. Thus the "kissing round" occurs within the framework of a "sitting together" (a system of spatial-orientational relationship referred to elsewhere as a "formation system"). "Sitting together," and the sub-systems such as "kissing rounds" that it integrates, is itself part of another level of behavioral organization which we might call "afternoon together" (a system of behavioral relationship which we might refer to, following Goffman 1971, as a "with"). Such an "afternoon together" may itself be a sub-system within a yet more inclusive system, which includes all the different occasions of togetherness M and F have with one another and which constitute their participation in a system of organization we might refer to as the "relationship" – here that of "couple" or "courtship." At each level in this complex hierarchy of systems we may identify a "working consensus" and different observational procedures and descriptive strategies will be needed at each level. Here we are confined to the level of the "kissing round" and its internal organization. We assume, however, that interactive systems, at whatever level, share similar principles of organization, so that a close analysis of a system at one level will throw light on principles that apply more generally.

A central problem in any investigation of interaction from this point of view will be to see how, in terms of the functioning of observable behavior, the "working consensus" for a given behavioral system is established and maintained. In particular, this means that we must identify those aspects of behavioral function which serve to control or regulate the behavior of the participants in relation to the currently established pattern of relationship. This requires that we look for regularities in behavioral relationship, but also that we look closely at places where these regularities change.

Of particular interest, then, from the point of view of more general principles of interactional organization, is the analysis of the sub-routines of the kissing round and the way in which these routines change. Thus we observed three sub-routines: Phase I, where F takes the initiative in orienting to M and approaching him; Phase III, where M assumes the initiative; and Phase V, where F re-assumes the initiative, though here M and F's behavior becomes much more symmetrical. In Phase I and Phase III, where two or three repetitive cycles of interaction could be observed, we saw how F's facial behavior appeared to function as a signal that confirmed the pattern of the current sub-routine. In the intervening Phases, Phase II and Phase IV, we were able to observe the way in which sub-routines of interaction may be changed. Thus in Phase II the change was brought about by a pre-enactment of the pattern that was to follow in Phase III. Here M initiated a turn to F which was a fragment of the complete sequence of actions he would perform in Phase III, while F responded to this by showing the facial display she was to use in Phase III. We suggested in this way that F confirmed the new pattern of behavioral relationship. Thus the "pre-enactment" of Phase II allowed M and F to agree upon a new set of rules to govern their interaction. In Phase IV F responded to an established pattern of behavior in M by a pattern of behavior that belonged to Phase I. In this way she established her intention to re-assume the initiative in starting periods of Involvement. Once again, we saw behavior which served to forewarn what later behavior was to be, and so again Phase IV allowed for a change in the prevailing rules of interaction.

A principle of importance that is here being illustrated is that an established routine in interaction is not simply changed, but that if a new routine is established its establishment is done as a joint achievement of the participants. This means that they must have a way of doing it, a way of each bringing the other to the point where they can begin together in terms of the new routine. The way in which this is done is for each to signal what his next mode of behavioral interrelating might be, before he actually begins to relate in this new fashion. Thus we can expect to see a pre-exchange before any exchange that is done according to new rules.

This feature of interactional organization has been demonstrated in some recent work on closings. The closing of an interactional system may be regarded as a special case of changing a routine and, like changing a routine, it is a joint achievement. Schegloff and Sacks (1973), in a study of conversational systems, have shown how such systems are brought to an end by a terminal exchange. This is a pair of utterances, such as "good-bye: good-bye," whose special function it is to bring both participants to the point that each does not respond to the end of the other's last utterance as if it is then his turn to speak. But Schegloff and Sacks show that such terminal exchanges cannot occur anywhere in a conversational system. They must have been preceded by a "closing section." Here $p$ announces, by a variety of devices (such as "O.K.," "we-el," "So-o" – to give their examples) that he is ready to close and the terminal exchange will not take place until $q$ has reciprocated, that is, matched $p$'s closing section initiation with a closing system completion. Similarly, mention may be made of some observations on the closing down of another kind of interactional system, the F-formation system described more fully in Chapter 7. This is a spatial-orientated system that participants in face-to-face conversations usually (though not always) establish and maintain and which they typically bring to a close concurrently with the closing of a conversation. In the observations reported it also appears that closing is accomplished in two steps: first we observe one of the participants to step away, turn out, or in some other way lapse in his contribution to the F-formation system. This is then reciprocated by the other, so that for a short time the system is not being fully sustained. The participants then re-constitute the system, whereupon they may jointly turn and step away from one another. Similarly, findings from the analysis of greetings presented in Chapter 6 may be mentioned here, for here it will be seen how greeting is often accomplished in two steps: a "distance salutation" and a "close salutation." Once again we have an exchange which allows the individuals involved to attune themselves to one another, so that they can then proceed together according to a new behavioral relationship.

If, in the present analysis, Phases II and IV have a functional status similar to the pre-phases of greeting and of conversational and facing-formation system closure, as we are suggesting, we may observe here, however, that in the present specimen, at least, these pre-phases are themselves foreshadowed. As we saw, the interaction in the kissing round could be segmented into periods of Involvement separated by periods of Disengagement. Within each period of Disengagement either

M or F will be the next to start a new period of Involvement. Whether this will be done in a new way, or not, and so whether a new Phase will be begun, is evidently indicated by how F behaves as she changes from Involvement to Disengagement. We pointed out how her action towards M in the last sub-phase of Phase I appeared to hint at her readiness for some change in routine. Likewise, as F moved away from the last period of Involvement in Phase III, her facial pattern was quite different from the one she showed at the end of the previous period of Involvement in Phase III, but it was one that belonged to a pattern of relationship we had already seen, namely one in which she takes the initiative in respect to M in beginning periods of involvement.

We have said that pre-exchanges and foreshadowings arise in interaction because the participants, having jointly committed themselves to a particular kind of behavioral relationship, must, if they are to change to a new one, have a means of changing together. In the case of the changes of routine in the kissing round we have examined here, it should be noted that what we have been concerned with are changes in routine *within* a kissing round. Another problem that arises for interactants when they change routines is that of maintaining (or changing) the boundaries of the system within which the change in routine is to take place. Thus, when a period of Involvement comes to an end, how do M and F ensure that this is not also the end of the kissing round, or how do they ensure that it is the end (as it is at the end of Phase V)? An important feature that these routine-changing phases (such as Phase II and Phase IV) must have, is a reference to the system of organization in which they are contained. In the present example we may find this, we believe in (a) the way in which behavior at the end of the previous Phase structures the context within which the next period of Involvement will begin, and (b) in the behavior pattern employed in the routine-changing Phase itself. We will discuss these two features in order.

The way a phase of Involvement is ended creates the context for repetition or change, but where it is to be changed it will also refer to the system of behavioral organization of which the ending sub-phase has been a part. When F leans her cheek against M's in the last sub-phase of Phase I we suggested that in doing so she no longer acts *on* M, but becomes passive in relation to him and so suggests a possible new mode of relation. However, the new mode of relation she is suggesting is one that is one of a kind of relation that can be incorporated into a kissing round. Thus any subsequent action that either of them takes will be responded to by the other as an action governed by the prevailing principles of the kissing round.

The behavior in the routine-changing phases can also be seen as having a reference to the system within which the change is to take place, and so contain the change within that level of organization. This is clear enough in Phase II where F's Fa B is here a signal for kissing to continue. Like the cheek lean, it proposes a pattern of behavior that is wholly within the framework of the kissing round. In Phase IV, however, which, as we have seen, does not foreshadow the pattern of organization of the next Phase, F behaves according to a pattern she has used in Phase I and so, we suggested, she hinted at her intention to regain the initiative in starting periods of Involvement. However, we may also note that by referring back to her behavior in Phase I, although she does not foreshadow the pattern of any subsequent Phase, this does once again serve to maintain the context as being that of the kissing round.

We may now compare what happens at the end of the kissing round. We may expect here that F will behave differently as she ends the last period of Involvement of the kissing round from the way she behaves at the end of a period of Involvement within the round. We can see an ending to a kissing round at the end of Phase V and also at the end of the kissing round recorded in the second segment.

At the end of Phase V, as F backs off from M, she shows Fa C, as already noted, and she also protrudes her tongue, as we have noted also. At the same time she rotates her head back to look behind her. In doing this, she looks in a direction she has not looked in before. In doing this, she looks out of the space that she and M have been using for the kissing round and, in so doing, looks to the wider surrounding environment and so hints at other variables to which her behavior may become linked. In this way she shows that the kissing round frame is over for her. This interpretation appears to be confirmed when, shortly thereafter, M initiates a turn to F. F responds to this by facing away very sharply.

The kissing round recorded in the second segment of the film ends with a Phase similar to Phase III. A period of Disengagement follows a period of Involvement that has the same structure as the periods of Involvement in Phase III, and this period of Disengagement is ended when M turns to F again. F responds with a part-turn to M as before but, as we noted above, she does not show Fa B, as she did earlier. Her lips are parted slightly, some exposure of teeth, and M does not continue his approach. F then pulls in her lower lip over her teeth and appears to lick it briefly and then, reverting to a smile with lips only very slightly parted, she glances over her shoulder. She again, thus, looks to the wider world just as she did at the end of Phase V. She then faces forward, whereupon M shifts posture, leaning toward her but, at the same time, bending his left arm at the elbow to bring his hand up so that he can lean his head on it.

We see, thus, that F behaves in a similar way at the end of the last period of Involvement of each of these two kissing rounds, but in a way that is quite different from the way she behaves at the ends of periods of Involvement within either of them. In referring, with her glance, to spaces beyond the space used for the kissing round, we suggest, she indicates that the frame of the kissing round is ended for her, that her behavior is no longer going to be governed by its principles. We may note that "looking out," in this way is something that is not uncommonly observed in individuals who are about to leave an F-formation system, as if one way of hinting an end to one's current involvement is to look at parts of the environment which are not incorporated into the focus of involvement one is currently related to.

In short, we may see how F's behavior appears to address itself not only to "what next," but also to the context within which that "what next" is to take place. This is done either by keeping behavior within the bounds of the current context, in which case that context can continue to operate, or by referring outside that context. This can be a signal to the other that the current context will now be terminated. M may thus be forewarned and so, jointly, again, a system of behavioral relationship can be brought to an end or changed.

### Differential functions of facial patterns

We started our analysis by listing a number of different facial patterns displayed by F and we have shown that, at least for some of these, we were able to see them repeated often enough for us to be able to compare the contexts of their occurrence and so propose what function they had within the interaction sequence we were studying. We may now raise the question: do the facial patterns we have observed in F occur in others and, if they do, within the context of other kissing rounds, do they have the same functions? With this question in mind we have reviewed the other filmed examples of kissing and related types of courting interaction that we have collected. This material is still very limited, but it does suggest that the features of F's facial behavior we have observed in the kissing round in C14.1 are not idiosyncratic. The main question we have been able to look into is whether or not "closed-lip" smile is characteristic of actual kissing, whereas "teeth smile" is characteristic of kissing round interactions where actual kissing nevertheless does not occur.

The material available to us for review consists of three series of film specimens: the CO Series and the C14 Series, comprising seventy-seven couples filmed in public parks in New York City, and two couples filmed in Australia (AN 1, AN 2). Of these, only eight specimens included examples of kissing or of a kissing round where it was also possible to examine facial behavior.

In the CO series we have three examples, CO 51, CO 59 and CO 75 where, as the couple walks along, F turns her face towards and up to M's, and M bends down and kisses her. In CO 51 and CO 59 F shows a facial pattern very similar to Fa B ("closed-lip smile"). In CO 75 F shows relaxed part-closed eyes and relaxed, parted, slightly protruded lips; a face pattern which, it may be noted, is very close to the one given by Eibl-Eibesfeldt (1971, p. 142) of a Waika Indian girl inviting a kiss.

Finally, in AN 1, a five-minute stretch of film of a seated couple, there are four instances when M and F orient to one another and where M moves his face in closer for kissing. In two of these instances kissing does not take place, F turning away as M completes his approach. In both of these instances F shows "teeth smile." In the two instances where kissing does occur, F shows no definitive smile, and she changes to a facial pattern very like Fa D ("kiss face I").

These few examples suggest, thus, that in kissing round contexts or contexts closely similar to this, if F shows "closed-lip smile" or some variant of slightly protruded, parted lips, in turning to M or when M turns to her, kissing is likely to occur. If F shows "teeth smile" at these same junctures, however, though M may begin an approach for kissing, actual kissing does not take place. The relationship between kissing or non-kissing and "closed-lip smiling" or "teeth smiling" that we had discerned in C14.1, thus, appears to obtain in other couples as well.

Several of the other facial patterns described for C14.1 may also be seen in other specimens, again in closely similar contexts. Thus Fa G (brows normal, upper lid lowered over eye, lips parted slightly with lower lip pushed forward slightly), which we see in F on two occasions in C14.1, as she turns from a kiss and where further kissing will follow, we also see in F as she turns from the kiss in CO 51 and CO 75. In both of these cases we may note that, as F turns her head away from the kiss, she also tilts it forward. Fa E, which we have already said could be described as a "passionate kiss face," is very well illustrated in C14.3 – a specimen of a couple who appear to be engaged in quite intense kissing.

These few examples, drawn as they are almost at random from among couples observed in urban park settings, do suggest that females, at least, have a repertoire of facial patterns which are common to them and which function in much the same way in kissing interactions, regardless of who the individuals are. We may well be able to build up a vocabulary of facial patterns that are used in kissing rounds, and be able to specify their functions within such interactions. An attempt along these lines will have to wait until a sufficiently large number of specimens have been acquired. For obvious reasons, this material is not very easy to obtain.

It should be clear, of course, that the facial patterns we have been describing here may not be confined in their occurrence to the context of kissing rounds. Fa C and its variants and Fa B, especially, occur much more widely. Thus we cannot infer, from the mere appearance of one of these facial patterns, what sort of an interactional context we are dealing with. A careful study of the range of contexts within which these different facial patterns can be observed to occur could be undertaken, and a systematic comparison of contexts might show that, for a given species of facial arrangement, the contexts of its occurrence all shared some underlying similarity or, perhaps, at least some "family resemblance." This could then, perhaps, be summarized in some single concept. This procedure has been followed, for human facial behavior, by Smith et al. (1974) in their study of tongue protrusion. As we have already mentioned, the common thread of all the contexts of occurrence of tongue protrusion studied by Smith and his colleagues was that $p$ was reducing, withdrawing from, or fending off interaction with others. Smith et al. infer from this common thread of contexts of occurrence that the information another could gain from observing tongue protrusion, without knowing anything of its context, is that of a tendency to withdraw from interaction. This information is referred to as the "message" of the behavior (Smith 1968; 1969a, b). "Meaning" is the way in which a recipient organism behaves in response to the behavior. Here, however, the recipient responds not to the "message" of the behavior but to its occurrence in a context. In Smith's terms, thus, in this chapter we have been attempting to give an account of the "meanings" of F's facial displays within the context of a kissing round.

## Implications for the study of human courtship

Courtship is the process by which a more or less stable relationship is formed between two individuals of the opposite sex, within which mating can take place. Since the relationship is to be one within which mating occurs, many of the behaviors which serve to establish and maintain the pair-bond that is the outcome of courtship are similar to behaviors that precede mating. An important feature of the behavior of courtship, indeed, appears to be that it should create some degree of sexual arousal in the partners. It seems that the "kissing round" of the sort we have studied in this paper, which is obviously so characteristic of a certain stage of courtship, has this function.

The detailed study of a single kissing round cannot allow us to draw any conclusions about this kind of interaction or its functioning in courtship. However, there are certain features of the organization of this kissing round that appear to illustrate a pattern of behavioral relationship that might be expected to be widely characteristic of courting interactions. From the point of view of the further study of human courtship behavior, therefore, the present analysis may suggest what may be looked for.

From this point of view, it is of interest to recall that throughout it is F's behavior, and particularly that of her face, that appears to function as a regulator, modulating the approaches and orientations of M. Thus the interaction of Phases III and IV may be characterized by saying that M makes a series of highly similar approaches to F, while what comes of those approaches – whether M continues into kissing F or not, that is – depends upon how F responds to them. In Phases I and V M does not initiate Involvement but waits for F to do so, and what he does then follows upon what F does. Throughout, thus, M's behavior appears to be guided by F. It is not surprising, therefore, that we find that F's behavior is also more highly differen-tiated than that of M.

This pattern, in which F appears to regulate and modulate the repetitive approaches of M is of interest because it seems that this is what we might expect on the basis of a more general picture of human courtship. One such general picture has been sketched by Crook (1972). In this picture, a female may appear attractive to a male (because of her various secondary sexual characteristics, both biological and cultural), however he will not approach her without some indication from her of her interest in him. In approaching her, however, the male must not only be sexually interested, he must at the same time be reassured that the female will not be aggressive to him. Certain characteristics of females, such as relative hairlessness, smooth complexion and voice tone which have a childlike character may contribute to this. They may also serve to dispose the male toward care-taking and protective behaviors which are important, not only as a reassurance to the female that she also will not be attacked upon approach by the male, but also in relation to the role the male will play in relation to the offspring that are the likely out-come of a successful courtship. However, once an association is estab-lished, specifically courting interaction may develop in which the male behaves toward the female in such a way as to arouse her sexually. However, how frequently and how extensively the male may do this will depend upon how the female responds. The male's behavior may con-sist in a succession of rounds of sexual advances – and this of course includes kissing – while the female will respond, in each round of sexual advances from the male, with behavior which serves to regulate this: she may show signs of sexual arousal, and so encourage the male to con-tinue or she may, in various ways, show a reduction in sexual respon-siveness and so discourage the male. However, in so encouraging or dis-couraging him, the female is faced with a delicate task. Her encouragements must be carefully matched to the stage that has been reached in the pair-bond that may also be developing. Her discourage-ments must also be carefully managed if she is not to drive the male off altogether. It will appear, thus, that from the point of view of successful courtship, we may expect that it will be the female who will show a high degree of differentiation in her behavior. In courtship interactions, thus, we may expect to see just the kind of behavioral relationship arising that we have found in the kissing round of C14.1

We have noted that F's face showed great variety in its behavior. M's face, in comparison, appeared relatively monotonous. Is this difference characteristic? If the above picture of human courtship has been sketched along the right lines, it would not be surprising if there were a tendency for females to be more varied and subtle in their facial behavior than males.


## Conclusion

We began this chapter by suggesting that in the study of the human face far too much attention has been paid to the face in its function in emotion and that our understanding of the role of the face in interaction remained almost unexplored. We have now seen how, by looking at the patterning of facial behavior in the context of interaction, we may arrive at some detailed notions of how it functions. We have seen how F's face appears to function as a feedback device, both regulating the relationship between M and F's behavior directly and also serving to refer to the wider context or frame within which this behavior is occurring, thus disambiguating F's actions and contributing to the maintenance of the current "working consensus" which governs the kissing round or its particular sub-phase, or contributing to the process by which this consensus is modified.

We may conclude by remarking on the superb efficiency of the face for these communicative functions. It allows for shared sets of expectations to be established or to be confirmed with extreme rapidity. If a device like the face was not available, coordination of action in interaction would be far less delicate and rapid. The possibility of each misreading the other's behavior would be much greater and the chances of maintaining one level of interactional organization as a change is made at another level would be much less. It appears that the delicate tuning device that the face is here seen to be, makes possible the development of the kind of highly complex hierarchy of systems of interrelationship that are characteristic of human social interaction. This, in turn, allows for the development of the elaborate systems of relationship in which individuals are enmeshed and which are so characteristic of human sociality. Thus we see how a detailed study of the interactional functioning of the face may help us to an understanding of the behavioral foundations from which the complexity and delicacy of human social life emerges.

## Postscript

At the time this study was published (1975), to the best of my knowledge, it represented one of the only attempts to analyze in detail just how patterns of facial behavior may function interactionally. In the introduction to the paper it is noted that the study of the face from this point of view had otherwise been undertaken almost exclusively in the context of interaction between infants and their adult caretakers. This continues to be the case. Since 1975 almost all of the studies of the interactive functions of the face that have appeared have been concerned with infants in interaction with their mothers (occasionally other caretakers). Malatesta (Malatesta 1985, Malatesta and Haviland 1982), Trevarthen (1977, 1979) and Fogel (1982) are exemplary, and anthologies such as Field and Fogel (1982), Tronick (1982), Lewis and Saarni (1985) and Zivin (1985) contain representative papers. There are far fewer studies of the interactive functions of the face in other contexts. Camras (1977) and Zivin (1977a, 1977b, 1982) are among those who have looked at the role of facial expression in interactions between children of nursery school age. Kraut and Johnston (1979) and Goldenthal, Johnston and Kraut (1981) have studied the social contexts of smiling in adults in natural situations and in field experimental situations. Ekman's (1979) paper on eyebrow movements also deserves mention here. In this paper he draws attention to some of the ways in which the eyebrows may be employed as gestures in association with speech. Finally, Fridlund (in press), in a critical discussion of work on facial expression in the light of considerations from ethology and evolutionary theory, argues for what he calls a "behavioral-ecology" view of facial expression. On this view, facial expressions are to be accounted for in terms of their functions as displays of social intention (affiliation, attack, withdrawal, and so on) rather than of "readouts" of emotional states. He urges an interactionist orientation in studying them and suggests that, alongside the sophisticated techniques that are now available for the description of facial action, such as Ekman's Facial Action Coding Scheme (Ekman and Friesen 1978) or Izard's Maximally Discriminative Facial Movement Coding System (Izard 1979), we need a "Facial Elicitor Coding System." That is to say, we need a way of studying the circumstances in which facial expressions occur, and their communicative functions. He argues that only if more attention is paid to this will we come to have a proper understanding of the adaptive significance of this highly complex aspect of human communicative behavior. The approach to the study of facial expression exemplified in this chapter, it will be seen, fits well with this view that Fridlund advocates.

# 6

## A description of some human greetings

### Introduction

In this chapter we describe certain instances of human greetings. The examples are all taken from films or video-tapes prepared for research on communicative behavior. They were all recorded in the eastern United States, among members of the professional middle class. Most of them were taken from a film made at an outdoor party held at a private house in a suburb of New York City. They include both greetings accorded to guests as they arrived at the party and also those that took place among the guests during the party.

The term "greeting" will be used to refer to that unit of social interaction often observed when people come into one another's presence, which includes a distinctive exchange of gestures or utterances in which each person appears to signal to the other, directly and explicitly, that he has been seen. Such an exchange may be as fleeting as an exchange of glances between strangers as they pass on the street, or it may be as prolonged and elaborate as the salutations that may sometimes be observed at airports or docksides, when loved ones are reunited after a prolonged absence

There are a number of reasons for choosing to study greetings. First of all, they have an important function in the management of relations

Jointly authored with Andrew Ferber. Originally published by R. P. Michael and J. H. Crook, eds., *Comparative Ecology and Behaviour of Primates*, London and New York: Academic Press, 1973, pp. 591–668. Reprinted with permission of the publishers. Thanks are due to all those who appeared in the films here made use of, for permitting themselves to be studied. Jane Ferber deserves special thanks for permitting the birthday party to be filmed. Financial support came from grants-in-aid from Ralph Freedman, Emory Kleiman and Mike Chernow, and from National Institutes of Health Grant No. 15977-03. Some of the film analysis equipment was bought with funds from the Van Amerigan Foundation grant to the project on Human Communication, Bronx State Hospital.

between people. It is by way of the greeting that a guest is made to feel
properly part of a party. It is by way of a greeting that friends acknowledge, and so confirm and continue their friendship. In the manner in
which the greeting ritual is performed, the greeters signal to each other
their respective social status, their degree of familiarity, their degree of
liking for one another, and also, very often, what roles they will play in
the encounter that is about to begin.

Secondly, since greeting occurs among people all over the world, it
would appear to be an excellent unit of social behavior to study if one is
to begin to examine systematically what is universal and what is traditional in human communicative behavior. The value of the greeting
for this kind of study has already been recognized by Eibl-Eibesfeldt
(1968, 1970, 1972b). Although no cultural comparisons are attempted
in this paper it is hoped that the detail we provide and the format we
have developed will prove useful in comparative studies.

Finally, greetings occur in animal species other than humans. If an
effective comparative ethology for human behavior is ever to be developed, we need to be able to make detailed comparisons between human
behavior and behavior of other animals. This, however, cannot be useful unless we are comparing behavior that occurs in contexts that can be
compared. It would seem that the greeting, as an interactional event,
provides us with a unit of behavior which occurs in closely similar contexts and thus makes comparisons between human and animal behavior meaningful. In this chapter we confine ourselves to description in an
effort to show that a common structure appears to characterize at least
those greeting transactions we have looked at, and also to show what
the repertoire of behaviors that occurs within such transactions
includes.

## Materials and methods of study

The specimens of greetings examined for this paper were taken from
films and video-tapes made for the purpose of studying communication
conduct. These included two films and a video-tape made specially for
this study. The films will be known herein as the *Birthday Party film* and
*Wedding.*[1] The video-tape will be referred to as the *Thanksgiving tape.*

[1] These films were made under the technical supervision of Jacques Van Vlack, Studies
in Human Communication Division, Eastern Pennsylvania Psychiatric Institute,
Philadelphia. Thanks are due to Paul Byers, Joseph Schaeffer and Sander Kirsch for

Use was also made of three other films made at other times for other purposes. These are known as *TRD Band*, *TRD Picnic* and *An Observation*. Details of all these films will now be given.

## Birthday Party film

As this was our principal document it will be described fully. The film consists of 4,800 feet of 16 mm color film, much of it with synchronized sound taken on an afternoon in early July 1969 at an outdoor birthday party held for the five-year-old son of one of the authors (AF). The party took place in the back garden and adjoining private beach of the boy's home in Westchester County, NY. Forty-five people were present, though not all of them at the same time. There were twenty-three adults and twenty-two children, aged between twenty-three and sixty-five years, and two and eleven years respectively. These included the parents of the five-year-old, his little sister; the parents, father-in-law, sister and her husband, of the boy's father; seven adults who were close friends of the boy's parents and their children; and several children who were schoolmates of the boy, together with their parents. The great majority of these people were of Jewish background and members of the professional middle class.

A sketch map of the site of the party is given in Fig. 16. The guests arrived by way of the brick walkway. In the early part of the party many of them were greeted on this walkway or on the lawns where, for a while, they remained. Eventually, however, all of the guests gathered on the beach. Latecomers or parents coming to fetch their children, thus had to walk all the way to the beach before being greeted. When all the guests were gathered on the beach, the birthday cake was brought out and cut and served from the beach deck. Before and after serving the cake, many of the children, and some adults, clustered at the water's edge, while some of the children were taken for rides in a small sailing boat. The others mostly remained near the beach deck, the source of food and drink. After about two hours had passed, the guests again gathered on the lawn, where the children played, or watched as the five-year-old opened his presents. The adults sat on the grass or in deck chairs, chatting. Then gradually, they began to leave.

acting as cameramen at the birthday party. Ronald Goodrich and John Frikor kindly assisted with filming the wedding.

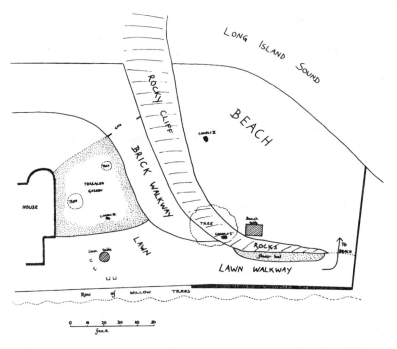

Fig. 16   Sketch map of the site of the Birthday Party to show its main
areas and the approximate locations of the cameras

In filming this event, three cameras were used. All filming was done
with 16 mm Commercial Ektachrome. Two cameras were fixed, one on
the beach to command a view of the walkway and the lawn. These
cameras were fitted with 1200 ft. magazines, to allow for up to half an
hour of continuous filming, if necessary. The third camera was hand-
held, and it was used to acquire a second angle on much that was filmed
by the two fixed cameras. A shot-gun microphone and synchronized
portable tape-recorder were used with the hand-held camera. A wireless
microphone worn by the hostess was tuned to the recorder synchronized with the lawn camera, while the microphone for the beach camera
was placed on the beach deck. The sound recording was not as successful as had been hoped, but some use of it has been possible.

The cameras were kept to the edges of the site, well away from people. Zoom lenses were used to compensate for this distance, but in filming, complete groupings of people were always kept in frame. No
attempt was made to film in close-up. This meant, of course, that we lost

details of the face. However, for the analysis of interactional events it is necessary to have all participants in the frame simultaneously as much as possible. Additional cameras would have to be used to get close-ups of faces, but these were not available to us.

At the beginning of the party the cameras were turned on as soon as a guest could be seen approaching down the walkway and were kept running until the guest finally parted from the host or hostess. Since a number of guests arrived in fairly quick succession, the first twenty minutes of the party were recorded by nearly continuous filming. The camera on the beach was allowed to run continuously for approximately forty minutes, from the time that the first guests were received there. Filming was resumed towards the end of the party, and an additional fifteen minutes of continuous filming was done.

No attempt was made to conceal the cameras, but since they were on the edges of the site at all times, they intruded very little. All of the guests knew that some filming was to take place. They knew that this was for research purposes, but they did not know that the main interest was in greetings. Nineteen of the adults and one of the children were interviewed afterwards in an attempt to find out, among other things, how they had reacted to the filming. Of these, three appeared to be totally unaware of the cameras, while the seventeen who reported they were aware of them, only four described their feelings as negative, ten said that the cameras made no difference at all, and three of them, including the child who was interviewed, felt excited and interested in the filming. These responses seem to confirm our observation of the guests. They appear in the film to be almost completely unaffected by the cameras, and there are very few instances in which someone is seen to look at the camera. This lack of camera effect is not really surprising. As we have said, the cameras were kept away from the people. Furthermore, the party was a real event. It had not been staged in any way for the purposes of the film. Furthermore, to most of those present the people and the site were all highly familiar. The event gathered its own momentum and proved to be absorbing enough for both adults and children for them not to care very much about the filming.

## The Wedding

This film was made at a wedding in Manhattan in March 1970. Footage was taken as the guests approached the chapel, and afterwards in the foyer of the chapel as they emerged from the ceremony. Filming was also done at the reception. This footage proved much more difficult to work with, mainly because we could not get far enough away from the people, and because it was so crowded. However, it has been possible to include some examples from this film in our corpus.

## Thanksgiving tape

This consists of one hour of video-tape made in a Manhattan apartment during a party held at Thanksgiving. It contains a sequence in which the successive arrival of the guests was recorded.

## TRD Band

Half-an-hour of high school adolescents in a parking lot waiting for a band practice. Filmed in a small town in Connecticut in 1964. It was made by Van Vlack at Eastern Pennsylvania Psychiatric Institute, as part of a project in the study of adolescent behavior.

## TRD Picnic

Footage shot in a picnic ground in a park near Philadelphia, when a local organization were having a picnic as part of Fourth of July celebrations. Two or three useful instances of greeting have been used from this film.

## An Observation

This consists of four hours of unstaged activity at a nursery school. It was made by the Child Development Center of the University of West Virginia, for the purposes of training students in child observation. Three examples have been used from this material.

The aim of this work was to develop a description of how people greet one another. We began by carefully watching and re-watching the examples available to us. The films were prepared for research by having a number printed on each frame which can be seen when the film is projected. We used an Athena L-W and a Bell & Howell 385 projector, converted to be operated by a hand-crank. In this way very small stretches of film could be examined at a time, and the events recorded could be analyzed in great detail. As a result of this process of intensive watching, we were able to formulate a list of behavioral units that appeared over and over again in the examples, and this formed the basis of a check-list which was used to record the presence or absence of these elements in the greeting studied. Additional specific procedures, such as how we analyzed behaviors such as gaze direction, will be given in the account of our findings.

The total number of greeting incidents that we have made use of in this study is ninety-two. However, it should be made clear that by no means all of these could be used for all parts of the analysis. In some of the examples only one participant in the greeting could be seen. In others we could see only a fragment of what was obviously a much longer event. Thus the size of the sample upon which our general statements are based may vary according to the statement being made. Where we have presented quantitative statements to show the distribution of a given feature of greeting within our corpus, no attempt has been made to evaluate these statistically. What we offer here is a synthetic picture of what we believe to be the main features of the organization of greeting interaction. It should not be taken as more than a guide for the more refined and systematic studies that undoubtedly should follow.

The greetings may be classified in various ways, according to the context of the greeting, its apparent function, and who was involved in it. Tables 10 and 11 present some of this data, so that a more complete picture of the sample we have worked with may be available.

## The structure of greeting interactions

The distinctive gestures and utterances that occur in a greeting inter-action will be referred to as *salutations*. In some greeting interactions the participants exchange salutations while there is considerable distance between them. Such a *distance salutation* exchange may be all that there is to the interaction, and afterwards the participants may go their separate ways. At other times it is a prelude to further interaction which occurs at close range. In these cases, which include most of the cases we are to consider in this paper, such interaction at close range is opened with another salutation exchange, here to be referred to as the *close salutation*.

As we shall come to see again later, it is characteristic of the close salutation that the participants enact it in a distinct location, and that

Table 10. *Types of greetings in the Birthday Party film*

| | |
|---|---|
| Total number of greetings | 63 |
| Number of greetings between | |
| host/hostess and guest | 31 |
| guest and guest | 32 |
| Number of greetings between | |
| adults | 56 |
| adult–child | 7 |
| males | 18 |
| male–female | 26 |
| females | 19 |
| members of same family | 20 |
| close friends | 15 |
| acquaintances | 28 |

they orient to one another in a way that is distinctive. Once the gestures of salutation have been completed, the participants then move away from the location taken for the exchange. If they continue in one another's presence as for instance when they remain together for conversation, they will adopt a different orientation to one another.

The close salutation may thus be said to occur within a distinct spatial and orientational frame. Obviously, the establishment of this frame is done jointly by the participants. The greeting interaction will be said to have begun once either of the participants has begun to move toward the other, whether or not any explicit interaction has taken place. The greeting interaction will be said to be over, for present purposes, as soon as the spatial and orientational frame of the close salutation is dissolved.

The diagram in Fig. 17 displays the structure of a typical greeting. This was a greeting, taken from the Birthday Party film, between two men, who were a considerable distance from one another at the outset. The converging lines in the center of the diagram represent the movement of the two men towards one another. Where the line is broken, the individual represented is in motion. Where the line is solid he is standing still. The arrows above and below these lines represent the orientation of the bodies of the participants in relation to one another. The outer oblongs, above and below the converging lines and arrows, represent

Table 11. *Number of individuals observed in the greeting examples and the number of times each was observed, for the Birthday Party film*

| Number of observations per individual | Number of individuals |
|---|---|
| 22 | 1 |
| 13 | 1 |
| 11 | 1 |
| 8 | 1 |
| 7 | 3 |
| 6 | 2 |
| 5 | 1 |
| 4 | 5 |
| 3 | 2 |
| 2 | 4 |
| 1 | 11 |
| 0 | 6 |
| 82 | 38 |

the segments of $p$'s[2] during which a given bodily orientation is sustained. Broken lines again represent movement through space, continuous lines represent standing still. The short blocks inside the outer oblongs represent short elements of behavior such as gestures of the arm or head, the occurrence of utterances, and so forth. These *actions*, as they may be called, are conceived of as occurring within the frame provided by the orientation of the whole body.

It will be seen from the diagram how, after an initial turn of the body in which each faces toward the other, the two men approach one another, and sustain a frontal orientation to one another. It will be noted that they both come to a halt (WF a little before JH) and while they are thus halted, facing one another, they engage in a handshake. The location each occupies and his orientation to the other at this point, constitutes the spatial–orientational frame of the close salutation that we spoke of above. Thereafter JH moves further towards WF, but as he does so he steps round him. WF takes a few steps backwards, also alter-

---

[2] Throughout this paper $p$ will be used to designate the individual whose behavior is being discussed, and $q$ will be used to designate the person he is in interaction with.

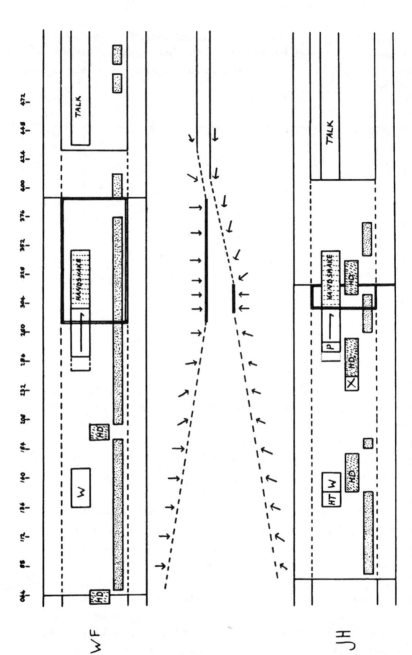

Fig. 17  Diagram of a greeting (for explanation see text)

ing his orientation. As they move into this side-by-side arrangement, they begin their conversation.

In this study, the greeting interaction in this example would be regarded as having begun at the point where WF turns towards JH. It would be regarded as over at the point where WF finally turns from the position he had adopted for the duration of the handshake. It will be seen that JH is engaged in the greeting interaction slightly later than WF, and that he begins to move into the phase of the interaction that follows the greeting slightly sooner than WF.

The frontal orientation of each greeter to the other, sustained through the approach and until the end of the close salutation, provides a frame within which a number of actions may be observed. In the present example we may note how, shortly after each has oriented to the other and begun his approach, they engage in a *distance salutation* exchange. This is the typical pattern. It will be noted, however, that there are certain conditions that must be established before the distance salutation can occur and these conditions are sometimes brought about by observable actions. Thus, before any greeting can begin, the participants must *sight* each other, and in so doing they must identify the other as someone they wish to greet. Sighting may sometimes be observed as a distinct action, though this is not usual in our sample. What we observe first, as a rule, is the orientation and the beginning of the approach of one participant to another.

It will be noted that $p$ will not begin an approach to $q$ unless he has some indication that he is aware of him and of his intention to greet. In some circumstances, for example where $q$ is preoccupied and $p$ is in a hurry to greet him, $p$ may announce his presence to $q$ explicitly. He may do this by calling his name, by coughing discreetly, or by knocking on the door. In the present example, as in most of those in our corpus, $q$ responds to $p$'s orientation to him by himself orienting to $p$ so no distinct announcement is apparent. We mention it here, however, for it may sometimes occur at a distinct step, and when it occurs it always precedes the distance salutation.

As the greeters continue to approach one another following the distance salutation, a number of different behaviors may be observed, some of which are illustrated in the example. Thus we note that people do not usually look at one another continuously as they approach one another, and they may often look sharply away just prior to the close salutation. We may also observe how they may touch their hair or adjust their clothing. Sometimes they may be seen to draw one or both arms across their own body in an action we refer to as the "body cross." This is seen in JH in the present example. These behaviors, which tend to occur toward the end of a long approach, are quite unformalized.[3] In their "withdrawing" character they contrast sharply with the behavior that occurs in the final stage of the approach, when the greeters are close enough to begin interaction with one another by means of speech.[4] Here, they characteristically look at one another, they usually smile, and they get ready for whatever gestures are to be involved in the close situation. Whether the unformalized "withdrawal" behaviors appear will depend in part upon how long the approach is. It will also depend upon the kind of relationship that exists between the greeters. Likewise, the behavior characteristic of the final phase of the approach may appear immediately after the distance salutation and be sustained thereafter. This also seems to depend upon the kind of relationship that obtains between the greeters.

Following the close salutation the greeters move out of the distinct spatial and orientational frame they established for it and the greeting is now said to be over. However, though what follows the close salutation is quite variable, there is one phase that is quite often observed, and in some circumstances has become quite formalized and should be described in any full treatment of greetings. We call this phase the *How Are You*. Here people engage in an exchange of information about one another. This commonly concerns their state of health, and is frequently highly formalized and quite brief. In some circumstances the exchange of information may be prolonged, however. People may relate news of one another and of mutual acquaintances, they may explain the purpose of their visit, or they may provide information about their identity. In our investigations to date we have done little more than merely note

[3] Behavior may be said to be "formalized" when it becomes stereotyped in form, conspicuous, sharply differentiated from other actions, and when it is explicitly addressed to another. Where it is known that the action in question has become formalized through tradition or habit, the term "conventionalized" may be used. We have used the term "formalized" throughout this paper since we do not commit ourselves as to which processes have been involved in the evolution of the behavioral forms we discuss. We are indebted to W. John Smith (unpublished material) for these terms.

[4] The distance within which individuals can sustain interaction by means of utterances which use interpersonal levels of voice projection (in contrast to public voice projection levels, or private levels – as in talking to oneself) will be referred to as the close interaction distance. It varies according to the situation and the kind of interaction taking place, but is probably rarely greater than ten feet. Cf. Hall's (1966) treatment of interpersonal distance and its relationship to interaction.

the existence of this phase. However, since it plays an important part in the process by which relationships are maintained and developed in any further study of greeting this phase will merit much more consideration.

In the rest of this paper we shall describe in more detail the behavior we have observed in each of the phases of the greeting as they have been sketched above, up to and including the close salutation. It should be noted that we are concerned with greetings between two people at a time. Sometimes such dyadic greetings occur within the context of a larger unit of interaction, as when several people are being greeted together. However, in this paper we shall not be concerned with the ways in which successive greeting exchanges may be related together, though there is much of interest here that could be described. It should also be noted that our descriptions are confined to greetings between adults, except in a few cases.

## The elements of greeting interactions and their interrelations

We now turn to an account of the behavioral elements that occur at the various stages of the greeting we have described above. To do this we shall describe examples which illustrate, for each phase, the behaviors we have observed in our corpus of filmed greetings.

### How greeting interactions begin: sighting, orientation, and the initiation of the approach

$p$ must first sight $q$ if he is to greet him. He must perceive him and identify him as the particular individual he may wish to greet. Sighting is a pre-interactional step. It need not be marked in any overt behavior. For example, $p$ may become aware of $q$'s presence in a passing glance, or by overhearing his voice. Once he has sighted him he must decide whether or not to initiate a greeting interaction. Whether he does so or not immediately upon sighting will depend upon (a) the urgency of $p$'s intention to greet $q$, (b) what $p$ is doing at the time of sighting, and (c) what $q$ is doing at the time of sighting.

If $p$ is already engaged in a conversation with someone when he sights $q$, he may have to postpone an initiation of a greeting with him until that conversation is ended. Similarly if, when he sights him, $q$ is busy, $p$ may have to wait until $q$ has completed what he is doing before initiating a greeting. How ready $p$ is to interrupt himself, and how ready he will be to interrupt $q$ will, of course, depend upon the importance of initiating a greeting with $q$, relative to the importance of other things. Sometimes $p$'s role in the situation may be that of a greeter, in which case his other involvements may all be interrupted the moment anyone who must be greeted appears. This was the case for the hostess at the birthday party, for example. At other times, $p$ may be prepared to interrupt himself to greet $q$ because it is the only opportunity he may have of doing so, or because he has not seen $q$ for a long time, or because $q$ is a valuable friend or a person of importance to $p$. How ready $p$ will be to interrupt $q$ will likewise depend upon a variety of factors. If $p$ is high in status in the gathering, he may be more likely to interrupt $q$, no matter what $q$ may be doing, than if he is low in status. $p$ may also have special rights in relation to $q$. For example, spouses or very close friends can interrupt one another for a greeting, whereas $p$ is less likely to interrupt $q$ if he does not know him well. In general, $p$ will only initiate a greeting if he is confident that the greeting will be returned. To be rebuffed or unrecognized is gravely embarrassing, and people rarely risk this.

The ways in which $p$ begins a greeting with $q$ in our corpus are quite various. Here we will cite a series of examples which illustrate how, at one extreme, $p$ may begin upon a greeting with another as soon as he has sighted him and how, at the other extreme, $p$ may not begin upon a greeting until he has received some explicit signal from $q$.

Where $p$ begins upon a greeting with $q$ without any prior interaction with him, we find that $p$ either has a special obligation to greet him or he has a special right to a greeting from him. First greetings between host and hostess and guests were initiated in this way. We also have instances of greetings between spouses that are begun by one of the pair without any prior interaction. Many of the greetings between guests, on the other hand, have a more tentative beginning. In these cases we see $p$ hinting to $q$ that he wants to approach him, for example by subtly synchronizing his movements with him, but not approaching him until this hint has been acknowledged with an explicit signal.

In the first few greetings recorded in the Birthday Party film, the hostess crossed the lawn and walked part of the way up the brick walkway where she would then stand and wait as the guests approached her. In these instances (G1, G2, G4, G5, G10), sighting could be observed as a distinct action. JF turns her face in the direction of the approaching guests, tilts back her head slightly and maintains this orientation for a perceptible length of time. Immediately following sighting she will begin her approach, usually combined with a distance salutation display. In these instances the hostess, upon sighting, would interrupt whatever else she might have been doing to embark upon the greeting. Greeting new guests was given priority over other involvements at this stage of the occasion, as befitted her role at the party as hostess. It may be noted here, however, that though the hostess did not depend upon any explicit signal from the approaching guests before she initiated an approach to them, she nonetheless would not begin her approach until they were close enough so that, upon walking toward them she would meet them at the edge of the site of the party. In the early stages of the party, where the guests could be seen from the lawn entering the gateway to the drive, JF would begin her approach upon sighting. In this way she had time to walk part of the way up the drive and stand and wait for them, when they were between fifteen and twenty feet away from her. Much later in the party, when the guests had all moved down to the beach, though a new arrival could be seen clearly from the beach as he walked down the grassy walkway, the hostess neither explicitly acknowledged him nor began her approach until the guest had turned on to the beach itself (G59, G57). The point at which she began her approach allowed her so to time her movement across the beach, that she could meet the guest at the edge of the gathering on the beach.

These examples reflect a general point that has to do with the location on the site of the occasion of the close salutation between host and newly arrived guest. In most of the examples this would take place at some point well removed from the center of the site of the occasion. In the above example the hostess took an active part in determining the location of the close salutation by timing the moment she began her approach. In other instances the arriving guests would not be seen by the hostess and they thus had an opportunity to fully penetrate the party's arena. In most of these cases they did not do so, however, remaining on the edge of the main area until they had been greeted by the hostess.

How freely a newly arrived guest will penetrate the site of an occasion and how far away from the center of it the host or hostess will move towards them, depends in a complex way upon the nature of the relationship between the guest and the host or hostess. In general, it would appear that the further the host moves from the center of the occasion's action, the greater the show of respect for the guest he creates.[5] The more fully the guest penetrates the arena of the occasion before being greeted, the greater is his familiarity with the host. Thus, at the birthday party, the guest who penetrated the site most fully before being greeted was the host's mother who, upon her arrival on the lawn, immediately set about some rearrangement of the furniture on the lawn, and gave some instructions to the host's maid, before being greeted either by the host or the hostess. On the other hand, guests who did not know the hostess or host well and who were not immediately greeted waited on the lawn until they were greeted. Only then did they move down to the beach, nearer the center of the occasion. However, it should also be noted that how far the host will move to the edge of the arena and how far the guest may penetrate the arena may also depend upon the stage the party has reached when the guest arrives. Later arriving guests typically get a less elaborate welcome than guests arriving early and, correlatively, guests arriving late may often enter more fully into the activities of the occasion before being greeted.

It will be noted that these expectations make it possible for hosts and guests to give expression to their attitudes toward one another. At the birthday party the host, piqued because his mother, father, and sister and her husband arrived much later than he expected, remained down on the beach and waited for them to come to him. He did not go to greet them, upon learning of their arrival. This little violation of etiquette was noticed by his wife who, as she left the beach to go up the lawn to greet them, called to her husband: "Aren't you going to come up and meet them?" with a sharp contrast in pitch over the last two syllables evidently expressive here of her pained surprise at his insistence on remaining on the beach.

In a number of the greetings between host or hostess and guest, the guest could be said to take the initiative. This occurred, for example, in G23a, G23b, and G62, where a guest was awaiting his turn for a close salutation from the host or hostess, while he or she was engaged with someone else. Here, what is observed is that the guest would begin his approach to the hostess or host, fully oriented to him and ready to engage in a close salutation, the moment the host or hostess began a behavioral element that would count as marking the beginning of the

---

[5] The host may also move to the edge of his territory to deal with intruders, of course, and how far he moves will be related to how threatening he perceives the intruders to be.

end of his involvement with the other. Here, thus, $p$ begins upon a greeting with $q$, not upon receipt of any signal addressed to him, but upon a change in $q$'s activity that is indicative of his relinquishment of his current involvement. He makes bold to approach here, either because he is clearly next in line (as was the case in G23a and G23b) or because, since he has a right to receive a greeting from the other, he can count on him to turn to him next, should the other be made aware of his desire for a greeting (G62).

For example, in G62 a recently arrived guest, MG, is chatting to the hostess while, about ten feet away, his host is engaged with another recent arrival, GG. MG, who has been standing with arms akimbo, his hands splayed on his hips, takes a step towards the host, extending his right hand first upwards in a little gesture by which he apparently indicates to her that he wishes to greet the host, and then forwards to the host in an offer of a handshake. By the time MG is near enough to the host to grasp his hand, the host has already turned to him, also with hand extended. Though the host has not looked at MG before this, he is nonetheless able to turn to him for a handshake coordinately with MG's approach. This was brought about, apparently, by the guest picking his moment to begin his approach to the host to coincide with a juncture in the host's conversation with the other guest. The first movement MG makes as he begins his approach is to lift his right hand away from his hip. He initiates this at frame number 72554. One frame before this the host had begun to lower his head, looking away from GG to attend to the plate of cake he is holding. MG, thus, though engaged in conversation with JF, was nonetheless sufficiently attuned to his host's behavior to identify the moment at which he began a pause in his conversation with GG, a moment at which he became more accessible to interruption than he would were he fully oriented to GG. Similarly, in G23a, JF the hostess, is engaged in a greeting with WF. BA, whom she next greets, is standing with her back turned about ten feet away from JF. As JF begins to step sideways, the first of the steps she takes to move out of the spatial and orientational frame she had been in for the close salutation with WF, BA turns and begins her approach to her. In this case, BA had presumably overheard the concluding utterance of the greeting exchange between JF and WF. And again, in G23b, BA's husband, HA, begins his approach to JF as she steps away from BA, though before she had begun to orient to him.

In contrast to these examples in which $p$ coordinates the beginning of his approach to $q$ with a movement, or a change in speech pattern that indicates that $q$ is going to relinquish a current involvement, there are a number of examples in which $p$ does not begin his approach to $q$ until he receives an explicit signal from him, a signal which may nonetheless be distinct from a salutation display. Whereas in the examples we have described so far, $p$ begins to approach $q$ as if on the assumption that $q$

will engage in a greeting with him, in the examples we shall now describe $p$ defers his approach until $q$ has directly signalled his readiness for an approach. The greetings in our corpus in which the approach was preceded by this "catching the eye" of the other are all between guests – between people, that is, who do not know each other very intimately and who do not have any special reason for greeting one another, as hosts and guests do.

Some examples of greetings initiated by an exchange of signals will now be described.

In G44 (see Fig. 22) CB is standing alone with his 5-year-old son, looking out to sea. Twenty feet away to his left DW is standing in conversation with HS and, like CB, he is facing the sea. DW's conversation with HS lapses and DW turns his head to direct his face to CB, though he does not turn his trunk or lower body towards him. Shortly thereafter CB turns his face in the direction of DW and then away again. He then looks at DW again, but this time smiling slightly, whereupon DW immediately throws back his head in a distance salutation. After CB has replied to this with a brief utterance and a much increased smile, DW then begins to turn his lower body and trunk to face CB, and then approach him. In G40 SW approaches the beach deck in front of which WF is standing, fully oriented to CB and BA who are talking together. SW stops about eight feet from this group, but stands so that she is fully facing at right angles to the axis between CB and BA, smiling, but looking down slightly. WF, who turned his head to her as she approached, but then resumes his orientation to CB and BA, now turns his head to her again, this time smiling. As she raises her head, apparently looking at him, he initiates his approach to her and directly thereafter they engage in a close salutation. In G41 SW, her encounter with WF over, turns to fully face the interactional axis between CB and BA. She remains in this position for two seconds and then begins to approach CB. Her approach here, however, begins only after CB has turned his face to her, away from BA. SW begins her approach one second after CB has looked at her, and as she begins her approach CB looks back at BA.

In these examples, we see $p$ orienting to $q$, but not approaching him until $q$ has oriented his eyes to $p$. $p$ by his orientation to $q$ may be said to announce his intention to approach, but he does not do so until $q$ has given his "clearance." It is to be noted that in two of these examples the initial orientation of $p$ is by a turn of the head only, the rest of the body being retained in $p$'s current orientation. This perhaps serves to give the initial move a certain tentativeness. If the other does not offer a clearance signal $p$ can easily turn his head in another direction and his look at $q$ can pass as a mere glance. To turn his whole body to $q$ is to commit himself much more fully to an approach to him, and this is less easily discounted if he is rebuffed. Correlatively, it is easier to ignore someone who merely turns his head in one's direction, than if he turns his whole body towards one.

Sometimes one may see what would appear to be an even more tentative form of beginning a greeting. Here $p$ avoids catching the eye of the other, but at the same time he synchronizes his movements with those of the other and he may also glance at the other fleetingly, looking away each time the other looks towards him, until the other actually directs a salutation display to him. An example of this kind of greeting is provided by G60:

Here MG is standing talking to JF while about eight feet away from him at JF's right GG is standing, arms folded, not engaged in any focused interaction. At frame 71340 GG turns his head left slightly, focusing on MG while, at the same time, MG turns his head, focusing his eyes on JF. GG thus looks at MG as MG looks away from GG. Then, MG rotates his head *away* from JF into an orientation in which he would catch GG's eyes. Simultaneously, GG looks away from MG. MG then directs a distance salutation to GG, who looks back at him and replies with a salutation. Here, thus, GG, by synchronizing his head turns with movements of MG may be said to have signaled his wish for contact. However, he consistently avoided catching MG's eye until MG offered him an explicit salutation. (See Fig. 23.)

Synchronizing one's movements with another but yet not meeting the other's eyes or in some way signaling a request for contact in an explicit fashion is commonly followed by explicit contact between $p$ and the person whose movements $p$ "picks up." An example within an established focused gathering has been described in detail by Kendon (1973). Initiating an explicit interaction with another person is always a somewhat risky business, since there is always the possibility that the other party does not wish to reciprocate. By simply picking up the rhythm of another person's movements one can establish a connection with him which, at the same time, does not commit one to a positive initiation. If, after having joined the rhythm of another, the other makes no move toward establishing explicit contact with one, one can continue to go about one's business as if one had not made the initiation attempt.

Another way in which a greeting interaction may begin should now be mentioned. This is where $p$ makes an explicit announcement of his presence. In the Birthday Party film all the greetings recorded took place in the open air, with relatively few barriers screening people from one another. Where $p$ is to enter someone's house or office, however, he must almost always announce his presence explicitly – as with the knock on the door or the bell-ring or, perhaps, the secretary who informs her superior of his visitor's presence. A few greetings in our corpus, however, were initiated by explicit announcements. For example, in G46, KH standing by the beach deck saw BA approaching the table, put down her cup and then immediately called out: "Why if it isn't BA." This was followed by BA orienting to her and a distance salutation was then exchanged. In G52 BA follows HR as he moves across the beach, runs around and confronts him, announcing her presence to him. In G4, G10, and G14 JF, upon sighting the approaching of children whom she is going to greet, calls out, as if to announce to anyone in earshot, who is coming. Following this she proceeds to approach and engage in a distance and close salutation.

Finally, there is the introduced greeting. In the examples in our corpus (G3, G18, G19, and G42) one member of the pair is accompanied by the hostess or host who then calls to the other announcing to him who she is with. In these instances a close salutation immediately follows the introduction. The introduction stands in for sighting, orientation, announcement, and distance greeting, since it serves to create the context in which a close salutation is possible.

## The distance salutation

At some point following $p$'s orientation to $q$, he is likely to address an explicit display to him, such as a call or a wave. This is generally reciprocated in kind by $q$. We refer to this as the *distance salutation* since it always occurs at such a distance that the greeters, if they continue to interact, move closer to one another afterwards. The absolute distance at which the distance salutation occurs is not fixed, of course. In some cases in the Birthday Party film it occurred at a distance of more than thirty feet. In some cases it occurred between greeters who were only a few feet apart. How far away the participants are when they engage in the distance salutation depends upon such factors as (a) how far $p$ is from $q$ when $p$ initiates his approach to him; (b) how eager $p$ is to greet $q$; (c) how crowded the setting is. In crowded settings, for example, $p$ may move closer to $q$ before he initiates a salutation with him than he does in less crowded settings.

In the distance greeting the greeters may be said to recognize one another explicitly and they thereby establish, both for each other and for anyone else within range, that they are now engaged to greet one another. We may expect, perhaps, that distance greetings are more likely to occur in settings such as the one at the birthday party, where there might be some ambiguity for $q$ as to whether $p$ was approaching him or someone else. However, as we shall see, two exchanges of salutation displays appears to be extremely common, even where the greeters are, from the outset, but a few feet from one another. We may expect, however, that the amount of time that separated the first salutation from the second will be greater, and that the first or distance salutation will be more vigorous in its enactment, in circumstances where there is more than one possible partner for a greeting exchange.

In the material we have examined we have observed several different kinds of distance salutation displays. These will now be described and we shall also indicate the characteristic contexts for the different forms we have observed, insofar as we know what these are.

(i)    *The headtoss.* The distance display most commonly observed in the Birthday Party film may be called the *headtoss display.* Its most characteristic feature is that the head is tilted back rapidly and then brought forward again. It is usually combined with a call – such as "hi" or "hi" followed by a name. Typically, the head is first raised and then, as it is lowered again, the call is uttered. As the head is raised, the mouth is opened and generally the lips are drawn back in a smile which tends to expose the upper teeth. In a few instances in our material we have been able to see enough facial detail to see that the eyebrows are raised sharply as the head is raised or tilted back, and they are then lowered again as the head begins to be lowered.[7] Commonly, only the head and face and voice are involved in this display, though in some instances the trunk and arms are involved as well. Here, as the head is thrown back there is an associated marked straightening of the trunk, it is often bent back at the hips, or the hips themselves may be thrust forward. At the same time, the elbows are extended, so that the arms are held straight at the sides of the body and drawn back at the shoulders so that they extend dorsally. There may also be some adduction at the shoulder so

---

[6] The display we have described here appears to be identical with that described by Eibl-Eibesfeldt (1968, 1970) in which the eyebrows are raised and lowered rapidly, together with a smile, commonly enough, and also a little toss of the head. According to Eibl-Eibesfeldt this display can be found to occur all over the world.

that the arms are spread somewhat to either side. The forearms may be rotated to a prone position, with the fingers of one or both hands extended, so that the palms of the hands are oriented so that they face towards the person to whom the display is addressed.

The occasions when the body and arms are involved in the display, as well as the head, face and voice, are rare in our corpus. When they are, the enacter seems to be somewhat excited. The headtoss display may thus be said to be enacted to varying degrees of intensity. At the very least we may have a slight raising of the head coupled with an almost imperceptible eyebrow raise. More usually, a definite toss of the head is observable. At the higher intensities the body and arms are also involved in the way we have described. An example of the headtoss display is seen in Fig. 21b.

The headtoss display does not appear to be reciprocated with a headtoss. In none of the eleven examples in the birthday party material in which a headtoss display occurred and in which both parties to a distance greeting could be clearly observed, was the headtoss display seen in both partners. In all but one of these instances, furthermore, the headtoss display was the first explicit greeting display to be observed – in other words, it was performed by the individual taking the initiative in the sequence of greeting display.

Other forms of the distance salutation display include the *head lower*, the *nod*, and the *wave*, which can itself take various forms. These are generally, though not always, associated with a smile and a call.

*(ii)    The head lower.* In the *head lower*, as the name we have given it implies, the head is lowered, or tilted forward, and it is distinguished from the nod only in its duration. In the head lower the head is tilted forward, held in that position, and then raised, whereas in the nod the head is lowered and then raised without a hold intervening. The head lower may be combined with a smile, but if it is, the smile is different from the open-mouth upper-tooth smile observed in the headtoss greeting. In the head-lower smile the mouth is not opened, or at least it is not opened widely, the lips are drawn back, sometimes so that both rows of teeth are exposed and the circum-orbital muscles of the eyes are much more likely to be involved, producing "crinkled eyes." The head lower may also be combined with a wave. In the instances in which we have observed this, the arm is not fully raised, the hand being lifted not much

above the top of the head. An example of the head lower is to be seen in Fig. 23c.

The head lower is commonly seen in response to the headtoss. However, we have also observed it in an initiator of a greeting exchange, but in these cases the initiator is either an adult greeting a child or, in a few cases, we have seen an older man greeting a much younger woman with this head action.

*(iii)* *The nod.* The *headnod* display, in which the head is lowered and then at once raised, is characteristic of greetings-in-passing. Here both parties to the greeting enact a nod. It is possible that the nod is closely related to the head lower. Whereas when *p* headtosses, he initiates contact with *q* and perhaps thereby invites further interaction, when *p* head nods he is not initiating but responding to the other. Where each responds to the other, but neither initiates, we have a greeting in passing. The headnod display is not often accompanied by facial involvement, or if it is this is relatively slight. Not uncommonly, a quiet vocalization, occurs such as "hi" or "good-day."

*(iv)* *The wave.* Waving is a common element in distance salutations, though the birthday party material provided us with only five examples. There are a number of different forms of waving. Here we shall describe the forms we have been able to observe from a variety of sources. No claims to exhaustiveness are made, however.

In waving, the hand and usually the forearm and upper arm as well are raised up. This may or may not be combined with flapping or wagging of the hand or limb. In all the waves we have observed, the fingers of the hand are extended at least partly. They may be either drawn together or spread, but the palm of the hand is always oriented toward the person being waved at.

Waves vary in the extent to which the limb is extended. Sometimes it is only the hand that is raised, sometimes it is only the forearm. At other times, of course, the whole arm is lifted, usually to a steep angle in relation to the vertical of the body, though occasionally the arm is held straight up above the head.

The wave may consist of a simple up-down movement of the hand or hand and arm. The hand, once raised, may be "flapped" – or it is moved from side to side or "wagged." Where it is "flapped," the wrist is alternately flexed and extended rapidly two or more times. In "flapped" waves, the hand is held high and flapped. Successive up-down movements of the whole arm are not observed. In "lateral" waves, the movements may be confined to a back-and-forth rotation of the forearm, with the wrist held somewhat extended, or the forearm, or sometimes the whole arm may be moved laterally back and forth.

The degree of limb extension in a wave is probably related in part to the distance over which signals are exchanged. Thus when people wave to one another at distances of fifteen feet or less they are not likely to do more than raise their hands by flexing their elbow, thus raising the hand to the level of the shoulder. At distances greater than this, however, the hand may be raised to the level of the eyes or above. At very great distances the arm is fully extended above the head. The degree of limb extension is also related to the vigor of the wave. The more vigorously the hand is "flapped" or "wagged" the more the rest of the limb is involved in the movement and the more it will be extended.

The simple wave, in which the hand is merely raised and lowered, seems to occur as a reply to a more elaborate wave, or as an acknowledgement of another's greeting. We also see the simple wave when the wave is part of a distance salutation that is performed while the individual is already approaching the person he will greet. "Flap" waves and "lateral" waves are characteristic waves where the waver is trying to catch another's attention. They also seem to occur where the waver is making contact with another, but will not or cannot thereupon proceed to have further close interaction with him. Whether there are any consistent differences in the contexts in which "flapped" waves as opposed to "lateral" waves occur, we do not yet know.

(v)   *Discussion.* The distance salutation occurs in all of the greeting interactions we have examined in which close interaction also occurs, with the exception of greetings preceded by an introduction. How far away the individuals are when they exchange a distance greeting is a matter of considerable variation, however. In some circumstances the distance greeting will occur as soon as the greeters come into one another's presence, in which case it will be followed by the close salutation almost directly. Thus, in the series of greetings recorded on the Thanksgiving tape, guests were entering the hallway of an apartment. As soon as they could be seen through the door they would greet the host or hostess who was already waiting for them. This greeting, which would include an utterance such as "Hullo, nice to see you" would then be followed by another greeting ritual such as a handshake, or an embrace. Similarly, in G60, in the Birthday Party film, where before the transaction occurs MG and GG are already within ten feet of one another, when GG catches MG's eye, MG initiates a headtoss greeting and GG responds with a head lower and a small wave. Then they lean forward to one another and shake hands (see Fig. 23). The distance salutation also occurs just prior to the close salutation where $p$ and $q$ are approaching one another in circumstances where they are bound to pass close to one another. For example, if $p$ sets off down a corridor at the other end of which he sights $q$, no distance greeting is likely until they are already close enough to begin close interaction. It occurs when the greeters are much more widely separated where, as frequently in the Birthday Party film, the greeters had sighted one another a considerable distance away, but where there were several different directions in which either of them could move, and often several other people about whom they might greet. Here the distance greeting serves, perhaps, as an official ratification of the partners into a greeting relationship, a move that is not necessary in the corridor situation and not possible in the hallway referred to above.

## The head dip

In many instances, one of the participants in the greeting transaction (though usually not both) will follow his distance salutation display with a *head dip*. Here the head is lowered by means of a forward bend of the neck. Examples may be seen in Figs. 21c and 22d. In the Birthday Party film, of the fifty separate distance salutations observed, twenty-five were followed by a clear head dip.

It may be noted that the head dip is not only observed in association with greetings. A number of observations of it have been recorded which have suggested to us the hypothesis that the head dip is associated with those points in an individual's flow of behavior where he is changing his attention, where he is changing from one major unit of involvement to another. This hypothesis led us to compare all the instances of distance salutations that are followed by head dips with those that are not, from the point of view of the location of the distance greeting in relation to changes in the greeter's direction of movement or orientation, and to changes in his activity or involvement.

As we have seen, some distance greetings occur just after $p$ has oriented to the other. At other times, the distance greeting occurs just before $p$ and $q$ begin to move close enough to one another for the close salutation. Distance greetings were classified according to whether they followed shortly upon $p$ changing his orientation to begin his approach to $q$ or whether they immediately preceded the close salutation phase. Whether a head dip followed the distance greeting or not was in each case noted. It was found that whereas no distance salutation that occurred during the final stages of the approach to the other were followed by head dips, sixteen of the distance salutations associated with head dips did occur just after $p$ had begun his new orientation and approach to the other. This would seem to support the hypothesis that the head dips here, as elsewhere, occurred in association with a change in $p$'s principal involvement. We suggest that it may mark a shifting of "attention gears."[7]

Whether the head dip has any regular signal function in greeting interaction or not we cannot, from our present corpus of material, determine. It is a conspicuous action, however, and insofar as it is regularly associated with the onset of new phases of activity in the individual, it could serve to forewarn others of this change. In the context of greetings it may perhaps serve to forewarn the recipient of a distance salutation of the greeter's firm intention to relinquish whatever he was doing before, and give his whole attention to the person he has just saluted. It is significant in this connection that a head dip does not follow a distance salutation which is *not* followed by further interaction. It is also significant that head dips do not follow distance salutations that immediately precede close salutations. In these cases, the individuals are already fully oriented to one another, and by this orientation, and by the other's previous approach, there is no ambiguity about who is attending to whom.

---

[7] To dip the head is to effectively cut visual input from the surrounding environment, except for the terrain immediately in front of one's feet. It is possible that this momentary cut-off of environmental input is associated with those internal processes by which an individual re-programs himself for the next unit of action, whatever this may be. In studies of changes in gaze direction in conversation, it was found that a conversationalist would look away from his partner, usually down, either just before beginning a long utterance or during hesitations in speech which, on other grounds, are supposed to reflect periods of planning in speech (Kendon, 1967, see Chapter 3).

## Approach

When people engage in a close salutation they always move to a distinct location to do so. Thus in any greeting which includes a close salutation we shall observe an approach, that is, a period during which the participants move toward one another to meet at a spot that is distinct from the one that either was occupying at the beginning of the transaction. How much each moves is, of course, a matter of considerable variation, depending upon the circumstances at the beginning of the transaction, such as how great a distance separates the interactants at the outset, and what each of them happens to be doing when sighting occurs. It is also to be noted, however, that the pattern of approach that is observed – whether one walks over to the other person, waits until they have approached instead, or whether each times his walk in the direction of the other so that each covers about the same amount of ground by the time they reach other – is also dependent upon tendencies of the individuals in their behavior toward one another which are not dependent upon the immediate situation. In other words, how far one "goes out of one's way" to meet another appears to have a communicational significance. As we noted in an earlier section, for instance, how far from the central area of the party the host moves to greet a new arrival at a party, can be taken as an indication of how important the new arrival is for the host.

The communicational significance of the mode of approach would appear to derive from the fact that, in moving from one location to another, an individual must perforce change the segment of the environment with which he can involve his attention. In moving away from one's current location, that is to say, one must necessarily give up whatever involvements were associated with it. In a greeting thus, the further $p$ moves from his location at sighting, in his approach to the other, the more fully will he be putting aside whatever his previous involvements were. He thus provides information about the relative importance he gives to various involvements.

The precise significance of the mode of approach in a particular greeting, of course, will depend upon the combination of circumstances in which it occurs. In the birthday party material approach patterns are quite various and few general statements appear to be possible. A more detailed attempt at working out the rules which govern approaches in greetings will be reserved for another report. Here we shall examine some of the behavior that may be observed during the approach.

*(i) Behavior during approach: facial orientation.* Earlier, in discussing how greeting transactions begin, we described examples in which $p$ did not begin his approach to $q$ until $q$ apparently looked at him. These examples support the observations of Goffman (1963) that an exchange of glances is one of the ways individuals give one another "clearance" for further interaction. In all of the instances of greetings in which we were able to observe both individuals from the outset of the transaction, there is a moment, early on, when each does appear to exchange glances with the other. This glance exchange is generally associated with the distance greeting by which the partners to the greeting may be said to give explicit acknowledgement to one another that they are such. After this moment of looking, however, one or other of the greeting pair, or sometimes both, look away, and they may continue to avoid looking at the other until they are almost close enough for the close salutation.[8]

We have investigated "looking" during the approach by recording changes in the orientation of the face. This can be seen readily in the films available to us, although in most cases we cannot arrive at a reliable estimate at the point of convergence of the eyes. Where an individual orients his face nevertheless indicates where he is most likely to be looking. Furthermore, in natural social interaction, it appears that a change in the direction of the glance from "looking at" one's partner to "looking away" from him, and vice versa, is almost always associated with a change in the orientation of the face (Vine 1971). In the present study, we shall confine ourselves to observations on whether the face is oriented in the direction of the other member of the transaction – in which case $p$ will be said to be "looking at" the other, or whether his face is oriented in some other direction – in which case $p$ will be said to be "looking away" from the other.

In examining face orientation or "gaze" during approach, all those greetings in the birthday party film were selected in which (a) at least ten feet separated the individuals at the start of the transaction and (b) at

[8] For both individuals to approach one another from a distance and sustain mutual gaze throughout is rare. When it happens we would probably say the relationship is very intense. The one instance in which we do see mutual face orientation over the whole length of the approach is in a greeting between JF and her two-year-old daughter.

least one member of the transaction could be observed from the beginning. The period of time during which observations could be made was
then divided into twelve-frame segments (half-second segments) and the
number of frames in each segment in which the individual had his face
oriented to the other was counted. The combined results of this analysis
are presented in Fig. 19. This gives an overall picture of "gaze" during
approach for a maximum of forty-seven individuals drawn from
twenty-five greetings. These individuals could be observed for between
two and fourteen seconds. All forty-seven of them could be observed for
the last two seconds of the greeting studied, twenty of them could be
observed for the last eight seconds, while seven could be observed from
the point at which the greeting transaction began. The later parts of the
curve are thus more reliable as an indicator of overall "looking" trends
than are the earlier parts.

The composite curve shows the proportion of time spent "looking
at" the other during approach at each of the twenty-eight twelve-frame
segments. The most outstanding feature of this curve is that although
within the half second immediately preceding the start of the close salutation almost all the greeters are "looking at" one another, during the
previous three seconds the proportion of time spent "looking" is
sharply lower. Thereafter the curve tends to rise, though irregularly,
until ten seconds before the close salutation the greeters are much more
likely to be "looking at" one another. In general, it would seem, we can
say that as the approach begins the greeters tend to look at each other.
It is here, at the beginning of the approach, that the distance salutation
tends to occur, and during the distance salutation the greeters look
directly at one another. This is often followed, as we have seen, by a
head dip, and it is this that no doubt accounts for the irregularities
observed in the early parts of the curve. Thereafter, some looking is
likely to occur, but less and less as the approach continues until, when
the individuals are within but a few feet of one another, as the curve
shows, they look comparatively little. This dip in the curve just before
the close salutation reflects a definite dip or turn of the head by which
gaze to the other person is sharply "cut off." This "cut off" tends to
occur when the individuals are just a little more than ten feet from one
another, a distance just a little greater than the one at which interaction
by means of utterance exchange can become possible (see Fig. 18).

This aversion of gaze just before the close salutation is observed
in 72% of the individual approaches examined. It may perhaps be

Fig. 18   Tracing to show the horizontal rotation of the head characteristic
of the exaggerated turning away of the face that often occurs just before
the greeters are close enough to begin the close salutation. From the
Wedding film

interpreted in terms of a theory of the role of the look in the regulation
of "intimacy" or degree of interpersonal involvement in social encounters (Argyle and Dean 1965).

First of all it may be noted that when $p$ looks at $q$ he may thereby be
said to reduce his behavioral distance from him. Conversely, to look
away is an act of withdrawal. In the situation studied here, in which two
individuals are physically approaching one another, we may expect that
the closer they get to one another the stronger will be any tendencies
either may have to withdraw from the other. We may expect, thus, that
behaviors associated with withdrawal will be more likely to appear the
closer the individuals get to one another.

This expectation seems to be fulfilled by the face-orientation data, if
we accept that to look away from someone is to partly withdraw from
him. Not only do we find that $p$ is more likely to look away from $q$ the
closer he gets to him, we also find that the partner who looks the least
in a given transaction is also the one who would expect to have stronger
withdrawal tendencies. The relevant data are given in Table 12. Here
we present the mean number of frames per twelve-frame blocks in
which $p$'s face was oriented to $q$, for the fifteen greetings in which this
could be observed simultaneously in both partners for three or more
seconds. It will be seen that in all but one of the seven greetings in which
the hostess was involved, the hostess spent substantially more time
looking at her approaching guests than the guest did looking at her. It
will also be seen that in the eight other greetings included here, in six of
these cases it is the individual who covers the least amount of ground in
his approach who looks the most. It seems that the partner to a greeting

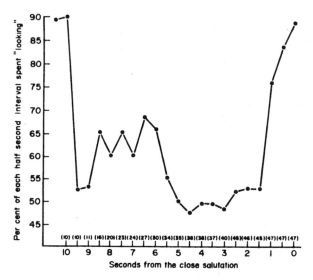

Fig. 19    Variation in the proportion of time spent in face orientation to other during approach. Abscissa: time intervals in seconds from the close salutation. Figures in parentheses are the number of individuals observed at each interval. Ordinate: proportion of each half second individual (in percent) spent in face orientation at other combined for all individuals observed at each half-second interval

who looks the least, is the one who must enter a space that is already occupied by the other.

However, as we see from Fig. 19, though looking away increases sharply in most cases just before the close salutation, thereafter looking at increases even more sharply. Almost everyone is looking directly at the other as he begins the close salutation. There is thus a reduction in withdrawal tendencies in the final phase of the greeting. This reduction, it is now suggested, may be brought about by the gaze aversion we have described. The very performance of an act of withdrawal may serve to decrease the tendency to withdraw.

Aversion of gaze may have the effect of facilitating further approach for two reasons, neither of which excludes the other. On the one hand, by looking away from $q$, $p$ sharply reduces stimulus input from him, and this may reduce his tendency to withdraw because it reduces the very input that is inducing that tendency. The aversion of gaze just prior to the close salutation thus could function as a "cut off" in the sense

Table 12. *Average "looking" time per twelve-frame block during the approach*

| | Hostess–guest greetings | | | | Guest–guest greetings | | |
|---|---|---|---|---|---|---|---|
| Greeting | Participants | Mean "looking" | No. of seconds observed | Greeting | Participants | Mean "looking" | No. of seconds observed |
| G1 | Hostess (JF) | 12.0 | 7 | G16 | Waits (MR) | 7.5 | 14 |
| | Guest (RG) | 3.7 | | | Approaches (DG) | 5.9 | |
| G2 | Hostess (JF) | 11.1 | 18 | G48 | Waits (WF) | 11.9 | 18 |
| | Guest (RC) | 6.2 | | | Approaches (JH) | 6.0 | |
| G5a | Hostess (JF) | 8.9 | 16 | G26 | Waits (DG) | 8.0 | 12 |
| | Guest (CB) | 8.9 | | | Approaches (RG) | 6.2 | |
| G6 | Hostess (JF) | 11.2 | 13 | G28 | Waits (MR) | 6.0 | 16 |
| | Guest (SK) | 3.9 | | | Approaches (AF) | 3.0 | |
| G10 | Hostess (JF) | 9.0 | 14 | G39 | Waits (CB) | 10.8 | 10 |
| | Guest (DG) | 5.4 | | | Approaches (HR) | 5.0 | |
| G17 | Hostess (JF) | 12.0 | 6 | G41 | Waits (CB) | 6.7 | 29 |
| | Guest (JR) | 0 | | | Approaches (SW) | 7.3 | |
| G24 | Hostess (JF) | 8.0 | 17 | G40 | Waits (SW) | 10.5 | 6 |
| | Guest (DF) | 6.1 | | | Approaches (WF) | 7.5 | |
| | | | | G44 | Waits (CB) | 7.1 | 21 |
| | | | | | Approaches (DW) | 10.5 | |

intended by Chance (1962). At the same time, of course, for $p$ to avert his gaze from $q$ as he gets closer to him, may make it easier for $q$ to remain where he is. This could come about because $q$'s tendency to remain is likely to increase with any manifestation by $p$ of his tendency to withdraw. A look directed at another is also, in many circumstances, a threat, and this, in another who is physically approaching $q$, might either frighten $q$ away or provoke him to attack. If, as he approaches him, $p$ averts his gaze, either of these agonistic tendencies in $q$ will be reduced.

*(ii)    Behavior during approach: the "body cross."* In several of our examples, at about that point in the approach where we see the sharp aversion of gaze, one of the members of the greeting transaction may be observed to bring one or both of his arms in front of him, "crossing" the upper part of the body. This may be done momentarily, or this arm position may be sustained, persisting either until the close salutation or, in some instances, persisting right through it. It may take a variety of forms. Either one arm may be moved across the mid-line of the body, or, in some examples, both arms are brought into play, the hands being clasped together in front. In other instances an object the individual is carrying may be raised up in front. In still other instances, which we have counted as examples, the hand is raised to the mouth or it is raised to grasp the neck. The body cross may be seen in Figs. 21 and 24.

In all of our examples, the body cross occurs in only one of the greeting partners. The one who does it is either the younger of the pair or he is entering a territory from the outside – as in the case of a guest entering the site of a party – or he is the one who covers the most distance in his approach. Of the three instances in which a body cross occurs when the greeting is between a male and a female, it is the female who body crosses in each case. Only two of our eighteen instances of body crosses occur in greetings between people of apparently the same age on what may be regarded as "neutral" territory.

This survey of the circumstances in which the body cross occurs in our sample of greetings suggests that it is likely to occur in the partner to the greeting transaction who may be expected to have the stronger tendency to withdraw. It seems to occur, in a word, in the more vulnerable of the two participants. It is tempting to describe it as a protective movement, and indeed a body cross may be observed as part of a pattern of rapid withdrawal, when an individual is confronted with a sudden and apparently dangerous situation.[9]

In all the instances of the body cross in our examples, the body cross is a very casual, unformalized movement. Nevertheless, we can still ask if it has any communicative function. From the data available to us, we cannot decide this question. We may suppose, however, that like the aversion of gaze we have already discussed, it may betoken non-aggressive intent, and so it may facilitate further approach. From the point of view of $p$, we may suppose that a protective move on his part may enhance his ability to approach more closely, for he is safer from any aggression that might occur. On the other hand, a protective display by $p$ may be reassuring to $q$. For $p$ to protect himself mildly as he approaches $q$ may signal to $q$ that $p$ perceives him as powerful. Thus the body cross could be a signal of subordination to $q$ and, like withdrawal of gaze, reduce the degree to which $p$ may appear threatening. $p$'s own tendencies to withdraw could thus thereby be reduced.

*(iii) Behavior during the approach: grooming.* Another action that may be observed during the approach is the "groom." We counted as a groom any instances where $p$ adjusts his clothing – straightening a sweater or a tie, for example; where he strokes or smooths his hair; scratches his head; pats himself or appears to brush something off himself; or rubs any part of his face. Such actions are typically unformalized, brief, and they are performed quite incidentally to the main flow of behavior.

In greeting sequences a groom is observed most commonly either just before or just after the distance salutation, or just before the close salutation. It may also be observed just before an individual is to leave a gathering, or just after he has left and after the parting ceremony is over. There are other circumstances in which grooming is observed besides these, of course, but these are the ones most pertinent to this study.

---

[9] For example, in a film in the collection of the Project on Human Communication at Bronx State Hospital, a couple may be seen seating themselves on a grassy hillock in Central Park in New York City. Just as the girl was settling, a pack of large dogs charged by, very close. As they did so, she drew up her legs, bent her body forward, and crossed her body with her arms. In the same film a girl is seen walking down some steps. As she does so she stumbles and, as she stumbles (but does not fall), she crosses her body. In the Birthday Party film, a small boy charges up to a nine-year-old girl, his fists raised as if to box with her. As he approaches, she lifts her shoulders and bends them forward, at the same time crossing her arms in front of her.

In the birthday party material relatively little grooming was observed. It seems to be characteristic of only a few individuals and each of them has a characteristic style of grooming. Thus CB usually strokes his beard, drawing the palm of the hand downwards towards the tip. He may be observed doing this repeatedly just prior to an engagement in interaction at close range. RC was observed either to touch the right side of her glasses or she would place the tips of the fingers of her right hand on the left side of her head, and draw the hand over her hair, in an apparent hair adjustment movement. HA would either pull down the sweater he was wearing, or he would run the fingers of his right hand through the long lock of hair that hangs over his forehead. DF's groom consisted in a brief patting of the buttocks.

In other material much more grooming has been observed. Thus, a study of grooming was made using the TRD Band film. This is a film of a gathering of about seventy adolescents who are milling around in a parking lot prior to a practice of their high school band. Conversational knots constantly form and break apart. During the first twenty minutes of the film over one hundred separate instances of grooming were recorded, and their occurrence was classified according to whether the groom occurred during interaction, just before it or as it was beginning, just after it or as it was ending, or when the individual was alone. It was found that 70% of the grooms observed occurred with the onset or off-set of interaction, while only 10% were observed in individuals who were alone. Thus, these preliminary findings suggest that it will be commonly observed where an individual is changing his involvement with others, as he is moving into interaction with another, or as he is moving out of interaction with him.

Whereas most of the examples of grooming we have observed are unformalized in character, formalized grooming does exist. One relatively well known form may be seen in females, where it seems to be part of the system of flirting gestures. Here, the head is tilted to one side, and, at the same time, the hand moves down the side of hair and it is so turned that the palm of the hand is oriented toward the person being addressed. In its full-fledged form it is accompanied by the eyebrow-flash and smile display, and also, if the individual is standing, by a sway of the hips. Fragments of this display are not uncommon. It has been described by Scheflen (1964) as part of what he calls "quasi-courtship," where he indicates that it has the function of heightening the attention of individuals to one another. Self-grooming has also been incorporated into the close salutational ritual in a few cultures. Among the Ainu of northern Japan, the traditional formal close salutation is reported to include stroking the beard and arms or, with women, smoothing locks of hair away from the forehead (Hitchcock 1891, pp. 464–465; Batchelor 1927). In Tibet, the salutation by which an individual of low station addresses someone of high station is reported to include opening the mouth and protruding the tongue, bowing forward slightly and scratching the back of the head (Bell 1946).

## The final approach

We noted, in the discussion of gaze during approach, that as the partners got closer to one another, they were increasingly likely to look away but that this aversion of gaze was highly likely to be followed by a phase in which each looked at the other. This phase immediately precedes the start of the close salutation. It generally begins when the greeters are within ten feet of one another, or less. It also appears to have certain distinctive behaviors associated with it, which are less likely to occur at earlier stages of the transaction. Thus vocalization is most likely to occur here. A distinctive facial display appears – almost always a smile in our data – and the greeters assume a set of the head that is distinct from the headsets they have adopted during earlier phases of the transaction. Finally, we have sometimes observed a distinct gesture in one of the hands, in which the palm of the hand is oriented toward the other. This gesture may precede or it may be combined with the movements associated with getting ready for the close ritual. These phenomena will now be discussed in more detail.

(i)   *Smiling.* The quality of the films available to us did not permit a fine-grained analysis of facial displays. However, it did prove possible to distinguish "smiling face" from "non-smiling face." Within the category of "smiling face," furthermore, we could distinguish "broad smiles" from other smiles on the basis of whether or not the teeth could be seen.

Smiling, as we have seen, is commonly associated with the distance salutation. Thereafter, however, the smile either rapidly fades in intensity, or even disappears altogether, until the participants are close to one another and once again are looking at one another. In some cases, to be sure, a smile could be clearly seen throughout the approach. This was

Table 13. *Observed smiling in the final phase of the approach for forty-three greetings in Birthday Party film*

|  | p's members of same family | p's not members of same family |
|---|---|---|
| No. showing tooth smiles | 1 | 20 |
| No. showing no-tooth smiles | 11 | 11 |

the pattern observed in the hostess when she was greeting guests as they entered the site of the party. Very often, however, a definite smile could not be distinguishable again until the final approach phase. In this phase, however, a smile was very common. Of the seventy separate observations of faces that were possible in this phase of the greeting transaction, only eight showed no smiling.

The distribution of smiles with teeth as compared to smiles without teeth is presented in Table 13. It will be seen that smiles with teeth ("broad smiles") were overall more frequent than smiles without teeth; males were somewhat less likely to show a smile with teeth than were females; smiling with teeth appears less often in greetings between family members than in greetings between friends and acquaintances. Thus, in the forty-three greetings in which the record was such that some smiling could be observed, twelve of these were between members of the same (extended) family, thirty-one between friends and acquaintances. In only one of the twelve family greetings was smiling with teeth observed in any party to the greeting, in contrast to twenty instances out of the thirty-one non-family greetings observed.

The only definite conclusion that seems to be warranted by these data is that smiling is a common feature of the greeting ritual. The distribution of the different types of smiling we have reported, however, does suggest that there will be much more to be said about smiling in greeting if a special effort is being made to study it.

*(ii)    Headset.* In the final approach phase, the greeters not only look at one another and smile, but as they do so they are likely to hold their head in a way that is distinct from the way they have been holding it at earlier phases of the approach.

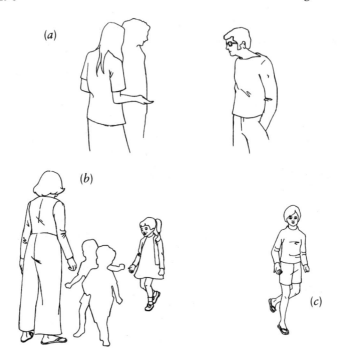

Fig. 20    Examples of palm presentations

(a) JS (left) turns to AF (right as AF approaches). Note JS's hand is extended toward AF with palm uppermost. AF shows head forward on neck, one of the headsets observed in the final phase of greeting inter-action

(b) A six-year-old girl approaching the hostess. Note how her right hand is open with palm oriented toward hostess

(c) A well-developed example of palm presentation in a five-year-old boy. Reconstructed from two views of KC in G2, from the Birthday Party film

The head positions of greeters in the final approach were classified into five categories: erect head, head tilted forward, head tilted back, head cocked to one side, and head held erect or forward, but with neck extended forward. Out of a total of eighty-three observations in the birthday party film, the forward position was observed thirty-five times while the cocked-to-one-side position was observed twenty times. It was further noted that eighteen of the cocked-to-one-side positions were performed by females, whereas twenty-seven of the forward positions were performed by males. Of the twenty-four females observed, nine adopted headcock at least once, in contrast to the nineteen males observed of whom only two adopted headcock in the final approach. It is our impression that this apparent tendency for females to adopt headcock in the final approach, in contrast to the male's erect or forward head position, appears to be more obvious in male–female greetings. Perhaps head erect or forward and headcock are kinesic gender markers of males and females, respectively. Head forward may be seen in Fig. 20a. Headcock may be seen in Figs. 21d, 24b.

*(iii)    The "palm presentation."* A gesture in which the palm of the hand is oriented toward the other, often with the arm extended forward or laterally, may sometimes be observed, either in association with a distance salutation or, more often, just before *p* prepares for the close salutation. This gesture will be referred to as the "palm presentation." Seventeen instances of it have been seen in our present material. It may appear in a conspicuous and well-developed form, though in most of the examples in our corpus it has a more fleeting character. It is also of interest to note that it may occur in quite small children. Two of our examples, one of them a very clear one, were enacted by five-year olds.

The palm presentation as a gesture of greeting has been recognized by Eibl-Eibesfeldt (1970) who reports that it occurs in greetings in many different parts of the world. The orientation of the palm to another has also been described by Scheflen (1964) in so-called "quasi-courtship" displays, which, according to him, function to heighten the attention of one individual upon another. When the gesture is performed, *p* is at the same time face-oriented to (or "looking at") the other. It is thus addressed to another. It is also associated with an increase in the closeness of interaction. It may thus be reasonably supposed that the palm presentation is a signal of openness to social contact – it may be seen perhaps both as a signal of *p*'s intentions and also, at the same time, as a signal to *q* serving to invite further approach from him. Palm presentation is illustrated in Fig. 20.

## The close salutation

The close salutation may be regarded as the culmination of the greeting transaction. Up till now, the participants have been reducing the distance between them. Eventually they stop doing this. They stand, often face to face, generally at a distance of five feet or less,[10] and engage in a highly formalized unit of interaction, usually recognizable as a hand-shake, an embrace, or some other well-known category of greeting rit-ual. It is this ritual which is usually thought of as *the greeting ceremony*. Insofar as greetings have been described by other writers, it is generally this part of the transaction that has been described. Most of what we have considered in this chapter so far can be regarded as having the function of preparing a context in which this close ritual may be per-formed.

Regardless of the actual form of the ritual, there are certain charac-teristics that are associated with all the close salutations we have observed. First, both partners to the greeting come to a halt as they per-form the salutation. Sometimes this halt is very brief, and key elements of the close salutation may be begun before it starts, or continued after one or both of the participants have begun to move again. But coming to a halt is always observed. Secondly, the participants, in coming to a halt, tend to face the ventral surfaces of their bodies toward one another, and each typically orients his face directly at the face of the other. Close salutations are not, as a rule, performed when the individuals are stand-ing side-by-side, both facing the same way, nor are they performed when the individuals are standing so that the angle of their bodies to one another in the horizontal plane is a right angle (such right-angle arrangements are commonly adopted in conversations). Thirdly, the position and orientation associated with the close salutation is not maintained after it is over. Both participants move away from the spot at which they came to a halt during the salutation, and both participants alter their orientation to one another. In many cases this is a large and obvious change – having shaken hands, the guest and hostess walk together to the center of the party, or the two greeters move into the room and sit down. In other cases the change may be slight as when, fol-lowing the close salutation, the two stand and talk, close to the location of their greeting. But even here the participants change their orientation and location in relation to one another, even if they do this by merely moving the position of a foot, or by shifting the distribution of weight in the body.

Since such a postural and positional change can always be observed

[10] The distance between people in greeting referred to here is the distance as estimated from pelvis to pelvis.

in association with the end of the gestures of salutation, and since following upon it some distinct kind of interaction is to be observed, we have taken this change as the point at which the close salutation may be said to be over. This is also the point at which, in the present study, we bring our analysis of the greeting transaction to a close.

There are many variations to be observed in the form of the close salutation. Here we shall describe what has been observed in our birthday party corpus under three main headings: close salutation which involves no body contact; handshakes; and kisses and embraces.

*(i)    Close salutation without body contact.* In some examples, the participants approach one another and stop, facing one another but, apart from speaking, do not appear to engage in any behavior distinctive of salutation.

Thus in G10, JF waits at the bottom of the brick walkway as DG, bringing up the rear of a group of four children, approaches down the walkway. When this group of guests is about twelve feet away, JF calls a greeting to each of them (a "hi" followed by the name) and then takes two steps backwards. The children come to a halt in front of her, as does DG. JF's face is oriented down and forward – she is apparently looking at the children. The children are looking either to their left or to their right. DG also looks down, apparently at the children, talking meanwhile. JF then turns and begins to tell them where to go as they go into the party, and they walk forward onto the lawn. Though both JF and DG stop in a face-to-face orientation, an orientation distinctive of greeting, no clearly distinguishable gestures of salutation can be observed. All the gestures of salutation – greeting calls by JF, and a smiling response from DG – were completed before the greeting parties stopped, facing one another.

More usually, in the non-contact close salutations we have observed, the greeters come to a halt in front of one another and simply sustain the head–eye orientation, the headset and the facial display they had already assumed when they were a few feet away from one another.

This is seen in GW1, for example, where a young woman crosses from some distance away to greet someone who is standing still. Here, as she approaches, she cocks her head on one side. She then stops within two feet of the person she is greeting, who holds her head erect. As the approaching woman comes to a halt, the other turns, so that she is now oriented at approximately right angles to the other (Fig. 21).

In this instance, stopping in the "salutational frame" (which here was only momentary) was not itself marked by any distinctive gestures. Sometimes, however, the participants do not assume the head orien-

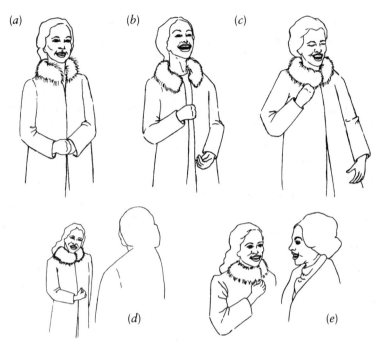

Fig. 21   Sighting, distance greeting, approach and close salutation in a
non-contact greeting. Sequence GW1 from The Wedding, BDF00170

(a) p sights q

(b) p showing headtoss display in distance salutation. Note the raised
eyebrows and the open-mouth smile

(c) Head dip following distance salutation. Note the eyes are now shut

(d) p is now closer to q and is looking at her. Note that p has her head tilted
to one side, an example of one of the headsets characteristic of the final
phase of the greeting encounter

(e) Following the salutation, p and q move out of their vis-a-vis orientation
into one in which their bodies are set more nearly at 90°. Note that p has
her arm across the front of her body, illustrating "body cross"

tations, headsets and facial display characteristic of the close phase of a
greeting, until they enter the salutational frame.

This is exemplified in G 44, where CB is approached by DW from a distance of
about twenty feet after an initial distance salutation. During most of the
approach DW looks at CB, while CB looks down and to the side. However,
when DW is within five feet of CB, CB orients his face to him. As he does so, DW
stops moving and cocks his head to one side. At the same time CB steps sideways
in such a way as to bring his body more fully into a frontal orientation to DW.

As he does so, his smile broadens, and he pronates his right forearm in what appears to be the beginning of a palm presentation (Fig. 22).

These examples are, perhaps, the most typical of the non-contact close salutations we have observed. Sometimes, however, gestures distinctive of the close salutational frame itself occur.

Thus in G18, MR headtosses three times to HS as HS bends forward at the trunk in a slight bow and then raises the cup he is holding as if to offer a toast to MR. He then nods three times. During this gestural exchange, MR is saying "Hi, I remember I met you at Jane's party" – HS probably makes some verbal reply here, but this cannot be heard. Likewise, in G6 SK headtosses twice to AF while AF stands before her with a slight headcock.

In these two examples, it will be noted, one member of the pair engages in repeated headtosses, while the other engages with nods or bows or with a headcock. Observations made outside the present corpus, without the aid of films, suggest that this is the typical pattern. We saw earlier, in the account of the distance salutations, that the headtoss is characteristically reciprocated with a head lower or headnod. The same seems to be true of the non-contact close salutations we have observed in which a gesture distinctive of the salutation frame occurs.

*(ii)   Handshakes.* In the handshake each extends, typically, his right hand to grasp that of the other and the joined hands are then squeezed or moved up and down one or more times. A common form in our corpus was for the hands to be raised and lowered three times, the first stroke of the handshake having much greater amplitude than those that follow. Just before the hand disengages there is a brief pause in the movement. In some instances, however, much more prolonged shaking occurred. As is well known, handshakes also vary in the strength of the grip. The handshake may also vary in that additional gestures may be associated with it. In our corpus we have observed it associated with head nodding (G3), with a marked forward tilt of the head combined with a headcock, or with a kiss. The handshake combined with a kiss is quite common, but occurs only between males and females, and generally speaking it is the female who offers her cheek which the male then touches with his lips. Where the handshake is combined with a head nod or forward head lower (as in G62), it seems to be performed by only one of the pair, not both. Another form of the handshake is when it is combined with a partial embrace. Here one member of the (usually male)

(a)

(b)

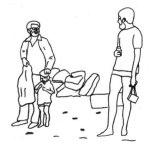

(c)

(d)

(e)

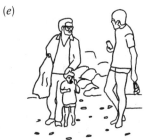

(f)

(g)

pair, places his hand upon the shoulder of the other. Finally, another form may be mentioned, in which one of the greeters takes the other's hand with both hands grasping with his right hand in the usual way, bringing his other hand to cover the back of the other's hand that he is grasping.

*(iii)     Embraces.* In our present corpus, seven instances of cheek kissing occurred, all except one of them in association with an embrace. In six instances this form of close salutation occurred between males and females, in one instance it occurred within an all female greeting.

The performance of the embrace is subject to some variation. We may note here what we have observed. In all the embraces between males and females, with one exception, the male's arms are lifted outwards, and placed around the female. The female lifts her arms and places her hands against the male's chest or waist, or she may slide her forearms under the male's arms to place her hands on his back. In the exceptional case (G22, JF/WF), JF placed her hands on WF's shoulders, but WF, instead of encircling JF with his arms, placed the palms of his hands under JF's chin. This gesture, it may be noted, is the close salutational gesture used by JF in greeting children. In this instance in some respects JF stands in relation to WF as a child, since she is his daughter-in-law.

In two instances of male–female embraces, the embrace had a two-phasic form. In the first phase, associated with a kiss by the male on the female's proffered cheek, the female placed her hands against the sides of the male's thorax. In the second phase, the hands of both greeters

Fig. 22    Pre-sighting, sighting, approach and close salutation in a non-contact greeting. G44 from the Birthday Party, BDF00269
(*a*) DW orients to face CB
(*b*) CB looks back at DW
(*c*) DW lifts head in "headtoss" for distance salutation
(*d*) DW begins his approach. Note his dipped head. CB has also turned his face away from DW
(*e*) CB and DW look at each other. DW stops approaching and sets head on one side
(*f*) CB walks forward and turns to face DW
(*g*) After the close salutation CB stepped back to his previous location and DW has come closer to him. They now stand with their bodies at approximately 90° to one another, a common arrangement for pairs of individuals as they stand and talk

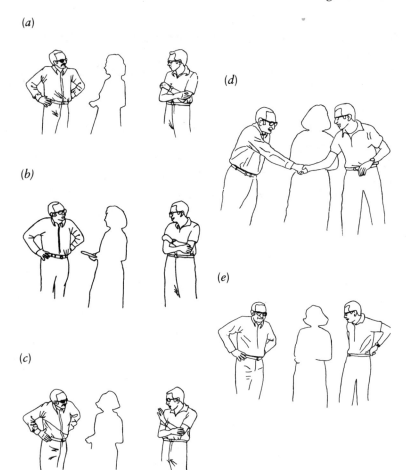

Fig. 23    Tracings from a sequence of stills from film of G60
(a) MG (on left) in conversation with hostess. DG (on right) looks at him
(b) MG offers a headtoss salutation to DG
(c) DG responds to MG's headtoss with a head lower and a raised hand
with an open palm
(d) MG and DG shake hands
(e) MG and DG step back. Note their symmetry in the handshake and in
the postures they assume afterward

Table 14. *Occurrence of close salutations of different types according to the sex of the participants*

| Type of CS | Male–Male | Male–Female | Female–Female |
|------------|-----------|-------------|---------------|
| No contact | 1         | 9           | 11            |
| Handshake  | 10        | 7           | 2             |
| Embrace    | 3         | 10          | 3             |

were placed on the other's back – each thus encircles the other with their arms, and they pulled each to the other in a hug, cheeks in contact.

*(iv)    Distribution of the main close salutational forms in the corpus.* The fifty-six instances of close salutation examined were divided into non-contact forms, handshakes, and embraces. The distribution of the forms so classified in relation to the sexes of the participants is given in Table 14. The figures suggest the following:

The most frequent forms of close salutation between males is the handshake, whereas between females the no-contact forms prevail. With cross-sex pairs, however, the frequencies of handshakes vs. no-contact forms is about equal. Though the figures of the present sample are small, this distribution is of interest because it exactly follows what would be expected on the basis of what is recommended as correct practice in leading North-American etiquette manuals. Thus *Emily Post* (Post 1965), *McCall's* (Bevans 1960) and *Vogue's* (Fenwick 1948) etiquette manuals are all agreed that men shake hands with men, but that women do not do so as a rule though "there is no reason why they shouldn't." Between men and women it is, according to these works, up to the woman to decide whether to shake hands or not, and thus the man should not offer his hand unless she offers hers first. In our corpus this is found to be the case. It seems unlikely that this distribution of close salutational forms has come about because the people observed in the corpus have studied etiquette manuals. Rather, it suggests that these manuals are accurate guides to what is, in fact, common practice.

As for the embraces and kisses, nine of the fifteen embraces occurred in male–female greetings, three occurred between females, and three between males. In these instances, one was between father and son (G33

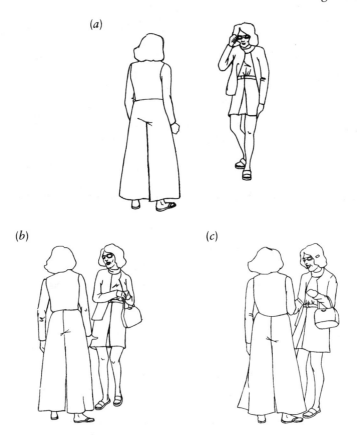

*(a)*

*(b)*                                   *(c)*

Fig. 24   Tracings from a sequence of stills from film of G2
(*a*) Guest is approaching hostess. Hostess stands and faces guest as she
approaches. Note guest is touching her hair ("groom") and has her head
tilted forward
(*b*) Just before guest offers her hand for the handshake. Note that her head
is on one side and her right arm is held across her body in a "body cross"
(*c*) Hostess and guest shake hands

AF/WF) and one between brothers-in-law (G30, HA/HF). It should be
noted that HA is Mexican, and Mexicans are said to follow the common Latin practice of mutual embrace combined with back patting.
This is exactly the form the close salutation in G30 takes. AF here, probably, is accommodating to HA's style.

## Conclusion: the study of greetings and the development of human ethology

Human ethology may be understood as a study of human behavior in which an attempt is made to throw light upon its evolutionary history. Such a study has to begin with a close analysis of what human behavior presently consists in. This means that the first task of a human ethologist, like that of an ethologist who sets out to study a bird or a fish or a monkey, must be systematic description. He must set out to see what behavioral structures the human being has, and how these structures are related to his mode of life. In doing this with people it would seem best to begin with those aspects of behavior which are most likely to be shared with other animals, for a comparison of human behavior with the behavior of related species will be an essential step in this inquiry. Thus while detailed analyses of language, or of perceptual and conceptual processes, must eventually find a place in a human ethology, these do not seem to be the best aspects of human behavior with which to start. Likewise, the more complex aspects of human social behavior, such as the development of self-image, mechanisms of leadership, the formation of attitudes, and all the other common topics of social psychology, are not appropriate aspects of behavior for a human ethologist to study. He must look for something more elementary. This is why the close analysis of communication conduct seems to offer so rich a vein. Since it is in his behavior in his immediate relationship to others that we most easily recognize similarities between human and animal behavior, it is here that an effective start on a human ethology may be possible.

The foregoing descriptive analysis of some human greetings may be understood as a contribution to this initial phase of human ethology. It is limited in many ways. There are many aspects of the behavior we have had to leave undescribed. We have been severely limited by the sample we have had available so that we have not been able to explore properly the contextual distributions of the various elements we have described. This has meant we have had to be extremely cautious in making statements about the signal function of these elements. Nevertheless it is hoped that the detail we have provided, and the format within which this detail has been set, will offer a guide to those who would follow with more rigorous observational and experimental studies.

In the analysis presented in this chapter, we have drawn a distinction between the structure of the greeting as an interpersonal transaction and the specific gestures and other actions that comprise its various stages. We suggest that the greeting transaction could be seen as a unit having certain general features, even though the salutational gestures might be different from greeting to greeting. Thus we suggested that greetings would have a pre-phase of sighting and announcement, a distance salutation, an approach phase and a close salutation; that the close salutation has a distinct location, and the participants as they engage in it orient themselves to each other in a way that is distinctive. Each of these components of the greeting transaction can be thought of as a spot in a program where one of a number of different actions can be performed. We expect that for each of these spots there will be a restricted class of actions that will be "selected" from. Thus the kinds of actions that will be observed in the distance salutation will comprise a rather different set from those that will be observed during the approach phase, and different again from those that will be observed in the close salutation.

From the point of view of an ethological study of greetings, the question of the diversity of salutational forms is one that must soon be faced. One may gather from reading such writers as Roth (1889) or Labarre (1964) that the forms of salutation are very diverse indeed. Yet, as Eibl-Eibesfeldt has shown, the display that we have here described as the headtoss display, appears to be universal to man. If the programmatic structure of greeting transactions is borne in mind, however, this seeming conflict is clarified, for it will be seen that whereas Eibl-Eibesfeldt has confined his observations to what we would call the distance salutation, such writers as Roth and Labarre have collected together descriptions of close salutational rituals.

It would seem, from what we have just said, that the range of gestures or other actions that occur in the greeting transaction is greater at some spots in the program than it is in others. Thus it appears that the range of variation in close salutational rituals may often be greater than is the range for distance salutations. This could well be due to the difference in function that these two steps in the greeting program have. Thus whereas the distance salutation often seems to function merely to establish that the two greeters have seen one another and that they are now ratified in a greeting relationship, the close salutation would seem to have several additional functions. These have to do with establishing or affirming the kind of relationship that the two greeters have to one another, both in reference to all the different situations in which they may meet, and in reference to the specific situation in which the greeting is taking place. Thus in the close salutation, we may expect that such aspects as relative dominance, friendliness, familiarity, and identity will be signaled. It would seem reasonable, therefore, that there should be greater variation in close salutational gestures than those of the distance salutation.

Even within a single culture, or indeed within a small sample from a single culture such as the one we have examined in this paper, we will encounter a good deal of variation in the kinds of greeting transactions performed. In understanding this variation we shall have to consider not only whether the greeters are friends, relatives or strangers; whether they are males or females; whether they differ greatly in social status; but also in what occasion the greeting occurs, and how long ago it was that the participants last met, if they have met before.

It is further to be noted that not only may the greeting transactions vary in what salutation or other actions are performed at any given spot in the program, but they will also vary in how much of the program is performed. Some transactions will include only a distance salutation. Others may include only a distance salutation and an approach. A few instances of this occurred in the Birthday Party where individuals were greeting one another for a second time. Mutual sighting would occur, followed by a distance exchange, followed by an approach in which the individuals moved directly into a formation in which conversation can take place. It will also be seen that for a given situation, how many stages of the greeting program are enacted will depend upon the kind of relationship that exists between the greeters. There are some with whom a mere distance exchange is all that is needed. There are others with whom one must engage in close salutation in addition. But again, this is related to the situation. For a given kind of relationship, there are situations in which all of the steps of the program will be appropriate, but others in which only some of them will be necessary. In situations where close interaction is to follow, for example, it appears that upon an initial encounter (i.e. the first time the two individuals encounter one another within the context of a given occasion) both a distance and a close exchange of salutation will occur. Upon subsequent encounters only a distance salutation is necessary. In some contexts where repeated encounters between the individuals are likely, all that is left of the greeting is the approach, and salutations appear to be omitted altogether.

Thus we see that which parts of the program are enacted is a function both of the situation that is prevailing, and also of the relationship that prevails between the greeters. It will be seen that insofar as $p$ can decide how much of the program to enact, he can take an initiative in defining the situation or the relationship between the participants.

Another question is: how can we account for the forms of action that do occur in the greeting? We might ask, for instance, why do we see the eyebrow flash and headtoss display in the distance salutation? Or we could ask about the origin of the palm presentation, the handshake, or any of the other forms.

To deal with this sort of question, three kinds of inquiry seem to be necessary. First, we must have a thorough understanding of the contextual distributions of the various forms. We need to know (a) at what stage in the greeting program the form is observed, (b) in what greeting *situations* the given form is observed, and (c) between what categories of person the given form is observed. Answers to these questions would enable us to infer much about the function of the given form in the greeting transaction. Second, we need to know, for a given form, whether it can be observed in other contexts besides that of greeting. If it can be observed in other contexts, is it different in any way, or is it clearly the same element in every respect? Third, we need to know its developmental history.

In this way, we may be able to see how a formalized action in the greeting has arisen from some unformalized form, such as in an intentional movement of contact, or of withdrawal, or of attack. With some elements, such as the smile, it will be found that it appears in the human being as a formalized display from the very first. In this case we would have to resort to comparisons between the various species of primates to understand its derivation (van Hooff 1972). Some of the other elements of greeting, however, appear to be only partly formalized in some cultures but not in others. Thus in the Ainu salutation, in which the participants stroke their own beards, we can entertain the hypothesis that the Ainu salutation is a formalized version of this action since we have noted that self-grooming in an unformalized form occurs in many greetings in so divergent a culture as our own. Why this element should have become formalized among the Ainu, and not among other peoples, is yet another kind of question. An answer to it will be suggested from an understanding of the place of this form of salutation in Ainu life, and also from an understanding of the nature of Ainu life as compared with life in other cultures. Needless to say, we are very far from such understandings.

These then, represent some of the further ways in which the human greeting may be investigated. A further step in the development of an ethology of greetings will be the comparison of the behavior of greetings in man with those observed in closely related species. As Jane Van Lawick-Goodall (1968) has shown, there are patterns of behavior in the chimpanzee that may reasonably be described as greetings, and there appears to be considerable overlap in the forms assumed by the actions that comprise these greetings. Until we know far more about the nature of human greetings and of those of the chimpanzee and other primates, little can be concluded beyond the rather general point that much in human greeting behavior appears to be phylogenetically quite ancient.

## Postscript

In 1972, when the work on greetings presented in this chapter was readied for publication, we had been able to locate only a few previous studies. Roth (1889) provided an account of the great variety of greeting behavior that may be found throughout the world but it appeared that an interest in greetings was otherwise a much later development. Systematic studies preceding 1973, and which were available to us at the time the paper was written, included Eibl-Eibesfeldt (1968, 1970), Schegloff (1968), Blurton-Jones and Leach (1972). Greetings had also been discussed by Callan (1970) and Goffman (1971). Goffman's suggestions that explicit focused interaction tends to be preceded by a kind of "unofficial" exchange of "clearance signals" (Goffman 1963, pp. 91–2) drew our attention to the importance of looking at what happened in the interaction prior to any engagement in explicit salutation exchanges. However the work presented in this chapter appears to have been the first attempt to deal with the greeting encounter as a complete interactional event, from the pre-greeting "sighting" phase and the phases in which the participants must indicate to each other their willingness to engage in salutations, all the way through to the point where they change from salutation exchanges to some other form of interaction.

Since 1973 a few other studies of greeting have examined the sequential organization of complete greeting encounters in a similar manner.

Thus Pitcairn and Eibl-Eibesfeldt (1976) discuss greetings recorded on film in the Tirol and Collett (1983) discusses greetings among the Mossi of West Africa. In both papers it is shown that the greetings studied have a sequential organization similar to that proposed in our own study. Furthermore, in both papers several behavioral details are described (such as patterns of head and gaze movement, "body crossing," and the like) which are similar to those described in the Westchester films. Youssouf, Grimshaw and Bird (1976), in an account of greeting practices between traveling Tuareg in the North African desert, and Schiffrin (1977), in an analysis of greetings among white middle-class Americans in urban Philadelphia, also discuss the sequential organization of greeting encounters and show that they unfold through a series of stages. These can be matched quite closely with those that are proposed in the present chapter. (See also Kendon 1980.)

A few workers have considered some of the specific gestures of salutation. Thus, the semiotic and ritual functions of "hat tipping" in American society have been discussed by MacCannall (1973) and the handshake has been discussed by Schiffrin (1974) and Hall and Hall (1983). Patterns of touching, including handshakes, embraces and kisses in greetings observed in American society have been studied by Greenbaum and Rosenfeld (1980) and Jones and Yarborough (1985). The eyebrow flash as a greeting gesture, first described by Eibl-Eibesfeldt (e.g. Eibl-Eibesfeldt 1972b) and also described in the present chapter, has been further discussed by Eibl-Eibesfeldt (1979), Ekman (1979) and Grammer, et al. (1988). Greeting gestures are also described for the Gonja and LaDogaa of West Africa by Goody (1972) and a comparative survey has been provided by Firth (1972, 1973).

Other work on greetings since 1973 has been done by linguists who have concentrated on the patterning of verbal salutations. Thus Irvine (1974) for the Wolof of West Africa and Caton (1986) for the inhabitants of the Yemen highlands have discussed the structuring of the spoken exchanges of salutation. Ferguson (1976) provides a useful general discussion, drawing especially on Syrian Arab spoken salutations for comparison with American English practices.

Several authors have discussed the way in which differences in how greeting exchanges are performed are related to such matters as the relative status of the greeters or degree of acquaintance between them. This has been discussed by Goody (1972) in comparing greetings among the Gonjaa and the LaDogaa, by Irvine (1974) for the Wolof, Kommenich

(1977) for greetings among Serbians and Montenegrins in Yugoslavia, Collett (1983) for greetings among the Mossi, and Caton (1986) for greetings as observed among "tribal" and "village" inhabitants in the Yemen highlands. Goody, Kommenich, Collett and Caton also discuss the way in which differences in greeting practices in different societies reflect differences in social structure. Caton emphasizes the way in which the forms of salutation employed can serve as the means by which people construct for each other particular social personae.

Several writers have noted the relationship between rituals of greeting and rituals of departure. Surprisingly, departures have received much less attention than greetings. Goffman (1971) suggested the term "access ritual" to refer to those rituals that are performed whenever persons alter their social access to one another. He comments on the apparent symmetry of greeting and parting ceremonial. This has been discussed in more detail by Deutsch (1979). Departure rituals or phenomena associated with the closing of encounters generally have also been discussed by Knapp, Hart, Friedrich and Shulman (1973), Schegloff and Sacks (1973), Adato (1975) and Albert and Kessler (1976, 1978). Other discussion relevant to the closing of encounters may be found in Goodwin (1981) and Heath (1986).

# 7

## Spatial organization in social encounters: the F-formation system

### Introduction

People often group themselves into clusters, lines, or circles, or into various other kinds of patterns. These patterns may be highly fluid or they may be relatively sustained. When such a pattern is sustained it will be referred to as a *formation*. In this paper we shall examine one kind of formation which will be called an *F-formation*. An F-formation arises whenever two or more people sustain a spatial and orientational relationship in which the space between them is one to which they have equal, direct, and exclusive access. Such a pattern can be seen in the circle of the free-standing conversational group. Here the participants stand so that they all face inwards to a small space which they cooperate together to sustain and which is not easily accessible to others who may be in the vicinity. The system of behavioral organization by which such a spatial–orientational pattern is established and sustained will be called an *F-formation system*. In this paper we shall explore some of the properties of this system and show how it may be delineated.

There are several reasons for studying F-formation systems. In the first place, as we shall argue, the F-formation system serves as an important means of maintaining the separate identity and integrity of an interactional situation. It provides a means by which the participants can maintain differential access to one another and it facilitates the maintenance of a common focus of attention. It is thus an important part of the means by which behavior is organized in occasions of face-to-face interaction such as conversations. Secondly, because it has this framing or bounding function, the F-formation system provides us with an excellent means of defining a social encounter as a unit for analysis. A central methodological problem in the study of the behavior of face-to-face interaction is that of defining the structural units in terms of which it is organized. In particular, it is of great importance to be able to delineate, in terms of the organization of observable behavior, distinct units of interaction which can then be analyzed into their components. The F-formation system provides us with a means of doing this. Thirdly, the F-formation is a system of behavior that organizes the spatial structure of face-to-face interaction. Any investigation into the relationship between social behavior and physical space will find it necessary to consider this organization.

In what follows, I shall offer some criteria for recognizing F-formation systems and I shall describe some of their properties. The account to be given draws heavily upon analyses of examples of F-formation systems recorded on film. Some of these examples will be given in detail as illustrations. We have drawn most heavily upon the Birthday Party film described in Chapter 6 (BDF 00269), but we have also drawn from other films as well, which will be noted when they are referred to.

### The F-formation system: definitions[1]

We have said that an F-formation system arises when two or more people cooperate together to maintain a space between them to which they all have direct and exclusive access. To make clear what is meant here, consider first how *individuals* maintain space.

Activity is always *located*. A person doing something always does it *somewhere* and his doing always entails a relationship to the space which has in it the objects or people with which the doing is concerned. Thus to write or to eat one sits at a table and immediately in front of one there is a space in which the writing or the eating is done. In watching television, one may sit on a sofa, let us say, and between oneself and the television set there is an unobstructed space which is the space within which television watching is done. We may imagine, thus, a space extending in front a person which is the space he is currently using in whatever his current activity may be. This space will be referred to as the

---

[1] In a previous paper, written in 1968 but not published until 1973 (Kendon 1973), I put forward the concept of *configuration*. This was defined as "the stable arrangement of bodies which characterizes the focused encounter." The term F-*formation* refers to the same phenomenon. However, here we have tried to define it simply as a system of spatial–orientational behavior. Furthermore, the term "configuration" seems now to be too static a label for something that must be actively maintained.

individual's *transactional segment*. It is the space into which he looks and speaks, into which he reaches to handle objects. He will endeavor to maintain this space, in the face of any intrusions, so long as he is engaged in the particular line of activity which requires it. As a rule, others respect this space, not entering it or crossing it. The size of this space is quite variable. A man sitting over a book has a narrow, highly circumscribed transactional segment. A man sprawled on a sofa watching television has a wide transactional segment that extends at least as far as the television set. The transactional segment, thus, is a space that is created and maintained by the individual's behavior.

The location and orientation of the transactional segment is limited by how the individual places his body, how he orients it and spreads his limbs. The location and orientation of the body thus serve as a frame, limiting the space to which the individual has immediate access and within which he carries out his current line of activity. Changes in whole-body location and orientation effect changes in this frame, and such changes occur whenever there is a major shift in the individual's line of activity.

When two or more persons come to do something together, they are liable to arrange themselves in such a way that their individual transactional segments overlap to create a joint transactional space. This joint transactional space, which is the space *between* the interactants over which they agree to maintain joint jurisdiction and control, will be called an o-space. Whenever such an o-space is created we have an *F-formation*. Where people cooperate together to maintain this o-space they establish a systematic relation in those aspects of their behavior that function to create the o-space and it is this system that we refer to as the *F-formation system* (see Fig. 29).

It is important to be clear that an F-formation refers to a spatial and orientational organization of participants where their spacing and orientation is measured in terms of the location and orientation of their *lower bodies*. When a person is standing, this is largely determined by the placement of his feet. Once an individual has adopted a particular bodily location and orientation he is still free to rotate his head and to some extent his shoulders through a considerable arc before he must begin to turn his lower body as well. The o-space of an F-formation is the overlap of the space that projects forward from the lower portion of the body, which is the space within which most of the individual's activity is carried out. An exact limit to this space is hard to establish.

However, if $p$ rotates his head so that a line projected from the midline of his face forms an angle of more than thirty degrees from the midline of his lower body, $p$ may be said to be facing out of his transactional segment. It is not uncommon for someone to look out of his transactional segment in this way – for example when someone looks over his shoulder. Such head orientations are rarely continued for long, however. Any sustained looking in such a direction is usually associated with a re-orientation of the lower body, so that the direction of the transactional segment again coincides with the direction in which the face is oriented.

Within a given F-formation, the participants can orient their heads in a number of different directions and when people are engaged in an utterance exchange they typically orient their faces repeatedly towards one another (see Chapter 4 and Kendon 1973). We may speak, thus, of a system of relationship in face orientations which may be referred to as a *face address system*. As a rule, in sustained conversations, the face address system falls within the overlap of transactional segments, the o-space. Under some circumstances, however, people may orient their faces toward one another and sustain an utterance exchange without sustaining an o-space. Again, this rarely lasts long and, if the conversation is sustained, the participants are highly likely to bring their bodies into an F-formation. An example of this is described later in this chapter, where a conversation is begun between adjacent participants whose individual transactional segments are oriented in quite different directions. As will be seen, as the conversation continues, the F-formation becomes established.

An F-formation *system*, it should be emphasized, is the system of spatial and orientational behavior which sustains an o-space. The circumstances that this creates, within which other systems of interactional behavior may be established, may be a consequence of the system, but are not part of its definition. It may also be noted that since an F-formation system is defined as a system of behavioral relations *between* individuals, any given instance of such a system lasts just as long as *these relations* persist. This means that a given F-formation system can change its participants, and still remain the same system. The F-formation system, thus, though it is a unit of behavior, is a unit of behavior at the interactional level of organization, not at the individual level.

The F-formation system is an obvious and commonplace phenomenon. Perhaps because of this it has received little systematic attention. Erving Goffman (1963), in discussing the behavioral arrangements of conversation, has referred to the "eye-to-eye ecological huddle [which] tends to be carefully maintained" (p. 95). Lyman and Scott (1967), in a very perceptive discussion of the various forms of human territoriality, have drawn attention to what they call "interaction territory," pointing out that people in talking together establish a joint space to which outsiders do not have access. Recently Knowles (cited in Knowles 1973) and Cheyne and Efran (1972) and Efran and Cheyne (1973) have reported some experimental studies in which they have begun to explore the circumstances under which outsiders will respect the space between talking individuals. The extensive work that has been done on spacing in social behavior in recent years, however, has considered it largely from the point of view of the individual, and the viewpoint followed here has been little explored. Reviews of this may be found in Sommer (1967), Patterson (1968), Vine (1973a, 1975) and Evans and Howard (1973).

## Spatial arrangements in F-formations

There are many different spatial patterns or *arrangements* assumed by F-formations. A circular arrangement is common in free-standing conversational groups of three persons or more, but it is by no means the only arrangement that may be observed. In F-formations of two individuals, for example, we may see a *vis-a-vis arrangement*, in which the two participants stand and face one another directly; an *L-arrangement*, in which the two participants stand so that the frontal surfaces of their bodies fall on the two arms of an L; or a *side-by-side arrangement*, where they stand close together, both facing the same way. In F-formations of more than two participants we may see linear, semicircular, or rectangular arrangements, as well as circular ones.

Which arrangement is maintained in an F-formation depends upon a number of different factors. First, it will depend upon the number of participants. A side-by-side arrangement, for example, is less likely to be sustained as an F-formation when there are more than three participants. The arrangement maintained will also depend upon the nature of the environment within which the F-formation occurs. In entering into an F-formation system, we suggest, participants enter a behavioral system which provides a frame within which some joint business is to be done. In situations where the physical environment can take over this framing function, for example in walled spaces such as rooms, or in

spaces well bounded by furniture or other such features and where the
participants are the only occupants of such a space, the F-formation
may be attenuated or occasionally dispensed with altogether. On the
other hand, in open spaces where each other's bodies are the only
objects the participants have available for delineating the boundary of
the encounter, F-formations are well articulated. In addition, the actual
arrangement maintained may be affected by the setting. Thus, in free-
standing dyadic F-formations in a pedestrian plaza, side-by-side
arrangements occur more commonly at the edges of the setting against
walls, vis-a-vis arrangements are more common on paths, while L-
arrangements are more common in open spaces (Ciolek and Kendon
1980).

Thirdly, the arrangement maintained in an F-formation is governed
by the other interactional systems that the given arrangement makes
possible. How people are spaced and oriented to one another places
important limitations on how they may interrelate their behavior in
other ways. Thus, Hall (1964a, 1966, 1968) has pointed out that at different distances the senses make available different kinds of information
and this has consequences for the kinds of actions that will be used in
interaction. Thus, at very close distances touch is available, whereas at
greater distances vision and hearing become more important and, as the
distance increases further, because the participants are able to detect one
another's behavior in a less fine-grained fashion, Hall suggests that
there will be shifts in the style of language used and in how listener
behavior is organized, and in the role of vision. Hall suggests, thus, that
because *how p* and *q* may relate their behavior alters according to the
distance that separates them, so the function of the transaction between
them will alter with distance so that different distances will be chosen by
interactants according to the kind of transaction they are going to have.
These suggestions of Hall's have never been directly followed up,
though the findings of studies such as those reviewed by Patterson
(1973) are in line with them.

Hall's analysis dealt only with distance, but angle of orientation also
influences how the two interactants may interrelate their behavior. For
example, Sommer (1965) showed in a questionnaire study that according to whether seated dyads were competing, cooperating, or engaged
in separate activities, there were definite preferences as to how they
would orient themselves. Competing pairs preferred face-to-face
arrangements, presumably because they could more easily monitor

each other's behavior. Cooperating pairs preferred an L-arrangement. Pairs acting separately chose arrangements in which they did not face each other. That is, in terms of the present study, they chose arrangements which avoided transactional segment overlap. Sommer's study has been repeated in England by Cook (1970), who found also that there were preferences for different arrangements according to the supposed activity of the pair, though the pattern of preference was somewhat different. Cook also investigated the relationship between social relationship and preferred arrangement and showed that whereas in hostile and competitive interaction subjects preferred a close face-to-face arrangement, interactants who were intimate friends of the opposite sex preferred a close side-by-side arrangement. As Cook points out, the kind of access a close vis-a-vis gives each to the other is different from the one made possible by side-by-side. Whereas the former is good for mutual monitoring and perhaps for threatening stares, the latter makes possible considerable physical contact which may also be combined with utterance exchanges.

Surprisingly, few attempts have been made to observe what arrangements people actually maintain when they are engaged in different sorts of interaction. Batchelor and Goethals (1972) have reported an experiment in which they showed that co-present individuals who worked on separate tasks sat so that they did not orient to one another, whereas an arrangement that was clearly of an F-formation was adopted when the task was cooperative. Heshka and Nelson (1972) observed distances adopted by static dyads in public spaces in London and showed that, in general, people who were friends stood closer to one another as they talked than people who were strangers. Thomas (1973) observed interpersonal distance in pairs photographed on a Brisbane beach and showed that distance was less in pairs where "sexual interaction" was likely. Cook (1970) reports a series of observations on pairs made in bars and restaurants which show that while the arrangement adopted is heavily influenced by the pattern of the available seating, there is a tendency for presumptive friendly couples to sit side by side.

It is to be noted that all of this work has been concerned with dyads. F-formations with more than two participants have been very little studied. However, Kendon (1973) has reviewed a number of studies in which it appears that the role of an individual in a group is related to his spatial position in the arrangement. These studies suggest that the distribution of speaking rights in a group are reflected in the arrangement maintained. Thus in circular arrangements these rights tend to be equal, whereas in arrangements where one individual is spatially differentiated from the others, as in a rectangular arrangement where there is a "head" position or as in the arrangement maintained in a lecture where one individual faces an audience that is arranged in rows facing him, the individual who occupies this spatially differentiated position has the right to do more speaking (which he usually exercises, it seems) than do the others.

It would appear, thus, that the arrangement maintained in an F-formation system is closely related to the other interactional systems that may be in operation within it. As we shall see later when, as can often be observed, an F-formation changes in its arrangement, these changes are concurrent with changes in the organization of these other interactional systems.

### Maintenance of the arrangement

The arrangement of an F-formation is something the participants cooperate to maintain. In many cases, of course, where the participants are seated, active cooperative maintenance is not observed, for the function of keeping the participants arranged is taken over by the furniture. In standing F-formations, however, individual participants may change their stance, orientation, or location quite often. Each such change affects the arrangement, however the other participants will also make changes in their stance, orientation or location which are compensatory, so that a given arrangement is maintained. One example may be cited.

In a film of three people standing and talking in a field,[2] several rounds of each compensatory fluctuation were analyzed. They maintained an arrangement in which two of them, M and G, were arranged in a V with the third, B, placed so he faced the space between them (Fig. 25a). One of the rounds of compensatory fluctuation may be described as follows: at Frame 289 B steps back. As he does so, G adjusts her stance in such a way as to bring herself slightly closer to B. Then G turns to face M rather more directly but, as she does so, M sways laterally away from her. This move by M increases her distance between herself

---

[2]  A film made by Sander Kirsch, on file at the film library of Eastern Pennsylvania Psychiatric Institute, Philadelphia. See Deutsch (1979) for a similar analysis of this film, with reproduced stills.

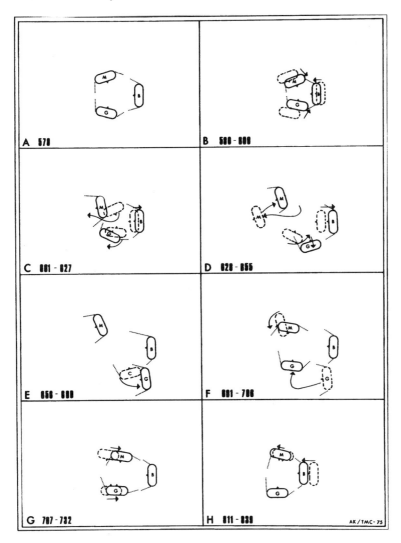

Fig. 25

and B, however, and concurrently, then, B steps in, bringing himself closer to M again. G now steps back and laterally, and again increases her distance from B. B then steps in again closer.

It will be seen how, in each case, the move of one appears to be compensated for by the move of another, so that the net effect is that the arrangement is maintained. When B moves back, G moves toward him.

When G re-orients to face M more fully, M moves laterally, thus reducing again, nearer to its previous value, the amount by which their transactional segments overlap. When G steps towards M, M moves back. When M moves away from B, B moves closer to her.

The movements just described are quite minor. From 578 to 866, the F-formation system in this example undergoes a vigorous oscillation. It may be of interest here to describe this in some detail to further illustrate the compensatory system of spatial relation participants in F-formations are involved in. A succession of diagrams depicting the various stages in this oscillation is given in Fig. 25. Each diagram represents a segment of what is, of course, a continuous process. The segments in the diagrams were chosen simply to facilitate the description.

The stable state of this F-formation is shown in Fig. 25a. Beginning at 580 G and M sway closer to one another and jointly in the direction of B, and beginning at 591 B also leans towards G and M. By 600 all three are now leaning towards one another and their o-space is now much smaller than it has been at any time hitherto. This state is depicted in (b). This joint leaning is associated with an utterance of G. This, as we shall see in a moment, is followed by a substantial change in the arrangement, and with vigorous laughter, particularly by M. G leans in closer, thus, as part of her means of emphasizing the final part of her utterance, and the other participants lean in to meet her.

At 601 all the participants begin to move rapidly away from one another – as if rebounding from their immediately preceding overcloseness. It will be apparent from (c) in Fig. 25, that each $p$ moves away to a different extent. B merely leans away, back to the position he was in before – his position as shown in (a). Both M and G, however, move well away from their original locations, G taking one step to the left, but at the same time facing away from M but towards B. M faces away from G and B, and takes several steps away from her original location as may be seen in (c).

This "overreaction" is now followed by a rather complex sequence of movements, the original arrangement not being restored until 870. As M continues to move away from her original position to the position depicted in (d), G steps towards B. In doing so, however, she steps past her original location, and thus reduces the distance between herself and B, below its original value. At the point where the G–B distance becomes less than the original value, B steps backwards, away from her. He moves as if to maintain his distance from G at the same value. At this point, however, M begins to move back again, towards her original location, but as she does so G steps backwards away from B. This is depicted in (d). Thus, when G "oversteps" toward B, B moves back, but when B moves back, this increases the distance between himself and M, who thereupon moves closer again. But M, in moving closer to B, reduces her distance from G, who now moves away from her. M remains facing away from both B and G, however, while G continues her backwards movement, changing her orientation as she does so. She continues in this until she is almost side by side with B, as may be seen in (e). She reaches her furthest point in this direction of movement and orientation at 680, whereupon she immediately commences to move on the path depicted for her in (f).

M, it will be seen, also begins to move and to change orientation, such that by 732 both M and G have returned to what are almost their original locations and orientations. However, M does not begin her return to her location and orientation until 690, and her turn towards G is so timed that she and G come to be exactly facing one another at the same moment, at 706 (see Fig. 25f). Thereupon they move jointly in the direction of B, from 707–732 (Fig. 25g). In other words, M times her reorientation to G so that it coincides with G's reorientation to M. Once their transactional segments are fully conjoined, they then move jointly to a stable location.

By 732 the original arrangement is thus nearly restored. Only B remains a little further away than he was before. From 810 he steps in closer, as if to correct this. M, coordinately, moves slightly away. Now we are back to virtually the same situation prior to 580, when M, G, and B maintained the arrangement depicted in Fig. 25a, with but intermittent compensatory adjustment.

It will be seen from this example how the locational and orientational movements of each appear to be coordinated about an equilibrial point. In the first segment described we noted minor compensatory adjustments. Beginning at 580, however, some incident in the utterance system impinged upon the F-formation system such that the locations and orientations of each went outside of the range that the participants had hitherto remained within (and within which they remained for a considerable period thereafter). When this happened, the arrangement was momentarily disrupted. It went from greatly reduced o-space size (580–600) to a dispersion of the participants (601–627). But as the participants moved away from one another two of them (M and G) went beyond the range of locations and orientations that had been adopted for the arrangement hitherto. What followed, then, could be seen as corrective maneuvering, but this, as we saw, caused some further corrective action before the original arrangement could be restored. Thus G, for example, turned (as in (d)), to return to her location, but over-oriented to B and stepped closer to him, as if correcting for her move away from B that preceded this.

It is also possible that this maneuver of G is related to the maneuver of M. M's orientational and locational deviation from the arrangement is the most extreme of all. G's movement and orientation toward B (in (c) and (d) in Fig. 25) can also be seen as the opposite of M's move here, so serving to counteract it.

In making her move in (c) and (d), however, G came closer to B and oriented her transactional segment more fully to him than before. B adjusts to this by stepping back, whereupon M moves closer to her original location, as we have already seen. G then turns fully out from the o-space, and it is upon her move back to it, as in (f), that M then turns in and rejoins it.

It may be that G's move here serves as a counter to her previous move. However, it may also serve another function. It may serve as a marker for her re-entry into the F-formation system. It is associated with the beginning of a new utterance by her. It is associated, thus, with a re-start of the utterance system to which the arrangement, in this example, is functionally joined. A new beginning in an interactive system is associated with the establishment of a new orientation, often of the trunk (thus readjusting the orientation of the transactional segment), or of the head. Such changes in orientation are commonly preceded by a sharp orientation away from the direction the new orientation will take. This is often accomplished by a marked rotation of the head but it may also include, as it does here, a marked turn-out of the trunk as well. This has already been reported in Chapter 6 in the study of the sequence of behaviors that leads up to an exchange of salutations. There, it will be recalled, it was reported that it was common to observe that, just before $p$ and $q$ become close enough to engage in the close salutation, one or other or both look, and sometimes turn, sharply away from one another. In other analyses, to be reported elsewhere, where $p$ makes a change in the orientation of his transactional segment in an F-formation system as a new arrangement is set up, such a change is often preceded by a sharp look away. We may also mention, in this connection, the observation given in Chapter 3 that, within a conversational system, $p$ tends to look away as he begins a new utterance. Such look-aways can be interpreted in a number of ways. Here we would like to suggest its function as a marker, a marker for the beginning of a new segment of involvement by $p$, a marker which will have considerable value insofar as it may serve to forewarn the other participants of the beginning of such a new segment by $p$. In this way the continued coordination of their actions with that of the other is facilitated.

We have dealt with this example at some length because we believe it illustrates well the way in which people do appear to so coordinate their locational and orientational movements in relation to one another, that it is appropriate to speak of $p$'s as parties to a *system*. We suggest that the F-formation system is appropriately referred to as such and that an account of the locational and orientational moves that occur within it is appropriately done in terms of the system of interdependency it appears to exhibit.

Spatial arrangements in an F-formation, thus, are entered into and sustained by cooperative maneuvering on the part of all the participants. We have seen that the arrangement is intimately linked to the other interactional systems the participants are also involved in. The arrangement maintained, thus, can be regarded as a behavioral manifestation of the "working consensus" (Goffman 1957, 1961, 1963) by which behavior in focused encounters is governed. So long as a given "working consensus" prevails to which all of the participants are jointly committed, we may expect that they will compensate for one another's positional deviations in the manner just described. Experimental studies on the maintenance of arrangements are rare. Reference may be made to studies by Sommer (1962), and McDowell (1972), however, which do show how an F-formation may adjust to variations in circumstance in such a way as to maintain a constant distance between the participants.

## Changes in the arrangement

In many cases the F-formation system maintains the same arrangement throughout its life. In other circumstances arrangement changes may be observed, and these are due to a number of different factors. Arrangement time changes often, though not always, occur when there is a change in participants in the system. Thus, in an instance where one participant left a system of three, the side-by-side that remained was then transformed into a closed L. An arrangement change will also occur if there is a change in the environment of the system, such as an increase in crowdedness of the setting or a change in activity of others nearby. For example, an L-shaped dyadic system became a side-by-side when an event in the vicinity occurred to which the two participants gave attention. Here the participants were also participants in a wider social occasion, in this case a ceremony of cake-cutting and singing *Happy Birthday* at a child's birthday party. As the singing got under way, the dyadic L-arrangement became a side-by-side as the two participants re-oriented slightly to face the table where the cake was and where the leader of the singing, the child's father, was also. In doing so, though they retained mutual access to each other's transactional spaces and so maintained the integrity of their F-formation system, they at the same time gave access to the wider event into which they were also incorporated. (BDF 002, 69, Cine Voice Roll II, 53960 to 54223, BA (yellow dress) SW (blue sweater).)

A change in arrangement will also occur if the other associated interactional systems within the F-formation system change. Thus in Chapter 6 we described how the participants in a salutational exchange such as a handshake or an embrace would always establish a distinct spatial–orientational frame, a distinct arrangement, that is, within which the salutation was performed. Once this was completed, the two greeters always stepped away from their respective locations and orientations, to form a new and different arrangement as they embarked upon the talk that followed. A change of arrangement here occurred, thus, as the participants changed from one kind of interaction to another. Typically, the close salutation is enacted with the two participants in a vis-a-vis arrangement. They both then step back and turn away from one another slightly to form an L or V-arrangement.

A specific example of an arrangement change which illustrates how it is coordinated with changes in other systems of interaction, is given in

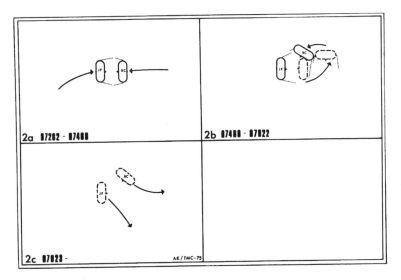

Fig. 26

Fig. 26. This example is taken from the Birthday Party film BDF 002 69, Auricon, 7290–72943. Here RC approaches JF, the hostess at the party, to tell her that she is leaving, and to ask her what time should she return to collect her small boy. Notice that she forms with JF a vis-a-vis arrangement (Fig. 26, 2a). This arrangement lasts until 7473, which is also the point at which the utterance exchange between RC and JF about the time the party was to end, also came to an end. RC now steps away, turning away from JF as she does so, and then she steps back again slightly to take up the position and location shown in Fig. 26, 2b. Within this L-arrangement, RC explains to SF something about some of the things her children have been doing. They then move away from one another, as shown in Fig. 26, 2c.

In this example we see, thus, a single F-formation, but two arrangements. Each arrangement is sustained for a given phase or topic of talk. The first, a vis-a-vis arrangement, is sustained during an utterance exchange in which *p* and *q* are negotiating directly about how they shall behave in relation to one another – in this case the question is, how shall RC behave in relation to the party of which JF is the hostess. The second, an L-arrangement, is sustained during an utterance exchange in which *p* and *q* are talking about some external topic.

A second example, also from the Birthday Party film (BDF 002 69,

Cine Voice Roll 1), provides further illustration of arrangement change in association with topic change. We shall also see, in this example, how the establishment of an F-formation is associated with the establishment of sustained conversation. The sequence of arrangements and maneuvers for this example is given in Fig. 27. BA is the wife of HA (who is Mexican), recently arrived in New York. CB is a close friend of BA's brother, the host of the party. The sequence analyzed took place on the beach, close to the beach deck (see Fig. 16, Chapter 6).

The initial situation may be seen in Fig. 27a. CB is seated, facing towards the sea, his back to the beach deck, a table on which food and drink is available. BA and HA arrive. BA faces the table, as shown, her husband stands directly behind her, while she mixes drinks for him and for herself. During this time, CB engages HA in a brief utterance exchange about "learning Mexican." Upon the lapse of this, CB stands up and turns, to assume the position and orientation shown in 27b. Here, it will be noted, CB has now joined BA and HA in a standing position, and further, he is oriented so that his transactional segment is directed towards them. A turn on their part can bring their transactional segments into overlap with that of CB. An F-formation including him can thus be formed very easily. CB's move here can thus be seen as having an invitational character. By relinquishing his previous position, and by assuming the one that he does here, he creates a potential for an F-formation. He confirmed this by a "filler" utterance – "hmm – wonderful" – which appears to serve as a further indication that he is fully open to addresses from BA and HA. As will be clear from Fig. 27, BA and HA do indeed turn to face CB, BA joining with CB in an F-formation system within which they sustain a fairly extended conversation. HA remains attached to this system, though not a full participant of it, as will be described later.

Utterance exchanges are resumed at 19660 when BA, at the same time as she completes mixing drinks, tells CB some news about her husband's new appointment and how this will mean that they will be staying in New York for an extended period. As BA turns to HA to hand him his drink (Fig. 27c), and as she then turns to face toward CB (Fig. 27d), she continues the conversation by asking CB if he knows anyone who has an apartment to sublet. This topic is continued with until 23750. During the closing utterances of this phase of conversation the vis-a-vis arrangement so far maintained begins to change to the second, L-shaped arrangement.

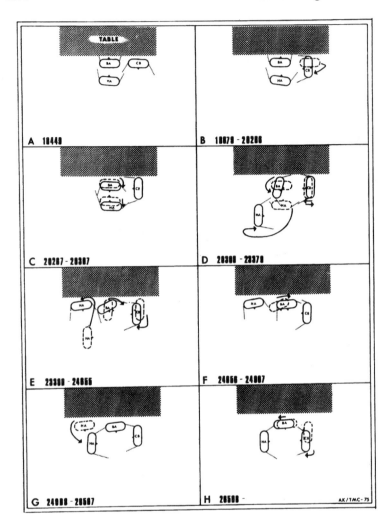

Fig. 27

Note that once HA has his drink he steps back and turns to overlap
his transactional segment with that of CB (at frame 20560) and, concurrently, BA also turns to face CB. As she does so, she sways forward
and back, slightly, in settling into her new stance. Concurrent with this,
CB also sways forward and back, adjusting his posture and orientation
slightly, to align the overlap of his transactional segment with those of

BA and HA more completely. The arrangement arrived at, and the maneuvers by which it was attained, are given in Fig. 27d.

It is to be noted here that CB makes no orientational adjustment until BA begins the move that brings her transactional segment into overlap with that of CB. Thus when she turns from her position in Fig. 27b to face HA and give him his drink, CB remains posturally and orientationally unchanged (Fig. 27c). The moment she begins the bodily turn that will lead to the inclusion of CB in her transactional segment, however, CB bows forward and back. This forward back bow is coordinated with a back–forward body sway by BA. Thus *as* the arrangement of the F-formation gets set up, CB and BA cooperate to jointly maintain a certain distance between them which, despite absolute changes in location of either of them, remains constant.

The same phenomenon may be seen again at 20611 where CB begins to step forward, closing the distance between himself and BA. He completes this by 20666. BA steps back, beginning at 20647, thus coordinating her move with his, and maintaining the previously established distance. HA, rather further off from CB, does not adjust to this maneuver.

We see in this example how the systemic relationship between the locational and orientational behavior phases of the participants comes about as they enter into the joint transactional space or o-space. Once they begin to do so, they immediately begin oscillating back and forth in a complementary fashion until their stances, distance, and orientation are stabilized.

It will be seen that the utterance exchange system in this example had become established before an F-formation was established. This, it appears, is a common course of events, though often, of course, the F-formation is established concurrently with greeting utterances rather than, as here, with utterances that belong to the conversation.

The arrangement reached by BA and CB is a vis-a-vis arrangement, and it is sustained until 23379, when the first of several changes occurs which lead to its transformation into a close L-arrangement. During the via-a-vis there are several periods in which CB and BA adjust their stances jointly, providing further illustration of the cooperative maintenance of the arrangement that we described in detail for another example earlier. It is of interest to note that HA does not take part in these adjustments. For much of the time he remains in a position in which, as may be seen, his transactional segment only partially overlaps with the o-space sustained by BA and CB. From time to time BA makes excursions to the table to pick up a piece of food. Occasionally he is addressed, however, and when he is he moves to the position shown in Fig. 27g, and he also becomes actively coordinated in his postural and locational movements with CB and BA. HA thus fluctuates between being a full participant in this F-formation system and being attached as what may be called an *associate* of the system (see below).

The vis-a-vis arrangement sustained by BA and CB lasts until 23379, as we have seen. The conversation within this arrangement was initiated by BA, as we have also seen, when she says to CB, as she moves into the position that complements that of CB, "D'you know any one with an apartment in the City they could sublet for ten months?" The conversation that follows includes queries by CB concerning when they want to come to the City, where they would like to live. BA explains how she expects to be in New York for only a year, because of the strong possibility that her husband will take up another appointment. BA explains this in an utterance which begins at 23277, and which is lengthy and is spoken rapidly. During it, CB steps sideways slightly, away from the table, and he brings his left foot down to the sand on the beach, stepping off a flat stone he has been standing on hitherto. This is shown in Fig. 27e. It is the first time, despite a number of fluctuations in his stance, that CB has actually changed his *position* in the arrangement.

When BA finishes her utterance (at 23505), CB summarizes the main conclusion of the conversation they have been having by saying: "So what you want is somebody . . . so what you want is somebody who is going away on a sabbatical. That ought to be possible to find." There is now a lapse in talk, during which CB takes a drink from the can of beer he is holding, while BA turns toward the table as she shelters herself from the wind to relight her cigarette. As she turns back to CB again she changes her stance slightly, to form a distant L-arrangement with CB, as also shown in Fig. 27e. Associated, thus, with the conclusion of this discussion about BA's needs for an apartment in New York, CB and then BA alter slightly the spatial arrangement they have been sustaining.

Sustained conversation begins again some thirty seconds later at 24562. This is initiated by simultaneous utterances, but BA's utterance continues after CB has finished and it is the topic that she raises that is discussed. BA indicates that she is familiar with the doorman of CB's apartment building, who is a Cuban and is notable because he reads a great deal. As CB laughingly confirms what BA has said, BA moves laterally, closer to CB, to form the close L-arrangement with him that may be seen in Fig. 27f. The conversation now pursues the question of different kinds of Spanish – Cuban, Puerto Rican, Mexican – a wholly new topic, thus, and one which, it will be seen, is framed by a new arrangement in the F-formation.

In summary, then, we may see from this example how an F-formation gets set up as it were in support of an utterance exchange system, and how the arrangement adopted is sustained for a given phase of talk. A new phase of talk, identifiable as a topic shift, is marked by a shift in the arrangement. Here, as CB closed off the first topic, he changed his position. As BA initiated a new topic, she also changed her position and the result was a new arrangement. Finally, we noted how coordinate spatial orientational movements characterize those who are also participants in an utterance exchange. This further suggests the coordination of the F-formation system with the utterance exchange system which typically goes on within it.

The alterations in arrangement described above all occurred in standing F-formations. Where the participants are seated the work of arrangement maintenance is largely taken over by the furniture and it becomes much less flexible and cannot be used for bracketing different phases of the associated interactional systems. Here, thus, it appears that postural changes take over this function. Scheflen (1964, 1973) has described this for psychotherapy groups; Blom and Gumperz (1972) have reported it for conversations (observed in Norway), and Erickson (1975) has observed it in counseling interviews. In all of these cases, major shifts in topic or changes from one phase of the interview or conversation to the next were marked by shifts in the postural arrangement of the participants.

### Changes in participants

An F-formation system may gain or lose participants. Indeed, a complete turnover of participants may occur in some instances without any discontinuity in the system itself. An example of this is provided in Fig. 28. Here, it will be seen, an initially dyadic system (Fig. 28) of WF and AF is joined by a third, HR. It will be seen how, upon HR's approach, AF steps back to give him access to the o-space, but he does so in such a way as to maintain the overlap of his transactional segment with that of WF, thus maintaining the continuity of the system (Figs. 28b, 28c).

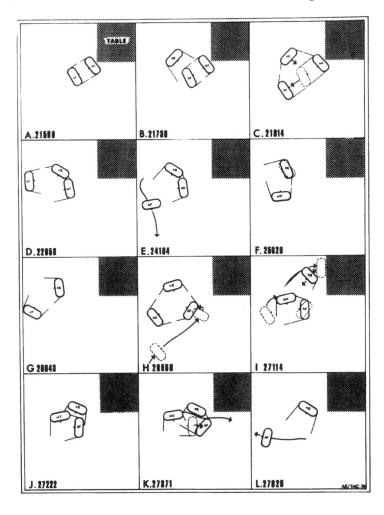

Fig. 28    A series of maps to show the spatial arrangements and movements of the participants in an F-formation system taken from the Birthday Party film, BDF 001 69, Cinevoice Roll 2, on file at the Eastern Pennsylvania Psychiatric Institute Film Library. The number following the letter identifying each diagram is the frame number of the film from which the diagram was made. The oval figures represent individuals, the dotted lines extending forward from either side of them are meant to suggest the transactional segment that extends forward from each person. Solid line ovals represent the established positions of individuals, dotted line ovals

Fig. 28 (*cont.*)

represent their previous positions, or positions they took up along a path of movement that led up to the position diagrammed within a given frame. Solid arrows represent the path of movement through space of an individual.

A. This shows the vis-a-vis arrangement assumed by AF and WF. It will be seen how their transactional segments overlap to create an o-space.

B. This shows the position taken by HR after he had approached AF and WF. Notice how his transactional segment does not overlap with the o-space between WF and AF and how he faces toward AF's body. HR's position here we term the Outer Position, and it is typical of the position taken up by those who are not members of an F-formation, but who are announcing themselves as candidates for membership.

C. AF steps back and so expands the o-space and thereby allows HR to contribute his transactional segment to it. Notice that AF steps back without changing his orientation, thus preserving his contribution to the o-space.

D. The F-formation now has three participants. It stabilizes the arrangement shown in this map.

E. AF departs, leaving HR and WF in an "open L" arrangement.

F. HR alters his orientation (in relation to the behavior of his small daughter who is not shown in these diagrams) and WF alters his position to create a closed L arrangement with HR within which conversation is established.

G. A further arrangement change occurs to produce the arrangement shown in this map. This comes about again as a result of HR altering his orientation in relation to the activities of his small daughter. WF alters his location and orientation to that shown in this map.

H. AF returns. It will be seen how AF approaches and stops at an Outer Position before turning and entering the F-formation, which he does here coincidentally with the change in orientation in HR and WF that will be noted here.

I. HR walks away to the table and turns to return almost immediately. In the meantime WF and AF rearrange as shown to establish a new arrangement.

J. HR returns and takes up an Outer Position as shown. Once again note how HR's transactional segment is obstructed by the bodies of WF and AF. He is thus not a participant in AF and WF's F-formation system, though he is attached to it and could be considered a member of a wider system that would include both HR and AF and WF.

K. AF steps back and re-orients slightly to admit HR to the o-space. Note that WF does not make a corresponding adjustment and virtually ceases to contribute to the o-space. From this point on he is no longer a member of the F-formation system. Shortly afterwards he departs, following the path shown by the arrow. Note that WF passes through the o-space of HR and AF, a very unusual path for anyone to take. This is probably

After a while AF departs, leaving HR and WF in a near side-by-side arrangement (Fig. 28d) which, however, is shortly changed into an L-arrangement (Fig. 28e). A further adjustment in the orientation of this arrangement then takes place (Fig. 28f). Then AF returns, and WF now adjusts his orientation so that AF gains access to the o-space, and again this is done so that continuity in the o-space is maintained (Figs. 28g, 28h). HR then departs – he goes to the table to get a drink – whereupon AF and WF move to form yet another arrangement (Fig. 28i). HR then returns and stands for a moment in the position shown, just outside the line AF and WF are standing on (Fig. 28j). It will be seen that he does not yet have direct access to the o-space and thus does not have membership in the system. However, AF steps back, away from WF, yet still maintaining the o-space with him, while HR steps forward and becomes a member of the system once again (Fig. 28k). WF then leaves, and shortly thereafter AF also leaves, leaving HR alone, though still in the location and orientation he had sustained during AF's presence. A short while later, HR turns and walks away, and the system is now finally ended.

The foregoing account has been considerably simplified, but it demonstrates how the system of behavioral relationship that sustains an o-space may be continued despite change in participants. It also exemplifies how the arrangement and even the location of an F-formation system changes as it adapts to these variations in participation.

A detailed study of how outsiders are incorporated into an ongoing F-formation system is of interest for it shows how both current members and outsiders cooperate in maintaining the integrity of the system's boundary. An outsider only becomes a member of an existing system through cooperative action between himself and members of the existing system. Some of the features of this process are illustrated when HR joins AF for the first time, in the above example.

It will be seen that HR approaches AF and WF but he stops a little

Fig. 28 (cont.)
related to what happened earlier in the interaction between AF and WF. Just before AF steps back to let in HR, as part of the terminal exchange in his conversation with WF, AF reaches out and pinches WF on the cheek. WF's passage through AF and HR's o-space may well be a reply to this rudeness. (It may be relevant to note at this point that AF is WF's son.)
  L. AF departs, leaving HR in the same position. A few moments later HR turns and walks away, thus bringing the F-formation to an end.

distance away, in a position where he does not have unobstructed access to the o-space. Here he bends down and sets down his small daughter (not depicted in Fig. 28), who he has been carrying. However, it is characteristic for outsiders to stop in such a position prior to entry. In many cases an outsider having reached this position, which will be referred to as the Outer Position, will then wait until a current member looks at him. An exchange of gestures or utterances then takes place which serves as the outsider's announcement of his wish to join in, and the insider's acknowledgement of this. This is then followed by a spatial–orientational move by an insider, with which the outsider coordinates a spatial–orientational move of his own, and which allows the outsider access to the o-space. This move, it is to be noted, is timed to coincide with some change in the outsider's behavior. That is, the insider conjoins his maneuver with the rhythmical structure of the outsider's behavior, thus establishing the behavioral coordination that is characteristic of participants in an F-formation system.

In the present example, no explicit exchange takes place between HR and AF or WF when HR arrives at the Outer Position. As in many other examples, merely to approach and stand at an Outer Position (facing toward the system) is sufficient for an announcement of intent to join the system. Here AF's step-back serves both to acknowledge HR's announcement and also to bring about HR's incorporation into the system. AF times the beginning of his step-back to coincide precisely with the moment HR begins to stand up, having let go of his daughter. That is, AF begins to get ready for his step-back at frame 21750, HR begins to unbend from his daughter at frame 21750. That is, just as HR begins to become free to participate in the F-formation system he has approached to become a member of, AF begins a maneuver that makes this participation possible. It is at this point also that greeting utterances begin, initiated by HR as he approaches WF with hand outstretched for a handshake.

The procedures of entry just described are seen where the outsider approaches an existing system on his own initiative. Where an outsider is called over by a current member, the members of the current system adjust their arrangement appropriately as the outsider approaches, and he does not stop at the Outer Position before entry. A member of a system who has been absent for only a brief period, likewise, may simply walk back to his position in the system without first stopping at the Outer Position, though if the system has readjusted during his absence then the entry procedure we have described will be repeated (as indeed we can see in the above example, where HR returns after leaving to get a drink).

In departures we may also see how the participants recognize the integrity of the F-formation system's boundary. Where a participant leaves for a short time, he may simply walk away. However, where the departure is permanent a more elaborate pattern is followed which, like the procedures of entry, probably serves to allow the participants to adapt to the state of the system that is to follow. In departing, the individual often first moves away from his position in the F-formation, sometimes even stepping away as if he is really leaving. He then steps back in, sometimes coming in closer to the others than before. At this point, salutations of departure occur. Thereupon, the departing individual turns and walks away. In walking away, he often moves from two to five steps in a direction that is different from his eventual direction. It is as if, as he leaves the F-formation, he undertakes first to leave it, so the walking away is *walking away* and, as such, is distinct from walking to some other focus of involvement.[3] It is towards the end of this walk-away that we may observe the backward glance that is not uncommon in departure and which is sometimes elaborated into a distance salutation of departure.

### Delineating the F-formation system in time and space

An F-formation system may be said to have begun as soon as the spatial–orientational cooperation which sustains an o-space can be observed. This is usually easy to determine, for when a new F-formation system is established the participants move towards one another in a decided fashion and they also move to a location that is new for all of them. The system then persists, notwithstanding changes in arrangement of participants, as we have seen, until the last of the participants moves away from the location from which he has made his contribution to the system. Once again, the end of an F-formation system is usually easy to determine. In many cases, all the participants disperse simultaneously. Sometimes it happens, however, that a single individual is left. In these cases this remaining individual does not remain in the same position or the same location for very long. Thus even where someone

---

[3] Mr. T. M. Ciolek first drew my attention to this phenomenon.

is left after everyone else has gone, we can still mark the end of the F-formation system in question at the point where the remaining individual changes his location to a new one or, in case he is seated, at the point where he changes his posture. We saw an example of this in the example illustrating participation turnover discussed above.

In delineating the space that an F-formation occupies it is necessary to be clear about who is to be counted as a member. A member of, or a participant in, an F-formation system is anyone whose transactional segment falls over the o-space without intersecting the body of any other individual and who takes part in the adjustments of spacing and orientation by which the o-space is sustained. It sometimes happens, however, that additional individuals become attached to an F-formation, as when someone is waiting for another as they have a conversation or where people gather to listen to a conversation or to watch a game that is being played. Such *associates* of the system, as they may be called, may adjust their spatial position relative to that of the system if it changes its location, but they do not take part in the various maneuvers by which the o-space is maintained. Furthermore, they can come and go without going through the procedures we described for exit and entry. Such associates, thus, do not meet the criteria of *participant* in an F-formation system and they are not included within its boundaries. We may, of course, want to consider associates and participants together as members of the same unit of spatial–orientational participation. If we do this, however, the unit we would then be considering, though it includes an F-formation system, is not the same as such a system.

## The domains of the F-formation[4]

An F-formation occupies an area of physical space and it may therefore be said to have a *domain*. In delineating the domain we may see that there are three kinds of spaces to consider. First, of course, is the area covered by the o-space. But around this we must recognize a relatively narrow space which is the space occupied by the bodies of the participants. This zone may be called the p-space. Beyond the p-space, however, we must recognize a further area which comes under the influence

---

[4] The terms for the spaces of the F-formation used here are intended to parallel those used by Scheflen in Scheflen (1977). Scheflen's analysis of what is here called the r-space is more detailed than the one given here, however.

of the F-formation. The extent of this space is rather ill-defined and it may be known as the r-space.

The r-space is postulated in the light of a number of observations on the relationship between F-formation systems and the behavior of others in their immediate vicinity. Thus in settings where several F-formations co-occur without any physical barriers between them, as on lawns or beaches or in large rooms, the F-formations tend to be spaced out. The amount of space by which they are separated is variable. It depends upon how crowded the setting is, obviously, but according to observations by Edney and Jordan-Edney (1974) it also depends upon how many participants a given system has (systems with more participants requiring less space around them than systems with fewer participants) and upon the kind of interaction that is going on within them. F-formations in which the interaction within them involved much mutual attention apparently may be spaced closer to adjacent systems than systems in which the interaction involves attention to things beyond its own boundaries. However, such inter-system spacing always occurs and adjacent F-formations actively cooperate with one another to maintain it. Each F-formation may be regarded, thus, as being surrounded by a region of space that functions as a buffer zone, insulating the system somewhat from what may be going on around it.

Further evidence for an r-space comes from observations of the behavior of outsiders. As we saw, when an outsider is going to become a member of an existing system, he approaches the system but stops a little distance away, before being invited in by the current participants. People who must pass by an F-formation generally give it a fairly wide berth but if, for any reason, they cannot do so, as they pass by they can often be seen to dip their heads or to look sharply away or to touch themselves. Also, as we mentioned in the discussion of departures, participants leaving an F-formation often change the direction of their walk after they have moved several steps away and, as they do so, they may sometimes look back and engage in a distance salutational exchange. Once again, this suggests that the F-formation system's influence extends beyond the outer limits of the p-zone.

An F-formation system, thus, generates three kinds of functional spaces: an inner space, the o-space; a narrow zone immediately around this called the p-space; and beyond this a much less well defined region or r-space which functions as a buffer, protecting the system from outside influences, and also as a kind of front hall or reception room in

Fig. 29

which visitors may be dealt with or newcomers greeted before they are fully incorporated into the system itself. In considering the extent of the domains occupied by an F-formation system, thus, it is necessary to consider these three kinds of spaces (see Fig. 29).

## Conclusion

The foregoing ideas were first formulated in the course of the study of greetings reprinted above as Chapter 6. A problem we faced early in this study was to establish what the boundaries were of the event we wished to study. It was easy enough to locate the central features of the event, for example a handshake, but it was less clear where our analysis should begin and where it should end. A solution was arrived at when it was discovered that the participants in a salutational exchange, such as a handshake, always established a spatial–orientational frame through the cooperative maneuvering of their whole bodies, and that this frame was altered as soon as the salutation was over. Thus the spatial–orientational frame and the movements that led up to its creation came to provide the outer boundaries of the event we were to study.

In a subsequent investigation, with Robert MacMillan, we were concerned with how members of a household used the space available to them within the living areas of their apartment. Their behavior could be studied *in situ*, for extended video-records had been made. The problem here was to develop criteria for a behavioral unit whose boundaries could be specified clearly not only in time but also in space and which was a unit of the observable structure of behavior and not one that was imposed arbitrarily. It became clear that for different activities individuals sustained different spaces, and that for things done jointly with several persons, joint spaces were sustained. The notion of the spatial arrangement of bodies as constituting a frame for a behavioral event, first developed in the greetings study, played an important part in the study of these video-tapes.

In the present study we have attempted to show that when people space themselves for a joint activity such as conversation they enter into a system of spatial–orientational behavior which can be conceived of as a unit of behavioral organization at the interactional level. We have suggested what some of the functions of this system may be and we have shown how this system organizes the physical space within which it takes place. We suggest that this spatial aspect of the behavior of interaction needs much further study if a full understanding of the ecology of social behavior is to be approached.

## Postscript

Work that is directly related to that reported in this chapter and which has appeared since it was written includes Scheflen (1975), Scheflen and Ashcraft (1976) and Deutsch (1977). Ciolek and Kendon (1980) explore the way in which the spatial organization of encounters shows adaptation to the wider environment in which the encounters occur. A useful discussion may be found in McDermott and Roth (1978). Other, related work includes McDermott, Gospodinoff and Aron (1978), Streeck (1984), Erickson and Shulz (1982, especially Ch. 4), Schulz, Florio and Erickson (1982) and Jones and von Raffler-Engel (1982). These studies all show the way in which spatial–orientational changes are related to changes in interactional context in encounters in the elementary school classroom, counseling interviews, at the family dinner table and service encounters, respectively. Bull and Brown (1977), in a study of seated dyadic conversations in the laboratory and Lockard et al. (1978), in an observational study of standing conversational groups, address similar issues and report compatible findings.

Aside from this, work on interpersonal spacing in interaction has not focused on it as an organizational property of the interactional occasion. Rather, the concern has mainly been with the distances individuals adopt in relation to their co-interactants as a function of their social role, status in the interaction, gender, age, cultural background and a variety of personality variables. Most of this work has been undertaken in the laboratory and there are few natural history studies of interpersonal spacing. The literature is now very large. Readers interested in surveying it further are referred to the comprehensive review by Miles Patterson and Joyce Edinger (1987).

# 8

---

# Behavioral foundations for the process of frame-attunement in face-to-face interaction

## Introduction

Unlike sticklebacks and herring gulls, at least as they are proverbially understood and, so it would seem, unlike baboons and even chimpanzees, humans are not constrained to respond to each other or to each other's actions in specific ways. For humans, any action of $p$ can be interpreted by another in a wide variety of different ways. By doing $X$, $p$ is in no position to be sure that $q$ will do $Y$. Furthermore, $p$ not only cannot be assured that $q$ will respond to a particular action of his in a particular way; he cannot even be sure that $q$ will apprehend his action in the same way in which he himself apprehends it. Yet it is impossible for $p$ to formulate a coherent program of action without some basis for supposing that it will be understood in a given way. To be able to act in the presence of others is to be able to assume that one's acts will be taken in a certain way. Whereas animals never seem to have any doubts, for human interactants there is always the possibility that each participant regards the other, his actions, and the interaction situation in quite different ways. This means that prospective participants are faced with the problem of establishing what each other's interpretative perspectives are. Interaction simply cannot proceed except insofar as participants are able to share at least some assumptions about the situation and each other's intentions in it. Thus we may expect to find that participants in interaction have ways of assuring themselves of how their co-participants are interpreting the situation and ways of communicating with

First published in G. P. Ginsburg, M. Brenner and M. von Cranach, eds., *Discovery Strategies in the Psychology of Action*. London: Academic Press, 1985, pp. 229–53. Reprinted with permission of the publishers.

one another about their interpretative perspectives so that a consensus between them may be arrived at and maintained.

The notion that coherent social interaction requires participants to share the same sets of assumptions has been expressed by several different authors in a number of different ways. For example, Garfinkel (1963) argued that coherence in social interaction requires that the participants all share a number of basic assumptions, including the assumption that these assumptions are shared. Such a condition he referred to as "trust," and he showed, through a series of demonstrations, the confusion, anger, and considerable anxiety that could very quickly be generated if a participant in an interaction acted as if one or more of these basic assumptions did not apply. Goffman (1955, 1957, 1961, 1963, 1974), in his analyses of face-to-face interaction, argued in a similar fashion. He distinguished what he referred to as occasions of "focused interaction": when two or more individuals openly join together to sustain a single common focus of concern as is done, most characteristically, perhaps, in occasions of talk. In such circumstances participants cooperate together to establish and maintain an official or common focus of attention on the topic at hand. Goffman pointed out that in any focused encounter a particular "definition of the situation" comes to be shared by the participants, which serves to define what will be considered, for the time being, as irrelevant as well as what is relevant. A *frame* comes to be placed around the actions and utterances of the participants, which both determines the sense in which they are to be taken and serves to define whole ranges of possible acts as irrelevant (as not to be included).

The question we wish to discuss in this chapter is how this shared frame, this common interpretative perspective, comes to be established. How do people come to know that they share each other's assumptions? As Garfinkel (1963) put it, "the constitutive expectancies of a situation" may be applied to different sets of events so that different constitutive orders of events are established. For coherent interaction to ensue, the participants must be agreed upon how these constitutive expectancies are to be applied. The question is, how is this accomplished?

It is seen that $p$ cannot wait to see what $q$ will do in response to anything that he does, because he needs to have some inkling of how $q$ will take any line of action he may offer in order to be in a position to begin a line of action in the first place. Thus communication about interpretative perspectives appears as a kind of prior in interaction. It seems that coherent interaction requires this commonality of interpretative perspectives to be established first. Yet, clearly, unless we are to admit the possibility of some sort of direct transmission of interpretative perspectives, the only way that $p$ can know how $q$ is taking the situation and how he will apprehend $p$'s own line of action is by observing what $q$ is doing. He must be able to see how $q$ is behaving in relation to his own behavior before being able to know what $q$'s interpretations of his actions are likely to be. $p$ is thus in something of a bind. He cannot formulate a line of action unless he knows how $q$ will take it. Yet he cannot know how $q$ will take any line of action he may produce, except by seeing how $q$ is indeed taking his line of action.

## Routinization

The resolution of this paradox is achieved in part through the routinization of interactional situations and events. Interactional situations are to some extent classifiable into types, and rules of conduct appropriate to each type come to be laid down in advance. Sometimes these rules are made quite explicit, and participants can be taught how to identify the kind of interactional situation they are in and the rules of conduct that apply. One comes to learn "how to behave" in church and at afternoon tea, how to ask for a drink in Subunun (Frake 1964), or how to enter a Yakan house (Frake 1975). Participants also operate in terms of categorizations of each other. As Goffman has reminded us (Goffman 1959), participants are able to establish selves for themselves in interaction, because they are able to manage their own appearance and manner according to established conventions that govern the significance of dress ensembles, patterns of conduct, grooming configurations, and the like. In this way, the range of possible interpretative frames a participant may expect to find being employed in a given situation or by the various people he may encounter within it can be considerably narrowed. Nevertheless, when a participant enters an actual encounter, when he comes to be called upon to take action in respect to others with whom he is in current interaction, there still remains considerable room for uncertainty. For example, if I am to offer you a greeting, how do I know that you will receive my salutation as I intend it to be received? If several persons are participating together in a conversation, how can any one participant count upon the continued participation of any of the others? What evidence can any of them provide for their continued participation without actually speaking? And, should any of them speak, how can the speaker know that his intended recipient is ready to receive his utterance, and how do the other participants know for whom the utterance is intended? Or consider the question of how occasions of focused interaction are brought to a conclusion. In maintaining themselves as participants in a focused interaction, the participants have negotiated a common perspective of relevance for each other's actions. For this to be changed or to be brought to an end, it is necessary for all of the participants to agree to the change or termination before it actually occurs. If such an agreement is not reached, then any action of $p$'s that, from his own perspective, belongs to a new frame of interpretation, will be interpreted by the other participants in terms of the currently prevailing frame and, accordingly, will be perceived as irrelevant, inconsistent, or in some other way disjunctive. For new actions to be perceived and responded to as meaningful, the frame of interpretation must be changed first. Thus for changes or termination to be accomplished in a well-managed fashion, participants must be able to communicate with one another about their intentions to change or to terminate before they actually do so. The question is, how is this accomplished?

## Differential attention in interaction

The processes by which participants are able to negotiate the *working consensus* of the interaction depend to an important degree upon the willingness of participants to allow that only certain aspects of behavior count as action. It appears that participants in interaction do not attend to all aspects of each other's behavior in the same way, and they do not accord all aspects of it the same significance. A distinction tends to be drawn in that certain aspects of another's stream of action are regarded as intentional and vehicles of explicitly intended messages, and certain other aspects are not regarded in this light. Such a distinction makes it possible for people to embark upon lines of action in respect to one another, and to observe each other's modes of dealing with those lines of action without, as it were, officially doing so. By making this distinction, by regarding only some aspects of behavior as intended (explicitly acknowledged action) whereas other aspects are regarded as unofficial, participants make it possible for themselves to explore one another's interpretative perspectives. They thereby negotiate some measure of agreement before either of them needs to address to the other any explicit action.

Goffman (1974) has drawn attention to this differentiation in the treatment participants in interaction accord various aspects of each other's behavior by his metaphor of *attentional tracks*. He suggests that in any social encounter there is always an aspect of the activity going forward that is treated as being within a *main-line* or *story-line track*. A domain of action is delineated as being relevant to the main business of the encounter, and it is oriented to as such and dealt with accordingly. Other aspects of activity are not included, but this does not mean that they have no part to play. Thus Goffman suggested we may also distinguish a *directional track*. Here, in Goffman's words, there is "a stream of signs which is itself excluded from the content of activity but which serves as a means of regulating it, bounding, articulating and qualifying its various components and phases" (Goffman 1974, p. 210). One may speak, too, of a *disattend track* to which are assigned a whole variety of actions not counted as being part of the interaction at all. Goffman mentioned here, in particular, various "creature comfort releases" – scratching, postural adjustments, smoking, and so forth – that are, so to speak, allowable deviations from the behavioral discipline to which all participants in a focused encounter are expected to conform. As Goffman himself made clear, and as a moment's reflection reminds us, it is, of course, not that the actions treated as being in the "disattend track" are not cognized and responded to by participants. On the contrary, they often play an important part in the very process of negotiating common perspectives that, as we have seen, is an essential part of what makes focused interaction possible. What I wish to suggest here, however, is that unless this kind of differential–attentional treatment is engaged in, the process of *frame-attunement* in interaction would not be possible.

Usually, there is considerable agreement among interactants as to how various aspects of behavior are to be assigned to these various tracks. One way in which this may be demonstrated very readily is to play the tame of "timmy" (Kendon 1978). In this game, one player, who may be called the Challenger, gets another, the Responder, to agree to imitate his actions. The Challenger says "do as I do" and he then holds up both his hands and, touching each fingertip of the left hand with his right index finger in succession, and saying "timmy" each time he does so, works his way from little finger to thumb and back again. After he has finished, he then lowers his hands and clasps them together in a resting position. The Responder is then expected to follow the Challenger's instruction to "do as I do," and what he does is to repeat the timmy performance just described. However, the Responder almost never imitates the resting position of the Challenger's hands. Since the Challenger, without any advance indication to the Responder, has included the resting position of his hands as part of the performance to be imitated, he is always able to maintain that the Responder has failed in his imitation.

This game shows us not only how interactants proceed in terms of the notion that their co-participants share the same set of assumptions as they do; it also shows us how consistent participants are likely to be in what they decide to treat as *background action* and *foreground* or *figure action*. The game works because the Challenger can be secure in his assumptions about what the Responder will include as relevant aspects of his behavior to be imitated.

The Challenger can rest secure in this assumption, in part, because it appears that some modes of behavioral organization are almost automatically assigned main-track status, simply by virtue of their nature. Thus it appears that vocalization and speech are specially oriented to and take a kind of first place in the attentional hierarchy. There is even evidence that suggests that humans are neurologically predisposed from the earliest age to give special attention to human speech (Cutting and Eimas 1975, Liberman 1979, Marler 1979). It also seems probable that certain patterns of organization of bodily movement are given main-track status simply by virtue of their character. Elsewhere (Kendon 1978) I have reported a preliminary study in which subjects were asked to report what they had observed of someone's actions after having watched a silent film of a man making a speech to a large gathering. It was found that all observers first reported only those movements that, they maintained, had to do with what the speaker was trying to say. Furthermore there was a very high degree of agreement between subjects as to which aspects of his movements were referred to in this way. Other investigators have reported findings in agreement with this. Freedman and Hoffman (1967), for example, have shown that naive observers can discriminate what they have termed *object focused movements* (movements of the forelimbs made in conjunction with speech) with a very high degree of reliability.

It must be seen, however, that if we are to understand how such significant acts function in interaction, we must understand how they become relevant for specific other individuals. It will be seen that, to understand what was going on in the timmy game, we need to ask not only about the features of the Challenger's performance that the Responder selects as relevant for imitation, but also how it was that someone came to regard the timmy performance as relevant for him and not for someone else, and how it was that the Challenger came to know that he had the Responder's agreement to play the game. Of course, the Responder might say "I agree." But how does the Challenger know when to start? Close observation of timmy games, as of other occasions of interaction, shows that the initiator of significant or main-track action does not begin just anywhere. He begins, characteristically, only when the attention of participants is properly organized. However, how does anyone know how the attention of another is organized? In terms of actual patterns of behavior that occur, how is the necessary alignment of attention accomplished?

## The communication of attention

An everyday example may allow us to identify some of the main components of this process. Consider a circumstance in which a child who has recently learned how to make a yo-yo perform a number of different tricks seeks to show these off to her father.

Father is sitting in the living room in his comfortable chair, reading the newspaper. His three children are in various parts of the room, all practicing with their yo-yos. Now one says, "Dad, watch all the tricks I can do," and she steps forward to a place somewhat in the middle of the room, stands fully erect, and fully faces Father and looks at him. Father is looking up and looking at Daughter, and Daughter begins to yo-yo. As she begins she looks down at the yo-yo, following its movements. She brings one yo-yo sequence to an end, looks up and then says, "Now watch" and yo-yos some more, again following the yo-yo with her eyes, not looking directly at Father. She does this several times. The yo-yoing is, thus, divided into segments or bouts, with each bout separately labeled and separated from the next bout by a pause in yo-yoing, during which Daughter looks at Father. After several such bouts of yo-yoing, Daughter again pauses. Father makes a remark and looks down at his paper, and Daughter turns away from him and moves to a different part of the room.

It is to be noted that in this sequence of yo-yo bouts the yo-yoing becomes the focus of a jointly focused interaction. In doing so, a distinctive spatial location and orientation is taken up. As the performance is announced the child moves to a location that she will occupy for the entire duration of the performance. Once the performance is over, she leaves that location. Within that location, again for the entire duration of the performance, she maintains an orientation of her body such that her front, rather than her back, can be seen by her father. For each bout of yo-yoing she assumes a distinct orientation and posture, and the yo-yoing itself it preceded and succeeded by a distinctive posture and orientation; it is also preceded and succeeded by looking at Father. Further, and this is very important to note, the yo-yoing itself gets underway only when Father has also oriented himself in such a way that he can be seen to be able to see the yo-yoing. If Father is looking at his newspaper, this will be remarked upon, and the yo-yoing will not commence until he is looking at Daughter.

We see, thus, in this example, how an activity such as yo-yoing comes to acquire main-track status in a focused interaction by virtue of it being provided with a locus in both space and time that sharply contrasts with what precedes and succeeds it. What is also crucial in providing the yo-yoing with main-track status, however, is that it should be done within the frame of an *address and its reciprocation*. That is, the behavior that has been provided a distinct spatial and temporal locus must be oriented to by another, and this orientation must be coordinated within the spatial and temporal boundaries of the activity that acquires this status. The actions that give the behavior that is to be given main-track status its delineation have, thus, an interactional significance as great as the main-track activity itself, for they make possible the "prior" orientation of the other to them; they make it possible for the other to know when and to what to orient. The yo-yoing does not begin until Father is looking at the child. If he does not look up when she calls out that she is going to do her yo-yo tricks, Daughter may even repeat one of her *framing actions*, such as stepping again to the location she will use for the performance, but this time stamping her feet to provide auditory evidence that she is moving to a new place. Thus what is required for focused interaction to get underway is that there be (1) aspects of behavior that serve in the process of providing spatial and temporal locus to the activity of the interaction, and (2) that these aspects of behavior be different from those aspects constituted as the main-track activity. It is seen, then, that for any analysis of an episode such as this, to focus simply upon the main-track actions of yo-yoing itself and Father's proffered comments at the end would be to miss completely the processes by which the episode is made possible at all.

## Spatial–orientational positioning

As we have just seen, the yo-yoing episode was demarcated by Daughter entering into and maintaining a particular spatial–orientational arrangement with Father. It appeared that, from her point of view, as long as she was in the spatial–orientational position she used for yo-yoing for Father, she was ready to yo-yo. Thus we can say her intention or plan to perform with her yo-yo for her father was indicated by her maintenance of this spatial–orientational position. This interpretation is borne out by the fact that when Father did not look up, Daughter made her stepping into position audible, by stamping her feet.

The yo-yo episode as a whole was characterized by a sustained spatial–orientational arrangement that was distinctive. Sub-episodes within the yo-yo episode were also marked by Daughter assuming repeatedly a particular posture and position for each bout of yo-yoing, alternating with a contrasting posture and position for each interval between bouts.

The establishment and maintenance of spatial–orientational arrangements, it seems, is one way that participants can provide one another with evidence that they are prepared to sustain a common orientational perspective. By arranging themselves into a particular spatial–orientational pattern they thereby display each to the other that they are governed by the same set of general considerations. By co-operating with one another to sustain a given spatial–orientational arrangement, they can display a commonality of readiness.

The spatial and orientational position of an individual can provide information about his interpretative frame or attentional domain in the following way.

First of all, it has to be recognized that a person's activity is always located somewhere. Any line of action that a person is pursuing is always carried out in a specific relation to a specific environment. If I am to write, I will organize myself in relation to environmental features such as a desk, in such a way that I have access to a little domain within which I can engage in writing and within which the various items needed for this line of action are to be found. If I am to watch television, I will organize myself in relation to appropriate environmental features so that again, a domain is available to me within which there is free space between myself and the television set. If I am to spend half an hour in quiet meditation, I will again organize myself in a way that fits that activity to an appropriate domain of space. At any moment, thus, there is a spatial consequence for any line of activity, and the individual is continuously re-adjusting himself in relation to his surrounds as he changes this line of activity. The spatial domain to which $p$ organizes himself to have easy and direct access for a given line of activity has been referred to as the individual's *transactional segment* (see Chapter 7). The transactional segment is the space into which the individual addresses his gaze as he carries out his line of activity, whatever it may be; it is the space from which he immediately and readily reaches for whatever objects his current project may require he manipulate; it is the space immediately in front of him that the individual projects forward and keeps clear if he is moving. In short, it is the space that the individual seeks to maintain clear for his own purposes.

An individual's transactional segment may be recognized by others from the position, orientation, and postural organization of his body. The body, it will be observed, can be viewed as an organization of segments, each one capable of a somewhat different orientation. However, the orientation of some segments sets limits upon the domain of the environment to which other segments may orient. Further, each of the segments of the body differs in the ease with which its orientation may be changed. Thus there is a kind of descending hierarchy of orientational mobility, from the eyes to the lower body, combined with an ascending hierarchy of orientational limitations, from the lower body upwards. Although the eyes can change very rapidly the direction in which they may point, the domain of the environment over which they may move is limited by the orientation of the head. The orientation of the head, which may be changed almost as easily as the orientation of the eyes, is itself limited by the direction in which the upper body is facing. The direction in which the upper body is facing can also be varied (an individual may twist his upper body to the left or right) but less easily, and it is limited in the changes it can make by the orientation of the lower body. Where a person seats himself, or where he may have planted his feet when standing, provides a frame within which he may then orient his upper body, and this, in turn, provides a frame within which changes in the orientation of the head and eyes may take place.

Changes in orientation of upper-body segments, such as the head and eyes, are characteristically done within the framework of limits set by the position of the lower body. Changes in the orientation of lower-body segments, therefore, have longer term implications for change in attention than changes in the orientation of upper-body segments and are seen as having more momentous implications for whatever new environmental domains are to become the concern of the individual.

It is seen, in short, how the hierarchy of priorities and longer and shorter term commitments in the organization of the individual's attention is directly perceivable by the way in which the various segments of the body are oriented. When this is taken in conjunction with the actual environmental settings in which these organizations occur, and with observation of the actual activities in which the individual is engaged, it will be seen that bodily orientation can be a source of quite detailed information about what is relevant for an individual at a given time and therefore what his interpretative frame may be.

## Formation arrangements

When two or more individuals are present, they are able to provide information about the relevance of each for the other according to how they space themselves and how they include or exclude each other in their respective transactional segments. Thus we find that people co-present in a setting tend to organize themselves into spatial patterns of various kinds, co-operating together to maintain them. We may therefore speak of people entering into various kinds of *formations*.

There are many different kinds of formation to be observed. Here I discuss only one type, one that commonly occurs when two or a few individuals enter together into a focused interaction, such as conversation. This type of formation, which we prefer to call an F-formation, has also been termed a *facing-formation*, or a *face-formation* (see Deutsch 1977, McDermott and Roth 1978, Scheflen and Ashcraft 1976). An F-formation may be said to arise whenever two or more individuals agree to position themselves in such a way that their transactional segments overlap, thereby establishing a space between them to which they have equal access. This space is an area over which all participants exercise control and for whose maintenance and protection from internal and external disturbances all are responsible. Thus whenever two or more individuals are placed close to each other, orienting their bodies in such a way that each of them has an easy, direct, and equal access to every other participant's transactional segment, and agree to maintain such an arrangement, they can be said to create an F-formation. The system of spatial and postural behaviors by which people create and sustain this joint-transactional space will be referred to as an F-formation *system*.

It is noted that by establishing such a system of spatial and orientational relations, individuals create for themselves a context within which preferential access to the other's actions is established. Furthermore, such a system of spatial and orientational relations provides for a visually perceivable arrangement by which participants in a given focused encounter are delineated from those who are outsiders. Indeed, it seems that the kind of arrangements that arise in the F-formation provide a means of clearly demarcating the "world" of the encounter from the rest of the "world." Entering into an F-formation, thus, is an excellent means by which interactional and therefore social and psychological "withness" may be established.

There can be considerable variation in the actual arrangements that individuals establish with one another within the framework that an F-formation provides. A roughly circular arrangement is common in free-standing groups of three or more people, where all are participating in the same conversation, but it is by no means the only arrangement that may be observed. In F-formations of two individuals, for example, we may see arrangements that vary from a direct face-to-face pattern, to an L-shaped pattern, or even a side-by-side pattern. In F-formations of more than two participants we may see semicircular or rectangular arrangements as well as circular ones.

## Interactional relationships

Different arrangements have different consequences for the kind of access that the participants have to each other. Thus different arrangements imply different kinds of interactional relationships. Hall (1964b, 1966, 1968) pointed out that at different distances the senses make available different kinds of information, and this has consequences for the kinds of actions that can be used in interaction. At very close distances, for instance, touch may be used, whereas at greater distances vision and hearing come to play important but varying roles. As distance increases, because the participants are able to detect one another's behavior in an increasingly less fine grained fashion, Hall suggested that there are shifts in the style of language used, how listener behavior is organized, and the uses to which vision is put in the interaction. Hall suggested, thus, that because of the way $p$ and $q$ may relate, their behavior alters according to the distance that separates them. The function of the transaction between them also alters with distance so that different distances are chosen by interactants according to the kind of transactions they are going to have.

Hall's analysis dealt only with distance, but similar considerations make it clear that the angle of orientation of the interactants also makes a difference in how they interrelate their behavior. Two people standing or sitting face-to-face, for instance, confront one another, and each, directing his eyes forward, looks at the other. The surrounding environment is less readily accessible. Two people standing or sitting in an L-arrangement, on the other hand, still sustain an exclusive interactional domain, but they also have ready access to the outside world, although which segment of the outside world each of them looks at is different. When two people are arranged in a side-by-side, both face toward the same outer world in the same way; they both can look simultaneously at the same segment of the outer world. They have a kind of mutual access to each other that is different from the access people in L-arrangements or face-to-face arrangements have.

Although studies of the relationship between the nature of the interaction and the spatial arrangement adopted by the gathering are sparse (see Batchelor and Goethals 1972, Kendon 1973, Sommer 1969), there are enough observations, it would seem, to show that there is a systematic relationship between spatial arrangement and mode of interaction. This means that $p$ will not only tend to adopt particular arrangements for particular kinds of interaction, but, by adopting a given spatial arrangement or by moving to a position and orientation that might suggest a spatial arrangement of a particular sort, he can thereby propose an interactive relationship of a particular sort. Spatial positioning is available as an expressive resource for interactants. It serves as a condition of interaction, and, for this reason, when used as an expressive resource by a participant to effectively propose an interaction of a certain sort, such propositions are treated as belonging to the unofficial or "not-counted" stream of action. Spatial and orientational positioning, thus, serves well as a device by which expectation and intention can be conveyed.

The function of spatial–orientational positioning in interaction is further illuminated by a consideration of the way in which spatial arrangements in F-formation may change. Such changes in arrangement occur in conjunction with changes in other aspects of the interaction, suggesting that they constitute one way in which frame changes in interaction are marked. It is common to observe that people maintaining an F-formation may alter their positions relative to one another, thereby changing the arrangement, sometimes several times, during the course of the encounter. These arrangement changes may be associated with external factors, such as a change in the environment of the encounter, or with changes in the participants of an F-formation. In the latter case they may be seen to reflect the adaptations to external changes through which the participants maintain or preserve the conditions of the interaction. On the other hand, such changes may also reflect rearrangements associated with changes in the interaction itself. As the kind of interaction the participants are engaging in alters, so the spatial–orientational framing appropriate for the interaction alters. This has been described elsewhere in analyses of opening encounters (see Chapter 6). Thus it has been observed how participants commonly frame their salutations with one spatial–orientational arrangement and move to another arrangement for the conversational interaction that follows. Examples have also been described in which shifts in conversational topic are accompanied by shifts in spatial–orientational arrangements. In these cases, it would seem, the shifts appear to serve not so much as a means whereby different interactive conditions are created, as much as a means whereby different phases of the conversation are marked as distinct phases.

It is now seen how participants may employ spatial–orientational maneuvers as a means of testing out each other's alignments to a given interpretative frame or as a means of finding out if the other is willing to change to a new one. A participant wishing to change to a new frame may precede any actual change by small maneuvers in the direction of the new position that would, if completed, constitute a position suitable for a different kind of arrangement. He may observe whether his co-participants will follow his lead. If they are willing to do so, instead of remaining in the same position or making maneuvers that would compensate for the new move that $p$ made, they will make incipient moves complimentary to $p$'s own, thus indicating that they will move to the same new position. Such preframe change negotiations can be observed especially when the closing of an encounter is being negotiated. Thus one may observe how one or other of the participants in a standing conversational group begins to step back, increasing the distance between himself and the others. Such a move may be taken as an announcement of a wish for closure. Step-backs by the other participants may follow, and these serve to acknowledge the closure bid, thus making it possible for all of the participants to move into the closing phase of the conversation together.

## Frame-attunement

By entering into and maintaining an F-formation, participants are able to keep each other continuously informed that they are present to a current occasion of interaction. Furthermore, as we have just seen, by showing themselves responsive to each other's adjustments in spatial–orientational positioning, participants can show whether they are ready or not for alterations in the frame of the situation. However, spatial–orientational positioning (or postural arrangements, in seated groups, as dealt with by Scheflen 1964, and McDermott et al. 1978), does not itself constitute the action of interaction. It functions as background. Spacing and orientation provide the scaffold for whatever it is that the interactants are to do together. It is for this reason that it can serve so well in the process of frame-attunement.

What interactants do together is accomplished through actions, such as utterances, either spoken or gestural, or manipulative actions, directed at the other, that are regarded by the participants themselves as moves of some sort in the interactive process they are engaged in. Such actions always have an address. We now discuss some aspects of what is involved in establishing address for such actions.

### Address

If $p$ is to address an action to another he commonly will not do so unless he has reason to suppose that there is an audience for its receipt. Although fellow participation in an F-formation in itself usually provides $p$ with good grounds for supposing that such a fellow participant will serve as an audience for any action he may address to him, it seems that usually more is required. Commonly what happens is that two or more participants establish an utterance exchange system between them such that any utterance produced within it by any of the participants is understood as being relevant for any other participant within the system. It is within such utterance exchange systems that we find the rules of turn-taking to have their application. Other sorts of action exchange may be set up, of course. One may compare, for example, the pattern of action in a "kissing round," as presented in Chapter 5. It will be seen that exchanges of kisses have a different sort of organization from exchanges of utterances. Likewise, systems of action that can be observed in dancing may be different (consider the reciprocated but simultaneous swaying in the courtship dance of the Melpa of New Guinea, as described by Pitcairn and Schleidt 1976). However, in these cases, as in the case of utterance exchanges, it would seem that the participants have to establish, within the frame of the agreement that is implied by the maintenance of an appropriate formation, a further agreement that their utterances or other actions are relevant for specific individuals in a particular way.

A number of studies have now been published which include detailed analyses of how utterance exchange systems are established and maintained. The main conclusions are summarized briefly here. It should be noted that all of the examples (Goodwin 1981, Kendon 1967, 1970, 1973) were taken from conversational occasions involving several people and concerning instances in which a speaker addressed his utterance to a specific other member of the gathering. Although all participants in the F-formation that constituted the gathering were able to hear what was being said, only two individuals were participants in the utterance exchange system at the time of the observation. What was at issue in these investigations was how speaker and recipient came to know that they were indeed together in a specific utterance exchange system.

It emerges from these analyses that participants in utterance exchange systems interrelate their behavior in a number of ways that are distinctive for them and different from the way their behavior is related to other participants in the gathering within which the utterance exchange system is contained. Typically both speaker and direct recipient orient their bodies at least partially toward one another so that one might say of them that they have established a sub-segment of their transactional segments in mutual overlap. They repeatedly focus their eyes upon one another and, from time to time, their eyes meet. The orientation of the body, especially the head, is toward one another, but it is the intermittent aiming of their eyes at one another that is one of the principal ways participants in utterance exchange systems indicate to whom their actions are addressed. It should be noted that it is insufficient to say of participants in utterance exchange systems that they "look at one another." The looking is rarely continuous, and sometimes it is very brief and takes up but a small proportion of the time that the exchange system lasts. At the very least we may expect to see such eye-address at the beginnings and endings of the system's establishment. What is characteristically observed, it should be noted, is that in aiming the eyes at another person, the speaker or listener's head repeatedly turns to the same position (oriented to the other member of the address system) and pauses. When the eyes are not directed to the other member of the address system, they are not directed to anyone else in the gathering. Indeed, one of the ways in which a recipient of an utterance may redirect the speaker to another recipient is by looking away from the speaker and towards another member of the gathering. Goodwin (1981) reported some closely analyzed examples that show how a speaker re-addresses his utterance in midstream if his initial recipient focuses his eyes elsewhere in the gathering. Sigman (1980) reported examples of what he called *conversational fission*: when two people speak at once, two separate utterance exchange systems may be set up within the same F-formation if other members of the gathering separately orient to the two speakers. I have studied a series of instances from a psychiatric case discussion film in which the chairman interrupts the case presentation from time-to-time to get complementary information on the case being discussed from the social worker who was involved. Having evoked replies from the social worker, he then redirects the address of these replies by himself looking elsewhere in the group to another member.

If the utterer, then, can begin marking the address of an utterance by patterning his gaze in such a way that his eyes are aimed repeatedly at his addressee, the recipient must cooperate by maintaining an appropriate patterning of orientation on his part. Recipients, furthermore, are commonly observed to display a heightened congruency of posture with that of the speaker, and they also tend to exhibit a particular set of gestures, such as headnods and changes in facial expression that are patterned in systematic relations with the structuring of the speaker's speech. If the recipient ceases to display these actions and, in particular, as we have seen, if the recipient alters the target of his eyes to that of another member of the gathering, the utterance exchange system will alter in who it includes or it will come to an end. Since only those within a current utterance exchange system have rights as "next speaker" within that system, if it changes its membership midstream, this also has implications for who may follow as next speaker.

*Rhythmical coordination*

A further feature of the relationship between participants in an utterance exchange system may now be noted. It has been reported by several observers that speaker and recipient in such a system often exhibit rhythmical coordination in their flow of action. In an earlier report (Kendon 1970, see Chapter 4), I described how, as an utterance exchange system got underway, the recipient's postural adjustments that ensued as he settled into a listening posture were rhythmically paced with the structure of the speaker's speech. Furthermore, as the speaker drew his utterance to a close, his recipient (who had evoked the utterance by a previous question) began to move again in time with the rhythmical organization of the speaker's speech, anticipating the precise moment the speaker completed his utterance.

Rhythmical coordination of action with that of another, it would seem, is also part of the way in which participants display that they share the same perspective on the interaction. Elsewhere (Kendon 1973) I have described an example of the establishment of an utterance exchange axis in which the participants established their orientations to one another prior to any exchange of utterance. What was at issue here was the observation that the headturns of the two participants were synchronized, as if the recipient of the first utterance in the system was already forewarned that she was to be the addressee. Close analysis showed how the recipient had begun to track the movements of the speaker well before he began to turn to her (while he was taking a drink from his coffee cup). Evidently, by following him in her movements, she was able to establish her attentiveness to him and thus establish her openness to an address from him. As we suggested there, moving into synchrony with another person is one of the devices by which a person can indicate to the other that he wishes to establish an action system with him, without making an explicit request (see also p. 171).

The point is that a person can modulate the rate at which he is carrying out any line of action that he may happen to be engaged in in such a way that it conforms to the rate of another. By allowing his actions to be performed at the same pace as those of another he lets the other know of his attentiveness and openness to him without in any way altering the nature of what he is doing.

## Salutations

Such rhythmic matching can also be seen between persons who are not members of the same F-formation but who merely happen to be co-present, and here it appears to lay the foundations for an exchange of salutations between people. As we saw in Chapter 6 where the aim was to analyze the way people organized their behavior as they carried out salutational exchanges, the question of how greeting sequences are initiated was examined in some detail. It was recognized that before $p$ could engage in a greeting with $q$, $p$ would not only have to sight $q$ and decide whether $q$ was sufficiently unengaged to be open to a greeting from him, but would also have to receive some indication from $q$ that $q$ was ready to receive a salutation from him. Careful examination of a number of filmed greetings, in which the film record included a record of the activities of both parties before any salutational exchange could be observed, showed that in a number of cases, coordination of behavior could be observed well before the salutational exchange. The greetings analyzed in the study were recorded at an open-air party. The greetings in which presalutational behavioral coordination could be observed took place between guests at the party who were not well acquainted and who were, thus, not in a position to be certain of how each would recognize the other.

In several examples we were able to see how, prior to any exchange of salutation, $p$ would place himself and orient himself in relation to $q$, but then not make any move toward $q$ or begin upon any address until after $q$ had begun to turn his head toward $p$. Often $p$ would allow his gaze to meet $q$'s gaze, and this seemed to provide the clearance $p$ needed to embark upon an approach and a salutation. However, one sometimes observes a carefully orchestrated eye-avoidance in which $p$, who has taken the initiative by orienting to $q$, leaves it to $q$ to begin the salutational exchange, but not until he has let $q$ know he is attentive to him by looking away from him synchronously with $q$'s looking at him. As an example, the reader is referred to Chapter 6, p. 171.

## Functions of salutational exchanges

The study of greetings just discussed showed that greeting encounters can be analyzed into a number of stages, from the initial perception of the other, through announcement of intention to greet, acknowledgement of this and the management of the mutual approach, to the procedures by which the gestures of the close salutation are enacted. Through these stages we can see how the attention of the two participants is progressively calibrated as they come to agree upon a greeting encounter and upon the precise form that the close-salutation will take.

The close-salutation of greeting itself has a number of characteristics that are worth remarking upon from the point of view of the theme of this chapter. Salutational exchanges, which can take a wide variety of forms, serve a number of functions. They serve to acknowledge a social relationship, and the form of the salutation itself also makes reference to the nature of the social relationship. They may be further modulated to reflect the degree of pleasure involved in the meeting of the greeters, the formality of the occasion, the amount of time that has elapsed since last meeting, and the like. We may also note that salutations also serve as a bracketing ceremonial. They come at a point of change in social access and often serve to establish the beginning of a social occasion of some sort. It seems that the peculiar character that salutations have is nicely adapted to this function.

First, we may note their very high degree of conventionalization. The forms that are employed for any given kind of greeting within a given communication community are highly restricted. There is a high degree of conventionalization of both gesture and verbal utterances. This has the important consequence of greatly reducing the degree of uncertainty of the participants about what may ensue at the moment of salutation. Second, it is to be noted that salutational forms, as acts, are often structured in such a way that the two participants do the same thing simultaneously (as in a handshake or an embrace) or in a closely coordinated sequential relationship (often observed in the verbal exchanges of salutation). Furthermore, the gestural forms of salutation often include rhythmically organized body contact such that the two participants come to share directly in the same rhythmical organization of action.

This has the consequence of rhythmically aligning the two individuals and, in consequence of the simultaneity of action, the salutational exchange is brought to a close simultaneously. This means that the two individuals are thereby placed upon an equal footing with respect to one another.

Not uncommonly, salutations are followed by utterance exchanges that, despite having the outward form of serving the exchange of information, either follow a set form or consist of informational exchange utterances concerning a topic on which all participants are already fully informed (as in weather conversation). Here again we may observe how use is being made of a ready-made format for interaction. The participants are thus able to further align the rhythmical organization of their actions and their expectations in regard to one another.

It is often said that greeting exchanges, because they are so highly conventionalized, are good examples of *phatic communion*: they do not serve any informational function. It should be pointed out, however, that because the forms of gesture and utterance are so highly conventionalized, the participants are able to pay careful attention to the manner of their performance, and from this much information can be derived. From the firmness or limpness of the handshake, from its prolongation or its curtailment, much can be inferred about the attitude of the other person. From the manner in which the conventional utterances are said and the readiness of responses, inferences can be made about many aspects of the person's social status, origins, background, current state of mind, and attitude in the present situation and toward his co-participant. This is a matter of widely held common knowledge in our own society, and etiquette books are fully aware of it, often providing quite detailed instructions on how to perform salutations so that the proper impression will be conveyed. Youssouf, Grimshaw and Bird (1976), in their account of Tuareg greetings, also bring this point out clearly. They show how the Tuareg, greeting one another in the lonely Sahara, follow a set routine. It is clear from their account, however, that this routine is of great informational value because it provides much opportunity for detailed observation of the other, thus allowing each to organize his expectations and thus his plans for action in the encounter that will follow.

When actions and interaction routines are conventionalized, they are provided with a detailed format for their performance. However, this format never amounts to a complete specification for action. The performer is always left with some latitude in how he may organize his actions in relation to the format. This means he has available to him a way of communicating in an explicit fashion that would not otherwise be open to him if the format were not conventionalized. Conventionalization of salutational forms has thus a specifically informational function that it gains by virtue of its conventionalization. By employing conventional forms, participants make available to each other a way of conveying information in just the manner that is needed if they are to convey to one another information about their interpretative frames.

## Gradients of explicitness

Hitherto we have written as if a sharp distinction is to be drawn between main-track action, on the one hand, and action that is treated as background and functions as communication "unofficially," on the other. It will be seen, however, that there is in fact no such sharp distinction. Spatial maneuverings and orientation changes, for example, can be performed in such a way that they are regarded as incidental to whatever else a person is doing. However, they may be performed in a way that makes them more salient than usual, that draws attention to them in their own right. They can become, thus, attended to and regarded as explicit. We may also observe that actions such as gestures, which are usually treated as main-track actions, may be modified in their performance in such a way that they are perceived as tentative, incomplete, or even so ambiguous in their form as to be treated as incidental. Morris et al. (1979) have described circumstances in which obscene or insulting gestures may be modified in form so that they are recognized as gestures only to the person to whom they are addressed but which, to an onlooker such as a policeman, may be explained away as an incidental, nongestural action. It would seem, in fact, that participants have considerable ability to modify their actions in such a way as to obscure them as merely incidental or to make them conspicuous as deliberately intended, officially meant actions to which the actor is officially committed. Participants may modulate their actions along what we might term *a gradient of explicitness*, according to circumstance.

We may sometimes observe such modulations of action along this gradient of explicitness when one member of a gathering wishes to induce a change in the working consensus of the interaction or, perhaps, to leave it altogether. Consider the circumstance where one participant wishes to leave ongoing interaction. We have already explained above why departures are sometimes very difficult to manage. The difficulty arises because participants become jointly responsible for maintaining the working consensus so that the withdrawal of any one person may lead to the collapse of the whole occasion. For someone to take their leave it first becomes necessary for them to alter the prevailing agreement in the group so that their departure will be appropriately interpreted. This means, as we have seen, that the person must engage in actions of some sort that announce his intentions in advance, so that the other participants may adjust their own expectations to the point where an explicit departure becomes possible. Under circumstances of this sort one often observes the individual who would like to leave perform a series of actions, each one more explicit than the next. At small social gatherings where food or drink is being consumed, one may often observe the following sort of sequence. The guest who wishes to initiate a departure may begin by finishing up whatever consumable he may have. Draining one's glass, stubbing out one's cigarette, and cleaning the last crumbs from one's plate can all serve to announce that one has finished consuming and that, accordingly, this reason for remaining is removed. Such actions may then be followed by shifting posture to a sitting position from which rising to one's feet could be very easily accomplished. Further actions might include looking at one's watch or glancing at one's spouse to indicate wish for departure. Such actions may, of course, be performed with varying degrees of conspicuousness. Eventually, if the guest does not succeed in getting any acknowledgement of these moves from the others, he may have to resort to much more explicit actions. However, the point to recognize is that there can be many steps between action that is considered to be completely incidental and action considered by others to be explicitly expressive. It seems evident that participants have a lively appreciation of these differences and often can be observed to exercise considerable delicacy as to the place on this gradient of explicitness that they choose to operate.

## Conclusion

Human interaction is built upon promises. As Peter Wilson (1980) wrote, because the human species is the most generalized of all primates, the forms of its social relationships are the least specified in advance.

In terms of adaptation, this means that it is possible for any individual to live with any others but, most important, it means that an enormous problem has to be met by all individuals, namely, that little information about another individual can be known in advance and hence an individual has little advance information that will help him coexist with others on a predictable basis . . . if the human individual is to coexist with other such individuals, he must arrive at some ground for expectation and reciprocation. He must work out some common form of agreement about actions and reactions, one with some degree of reliability. (p. 43)

In this chapter we have sought to show how various features of observable behavior in face-to-face interactional contexts can function as a way of providing the advance information that anyone proposing to interact with another has to have. We have suggested that, in a number of different ways, people can make manifest their intentions, and they can reveal which of the situational principles they are responding to in advance of their taking any action that is explicitly addressed to another and would count as making a definite move in an interactional sequence. We have argued that for this to be possible, people must be able to deal with each other's behavior either as fully intended and explicit or as unintended and inexplicit, and to treat the information they receive in this way as unofficial. There seems to be a tacit understanding that certain behavioral forms shall be treated in this way even though, as we have seen, participants are fully able to control much of their own behavior that is treated as unintended; they are fully aware that the information that it may make available can be deliberately provided. It is our contention that the willingness and ability to treat each other's behavior in this differential fashion is an essential component in the skill or competence of any normal participant in face-to-face interaction.

# Films cited

Listed here are those research films that are discussed in the chapters in this book which exist in archives available to scholars. Some other film and video material is also mentioned which has either been lost or is not available in any archive and this is not listed here.

Bateson, G. GB-SU-005, "Doris" in conversation with Gregory Bateson, 1956. This is the film that was used in the "Natural History of an Interview" study. Copy at Annenberg School of Communications, University of Pennsylvania, Philadelphia

Bateson, G. GB-SU-008, "Doris" and her therapist, *c*. 1956. Copy at Annenberg School of Communications, University of Pennsylvania, Philadelphia

Birdwhistell, R. L. and Van Vlack, J. ISP 001 61. Teaching of Psychotherapy V. Commonwealth of Pennsylvania, Eastern Pennsylvania Psychiatric Institute, Studies in Human Communication. 1961. Copy in Human Studies Film Archive, Smithsonian Institution, Washington, DC

Birdwhistell, R. L. and Van Vlack, J. TRD 009, English Pub Scene. Commonwealth of Pennsylvania and Institute of Intercultural Studies, 1961. Copy in Human Studies Film Archive, Smithsonian Institution, Washington, DC

Jones, P. What's in a Face. BBC Television, 1973

Kendon, A., Ferber, A. and Van Vlack, J. Birthday Party Film, BDF 00269. 6 reels (Bolex I, II and III, Cinevoice I, Auricon I and II). Studies in Human Communication Division, Eastern Pennsylvania Psychiatric Institute, Philadelphia, 1969. A copy of this film is lodged with the Human Studies Film Archive, Smithsonian Institution, Washington, DC

Kendon, A., Ferber, A. and Van Vlack, J. Manhattan Wedding, BDF 00170. A copy of the roll used as source material in Chapter 6, known as "Foyer After Service" is lodged with the Human Studies Film Archive, Smithsonian Institution, Washington DC

# References

Adato, A. 1975. Leave-taking: a study of commonsense knowledge of social structure. *Anthropological Quarterly*, 48: 255–271

Albert, Stuart and Kessler, Suzanne. 1976. Processes for ending social encounters: the conceptual archaeology of a temporal place. *Journal for the Theory of Social Behaviour*, 6: 147–170

1978. Ending social encounters. *Journal of Experimental Social Psychology*, 14: 541–553

Ambrose, J. A. 1961. The development of the smiling response in early infancy. In B. M. Foss, ed., *Determinants of Infant Behaviour*. London: Methuen, pp. 179–201

Andrew, R. J. 1963a. The origin and evolution of the calls and facial expressions of the primates. *Behaviour*, 20: 1–109

1963b. The evolution of facial expressions. *Science*, 142: 1034–1041

Arensberg, C. 1972. Culture as behavior: structure and emergence. *Annual Review of Anthropology*, 1: 1–26

Argyle, M. and Cook, M. 1976. *Gaze and Mutual Gaze*. Cambridge: Cambridge University Press

Argyle, M. A. and Dean, J. 1965. Eye contact, distance and affiliation. *Sociometry*, 28: 289–304

Argyle, M. A. and Kendon, A. 1967. The experimental analysis of social performance. In L. Berkowitz, ed., *Advances in Experimental Social Psychology*, Volume 3. New York: Academic Press, pp. 55–98

Argyle, M. A., Laljee, M. and Cook, M. 1968. The effect of visibility on interaction in a dyad. *Human Relations*, 21: 3–17

Arndt, H. and Janney, R. W. 1987. *InterGrammar: Toward an Integrative Model of Verbal, Prosodic and Kinesic Choices in Speech*. Berlin: Mouton de Gruyter

Atkinson, J. M. and Heritage, J., eds. 1985. *Structures of Social Action: Studies in Conversation Analysis*. Cambridge: Cambridge University Press

Bales, R. F. 1950. *Interaction Process Analysis*. Reading, Mass.: Addison Wesley

Barker, R. and Wright, H. F. 1951. *Midwest and its Children*. Evanston, Illinois: Row, Peterson and Co.

Batchelor, J. 1927. *Ainu Life and Lore: Echoes of a Departing Race.* Tokyo: Kyobunkwan

Batchelor, J. P. and Goethals, G. R. 1972. Spatial arrangements in freely formed groups. *Sociometry,* 35: 270–279

Bateson, G. 1955. A theory of play and fantasy. *Approaches to the Study of Human Personality.* American Psychiatric Association Research Reports, No. 2, pp. 39–51

1956. The message "This is play." In B. Schaffner, ed., *Group Processes: Transactions of the Second Conference.* New York: Josiah Macy Jr. Foundation, pp. 145–242

1958. Language and psychiatry: Frieda Fromm-Reichman's last project. *Psychiatry,* 21: 96–100

1971. Communication. In N. A. McQuown, ed., *The Natural History of an Interview.* Microfilm collection of manuscripts on Cultural Anthropology. Fifteenth Series. Chicago: University of Chicago Joseph Regenstein Library, Photoduplication Department, pp. 1–40

Bateson, G., Jackson, D. D., Haley, J. and Weakland, J. 1956. Toward a theory of schizophrenia. *Behavioral Science,* 1: 251–264

Bateson, G. and Mead, M. 1942. *Balinese Character: A Photographic Analysis.* New York: New York Academy of Sciences, Special Publication, Volume II

Bauman, R. and Sherzer, J., eds. 1974. *Explorations in the Ethnography of Speaking.* Cambridge: Cambridge University Press

Bär., E. 1974. Context analysis in psychotherapy. *Semiotica,* 10: 255–281

Beebe, B., Stern, D. and Jaffe, J. 1979. The kinesic rhythm of mother–infant interactions. In A. W. Siegman and S. Feldstein, eds., *Of Speech and Time.* Hillsdale, NJ: Lawrence Erlbaum, pp. 23–34

Bell, C. A. 1946. *Portrait of the Dalai Lama.* London: Collins

Bennett, A. T. 1980. Rhythmic analysis of multiple levels of communicative behavior in face-to-face interaction. In Walburga von Raffler-Engel, ed., *Aspects of Nonverbal Communication.* Lisse: Swets and Zeitlinger B.V., pp. 237–251

Bevans, M. 1960. *McCall's Book of Everyday Etiquette.* New York: Golden Press

Birdwhistell, R. L. 1952. *Introduction to Kinesics: An Annotation System for the Analysis of Body Motion and Gesture.* Washington, DC: Foreign Service Institute, U.S. Department of State

1962. Critical moments in the psychiatric interview. In T. T. Tourlentes, ed., *Research Approaches to a Psychiatric Problem.* New York: Grune and Stratton, pp. 179–188

1970. *Kinesics and Context.* Philadelphia: University of Pennsylvania Press

Blom, J.-P. and Gumperz, J. J. 1972. Social meaning in linguistic structure: Code-switching in Norway. In J. J. Gumperz and D. Hymes, eds., *Directions in Sociolinguistics: The Ethnography of Communication.* New York: Holt, Rinehart and Winston, pp. 407–434

Blurton-Jones, N. G. 1967. An ethological study of some aspects of social behaviour of children in nursery school. In D. Morris, ed., *Primate Ethology*. Chicago: Aldine, pp. 347–368

1971. Criteria for use in describing facial expression of children. *Human Biology*, 43: 365–413

Blurton-Jones, N. G. and Leach, G. M. 1972. Behaviour of children and their mothers at separation and greeting. In N. G. Blurton-Jones, ed., *Ethological Studies of Child Behaviour*. Cambridge: Cambridge University Press, pp. 217–247

Bowlby, J. 1969. *Attachment and Loss*. Vol. 1: *Attachment*. New York: Basic Books

Boyd, H. B. and Banks, S. W. 1965. *An Outline of the Treatment of Fractures*, 8th Edition. Philadelphia: W. B. Saunders and Co.

Brannigan, C. R. and Humphries, D. A. 1972. Human non-verbal behaviour, a means of communication. In N. G. Blurton-Jones, ed., *Ethological Studies of Child Behaviour*. Cambridge: Cambridge University Press, pp. 37–64

Broadbent, D. E. 1958. *Perception and Communication*. Oxford: Pergamon Press

Bruner, J. S. and Taguiri, R. 1954. The perception of people. In G. Lindzey, ed., *Handbook of Social Psychology*, Vol. II. Reading, Mass.: Addison-Wesley, pp. 634–654

Bull, P. E. and Brown, R. 1977. The role of postural changes in dyadic conversations. *British Journal of Clinical and Social Psychology*, 16: 29–33

Button, G. and Casey, N. 1984. Generating topic: the use of topic initial elicitors. In J. M. Atkinson and J. Heritage, eds., *Structures of Social Action: Studies in Conversation Analysis*. Cambridge: Cambridge University Press

Callan, H. 1970. *Ethology and Society*. Oxford: Clarendon Press

Camras, L. 1977. Facial expressions used by children in a conflict situation. *Child Development*, 48: 1431–1435

Caton, S. U. 1986. *Salam taniya*: Greetings from the highlands of Yemen. *American Ethnologist*, 13: 290–308

Chance, M. R. A. 1962. An interpretation of some agonistic postures: the role of "cut-off" acts and postures. *Symposia of the Zoological Society of London*, 8: 71–89

Chapple, E. D. 1940a. Measuring human relations. *Genetic Psychology Monographs*, 22: 3–147

1940b. "Personality" differences as described by invariant properties of individuals in interaction. *Proceedings of the National Academy of Sciences*, 26: 10–16

1953. The standard interview as used in interaction chronograph investigations. *Human Organization*, 12: 23–32

Chapple, E. D. and Coon, C. W. 1942. *Principles of Anthropology*. New York: Henry Holt

Chapple, E. D. and Donald, G., Jr. 1946. An evaluation of department store sales people by the interaction chronograph. *Journal of Marketing*, 12: 173–185

Chapple, E. D. and Lindemann, E. 1942. Clinical implications of measurements of interaction rates in psychiatric interviews. *Applied Anthropology*, 1: 1–11

Chevalier-Skolnikoff, S. 1973. Facial expression of emotions in non-human primates. In P. Ekman, ed., *Darwin and Facial Expression: A Century of Research in Review*. New York: Academic Press, pp. 11–89

Cheyne, J. A. and Efran, M. G. 1972. The effect of spatial and interpersonal variables on the invasion of group controlled territories. *Sociometry*, 35: 477–489

Chomsky, N. 1957. *Syntactic Structures*. The Hague: Mouton and Co.

Ciolek, T. M. and Kendon, A. 1980. Environment and the spatial arrangement of conversational interaction. *Sociological Inquiry*, 50: 237–271

Coleman, J. C. 1949. Facial expression of emotion. *Psychological Monographs*, Whole No. 296, 49: 1–36

Collett, P. 1983. Mossi salutations. *Semiotica*, 45: 191–248

Collins, O. and Collins, J. M. 1973. *Interaction and Social Structure*. The Hague: Mouton and Co.

Collins, R. 1981. Erving Goffman and the development of modern social theory. In J. Ditton, ed., *The View from Goffman*. New York: St. Martin's Press, pp. 170–209

1988. Theoretical continuities in Goffman's work. In P. Drew and A. Wootton, eds., *Erving Goffman: Exploring the Interaction Order*. Cambridge: Polity Press, pp. 41–63

Collis, G. M. 1977. Visual co-orientation and maternal speech. In H. R. Schaffer, ed., *Studies in Mother–Infant Interaction*. London: Academic Press, pp. 355–375

Condon, W. S. 1976. An analysis of behavioral organization. *Sign Language Studies*, 13: 285–318

1977. A primary phase in the organization of infant responding. In H. R. Schaffer, ed., *Studies in Mother–Infant Interaction*. London: Academic Press, pp. 153–176

1979. Neonatal entrainment and enculturation. In M. Bullowa, ed., *Before Speech: The Beginning of Interpersonal Communication*. Cambridge: Cambridge University Press, pp. 131–148

1982. Cultural microrhythms. In M. Davis, ed., *Interaction Rhythms: Periodicity in Communicative Behavior*. New York: Human Sciences Press, pp. 53–77

Condon, W. S. and Sander, L. W. 1974a. Neonate movement is synchronized with adult speech: interactional participation and language acquisition. *Science*, 183: 99–101

1974b. Synchrony demonstrated between movements of the neonate and adult speech. *Child Development*, 45: 456–462

Condon, W. S. and Ogston, W. D. 1966. Sound film analysis of normal and pathological behavior patterns. *Journal of Nervous and Mental Disease*, 143: 338–347

1967. A segmentation of behavior. *Journal of Psychiatric Research*, 221–235

Cook, M. 1970. Experiments on orientation and proxemics. *Human Relations*, 23: 61–76

Cooley, C. H. 1902. *Human Nature and the Social Order*. New York: Scribner's

1909. *Social Organization: A Study of the Larger Social Mind*. New York: Scribner's

Cott, H. B. 1957. *Adaptive Coloration in Animals*. London: Methuen

Craik, K. J. W. 1947. Theory of the human operator in control systems. I. The operator as an engineering system. *British Journal of Psychology*, 38: 56–61

1948. Theory of the human operator in control systems. II. Man as an element in a control system. *British Journal of Psychology*, 38: 142–148

Cranach, M. von, Foppa, K., Lepenies, W. and Ploog, D., eds. 1979. *Human Ethology: Claims and Limits of a New Discipline*. Cambridge: Cambridge University Press

Crook, J. H. 1972. Sexual selection, dimorphism and social organization in the primates. In B. Campbell, ed., *Sexual Selection and the Descent of Man 1871–1971*. Chicago: Aldine, pp. 231–281

Crossman, E. R. W. F. 1956. Perception study – a complement to motion study. *The Manager*, 24: 141–145

Crossman, E. R. W. F., Cooke, J. E. and Beishon, R. J. 1964. Visual attention and the sampling of displayed information in process control. Unpublished manuscript. Human Factors in Technology Research Group, Department of Industrial Engineering, University of California, Berkeley, California

Cutting, J. E. and Eimas, P. D. 1975. Phonetic feature analyzers and the processing of speech in infants. In J. F. Kavanagh and J. E. Cutting, eds., *The Role of Speech in Language*. Cambridge, MA: The MIT Press, pp. 127–148

Darnell, R. 1990. *Edward Sapir: Linguist, Anthropologist, Humanist*. Berkeley: University of California Press

Darwin, C. 1872. *The Expression of the Emotions in Man and Animals*. London: John Murray

Davis, R. 1948. *Pilot Error*. Air Ministry Publication AP.3139A, London: H.M.S.O.

Davitz, J. R. 1964. *Communication of Emotional Meaning*. New York: McGraw Hill

Deutsch, R. D. 1977. *Spatial Structurings in Everyday Face-to-Face Behavior: a Neurocybernetic Model*. Orangeburg, New York: Association for the Study of Man Environment Relations

1979. On the isomorphic structure of endings: an example from everyday face-to-face interaction and Balinese Legong dance. *Ethology and Sociobiology*, 1: 41–57

Duncan, S. 1969. Nonverbal communication. *Psychological Bulletin*, 72: 118–137

1972. Some signals and rules for taking speaking turns in conversation. *Journal of Personality and Social Psychology*, 23: 283–292

1973. Toward a grammar for dyadic conversation. *Semiotica*, 9: 20–26

Duncan, S. and Fiske, D. W. 1977. *Face-to-Face Interaction: Research, Methods and Theory*. Hillsdale, NJ: Lawrence Erlbaum

Edney, J. J. and Jordan-Edney, N. 1974. Territorial spacing on a beach. *Sociometry*, 37: 92–104

Efran, M. G. and Cheyne, J. A. 1973. Shared space: the cooperative control of spatial areas by two interacting individuals. *Canadian Journal of Behavioural Science*, 5: 202–210

Eibl-Eibesfeldt, I. 1968. Zur Ethologie des menschlichen Grussverhaltens. I. Beobachtungen an Balinensen, Papuas und Samoanern nebst vergleichenden Bemerkungen. *Zeitschrift für Tierpsychologie*, 25: 727–744

1970. *Ethology: The Biology of Behavior*. New York: Holt, Rinehart and Winston

1972a. Similarities and differences between cultures in expressive movements. In R. A. Hinde, ed., *Nonverbal Communication*. Cambridge: Cambridge University Press, pp. 297–312

1972b. *Love and Hate: On the Natural History of Basic Behaviour Patterns*. London: Methuen

1979. Ritual and ritualization from a biological perspective. In M. von Cranach, K. Foppa, W. Lepenies and D. Ploog, eds., *Human Ethology: The Claims and Limits of a New Discipline*. Cambridge: Cambridge University Press, pp. 3–55

1989. *Human Ethology*. Berlin: Mouton de Gruyter

Ekman, P., ed. 1973. *Darwin and Facial Expression: A Century of Research in Review*. New York: Academic Press

1979. About brows. In M. von Cranach, K. Foppa, W. Lepenies and D. Ploog, eds., *Human Ethology: Claims and Limits of a New Discipline*. New York: Cambridge University Press, pp. 169–202

1982. Methods for measuring facial action. In K. R. Scherer and P. Ekman, eds., *Handbook of Methods in Nonverbal Behavior Research*. Cambridge: Cambridge University Press, pp. 45–90

Ekman, P. and Friesen, W. 1969. The repertoire of nonverbal behavior: Categories, origins, usage and coding. *Semiotica*, 1: 49–98

1976. Measuring facial movement. *Environmental Psychology and Nonverbal Behavior*, 1: 56–75

1978. *The Facial Action Coding System*. Palo Alto, California: Consulting Psychologists Press

Erickson, F. 1975. One function of proxemic shifts in face-to-face interaction. In A. Kendon, R. M. Harris and M. R. Key, eds., *The Organization of Behavior in Face-to-Face Interaction*. Chicago: Aldine; The Hague: Mouton, pp. 175–187

1979. Talking down: some cultural sources of miscommunication in interracial interviews. In A. Wolfgang, ed., *Nonverbal Behavior: Applications and Cultural Implications*. New York: Academic Press, pp. 99–126

1982. Money tree, lasagna bush, salt and pepper: social construction of topical cohesion in a conversation among Italian-Americans. In D. Tannen, ed., *Analyzing Discourse: Text and Talk*. Washington, DC: Georgetown University Press, pp. 43–70

Erickson, F. and Mohatt, G. 1982. The cultural organization of participation structures in two classrooms of Indian students. In G. Spindler, ed., *The Ethnography of Schooling: Educational Anthropology in Action*. New York: Holt, Rinehart and Winston

Erickson, F. and Schultz, J. 1981. When is a context? Some issues and methods in the analysis of social competence. In J. L. Green and C. Wallat, eds., *Ethnography and Language*. Hillsdale, NJ: Ablex Press, pp. 147–160

1982. *The Counselor as Gatekeeper: Social Interaction in Interviews*. New York: Academic Press

Evans, G. B. and Howard, R. B. 1973. Personal space. *Psychological Bulletin*, 80: 334–344

Ex, J. and Kendon, A. 1964. A notation for facial positions and bodily postures. Progress Report of the Social Skills Project to the Department of Scientific and Industrial Research, Appendix to Appendix II, Institute of Experimental Psychology, University of Oxford

Exline, R. V. 1963. Explorations in the process of person perception: visual interaction in relation to competition, sex and need for affiliation. *Journal of Personality*, 31: 1–20

1972. Visual interaction: the glances of power and preference. In M. R. Jones, ed., *Nebraska Symposium on Motivation*. Lincoln, Nebraska: Nebraska University Press

Exline, R. V. and Fehr, B. J. 1978. Applications of semiosis to the study of visual interaction. In A. W. Siegman and S. Feldstein, eds., *Nonverbal Behavior and Communication*. Hillsdale, NJ: Erlbaum, pp. 117–157

1982. The assessment of gaze and mutual gaze. In K. Scherer and P. Ekman, eds., *Handbook of Methods in Nonverbal Behavior Research*. Cambridge: Cambridge University Press, pp. 91–135

Exline, R. V. and Winters, L. G. 1965. Affective relations and mutual glances in dyads. In S. Tomkins and C. Izard, eds., *Affect, Cognition and Personality*. New York: Springer, pp. 319–350

Exline, R. V., Gray, D. and Schuette, D. 1965. Visual behavior in a dyad as affected by interview content and sex of respondent. *Journal of Personality and Social Psychology*, 1: 201–209

Exline, R. V., Thibaut, J., Brannan, C. and Gumpert, P. 1961. Visual interaction in relation to Machiavellianism and an unethical act. Paper read to the American Psychological Association

Fehr, B. J. and Exline, R. G. 1987. Social visual interaction: a conceptual and literature review. In A. W. Siegman and S. Feldstein, eds., *Nonverbal Behavior and Communication*, Second edition. Hillsdale, NJ: Erlbaum, pp. 225–326

Fenwick, M. 1948. *Vogue's Book of Etiquette*. New York: Simon and Schuster

Ferguson, C. A. 1976. The structure and use of politeness formulas. *Language in Society*, 5: 137–151

Field, T. 1982. Affective displays of high risk infants during early interactions. In T. Field and A. Fogel, eds., *Emotion and Early Interaction*. Hillsdale, NJ: Erlbaum, pp. 101–125

Field, T. and Fogel, A., eds. 1982. *Emotion and Early Interaction*. Hillsdale, NJ: Erlbaum

Firth, R. 1972. Verbal and bodily rituals of greeting and parting. In J. S. La Fontaine, ed., *The Interpretation of Ritual: Essays in Honour of A. I. Richards*. London: Tavistock Publications, pp. 1–38

   1973. *Symbols Public and Private*. London: George Allen and Unwin, Ltd.

Foerster, H. von, Mead, M. and Teuber, H. L. 1949–1953. *Cybernetics: Circular, Causal and Feedback Mechanisms in Biological and Social Systems. Transactions of Conferences*, 5 volumes. New York: Josiah Macy Jr. Foundation

Fogel, A. 1977. Temporal organization in mother–infant face-to-face interaction. In H. R. Schaffer, ed., *Studies in Mother–Infant Interaction*. London: Academic Press, pp. 119–152

   1982. Affect dynamics in early infancy: affective tolerance. In Field, T. and Fogel, A., eds., *Emotion and Early Interaction*. Hillsdale, NJ, Erlbaum, pp. 25–56

Fraiberg, S. 1979. Blind infants and their mothers: an examination of the sign system. In M. Bullowa, ed., *Before Speech: The Beginning of Interpersonal Communication*. Cambridge: Cambridge University Press, pp. 149–169

Frake, C. O. 1964. How to ask for a drink in Subanum. *American Anthropologist*, 66, Part 2, pp. 127–132

   1975. How to enter a Yakan house. In M. Sanches and B. Blount, eds., *Sociocultural Dimensions of Language Use*. New York: Academic Press

Freedman, N. and Hoffman, S. P. 1967. Kinetic behavior in altered clinical states: approach to objective analysis of motor behavior during clinical interviews. *Perceptual and Motor Skills*, 25: 527–539

Fridlund, A. J. In Press. Evolution and facial action in reflex, social motive and paralanguage. In P. K. Ackles, J. R. Jennings and M. G. H. Coles, eds., *Advances in Psychophysiology*, Volume 4. London: Jessica Kingsley

Fridlund, A. J., Ekman, P. and Oster, H. 1987. Facial expressions of emotion: review of literature, 1970–1983. In A. W. Siegman and S. Feldstein, eds., *Nonverbal Behavior and Communication*, Second edition. Hillsdale, NJ: Erlbaum, pp. 143–224

Fries, C. C. 1952. *The Structure of English*. New York: Harcourt, Brace and Co.

Frijda, N. H. 1953. The understanding of facial expression of emotion. *Acta Psychologica*, 9: 294–362

Garfinkel, H. 1963. A conception of, and experiments with, "trust" as a condition of stable concerted actions. In O. J. Harvey, ed., *Motivation and Social Interaction*. New York: Ronald Press, pp. 187–238

Gatewood, J. B. and Rosenwein, R. 1981. Interactional synchrony: genuine or spurious? A critique of recent research. *Journal of Nonverbal Behavior*, 6: 12–29

Gibson, J. J. and Pick, A. D. 1963. Perception of another person's looking behavior. *American Journal of Psychology*, 76: 386–394

Gilliland, A. R. 1926. A revision and some results with the Moore–Gilliland Aggressiveness Test. *Journal of Applied Psychology*, 10: 143–150

Goffman, E. 1953. *Communication Conduct in an Island Community*. Thesis submitted in partial fulfillment of the requirements for Doctor of Philosophy, University of Chicago, Chicago, Illinois

1955. On face-work. *Psychiatry*, 18: 213–231

1956. The nature of deference and demeanor. *American Anthropologist*, 58: 473–502

1957. Alienation from interaction. *Human Relations*, 10: 47–59

1961. *Encounters: Two Studies in the Sociology of Interaction*. Indianapolis: Bobbs-Merrill

1963. *Behavior in Public Places*. New York: The Free Press

1967. *Interaction Ritual: Essays in Face-to-Face Behavior*. Chicago: Aldine

1971. *Relations in Public: Microstudies in the Public Order*. New York: Basic Books

1974. *Frame Analysis: An Essay on the Organization of Experience*. Cambridge, Mass.: Harvard University Press

1983. The interaction order. *American Sociological Review*, 48: 1–17

Goldenthal, P., Johnston, R. E. and Kraut, R. E. 1981. Smiling, appeasement and the silent bared teeth display. *Ethology and Sociobiology*, 3: 127–133

Goldman-Eisler, F. 1954. On the variability of the speed of talking and on its relation to the length of utterances in conversations. *British Journal of Psychology*, 45: 94–107

1958. Speech analysis and mental processes. *Language and Speech*, 1: 59–75

1961. The distribution of pause durations in speech. *Language and Speech*, 4: 232–237

Gonos, G. 1977. "Situation" versus "frame": the "Interactionist" and the "Structuralist" analyses of everyday life. *American Sociological Review*, 42: 854–867

Goodwin, C. 1981. *Conversational Organization: Interactions Between Speakers and Hearers*. New York: Academic Press

1984. Notes on story structure and the organization of participation. In J. M. Atkinson and J. Heritage, eds., *Structures of Social Action: Studies in Conversation Analysis*. Cambridge: Cambridge University Press, pp. 225–246

Goody, E. 1972. "Greetings," "begging," and the presentation of respect. In J. S. Fontaine, ed., *The Interpretation of Ritual*. London: Tavistock, pp. 39–71

Grammer, K., Schiefenhövel, W., Schleidt, M., Lorenz, B. and Eibl-Eibesfeldt, I. 1988. Patterns on the face: the eyebrow flash in cross-cultural comparison. *Ethology*, 77: 279–299

Grant, E. C. 1961. An ethological description of non-verbal behaviour during interviews. *British Journal of Medical Psychology*, 41: 177–184

1969. Human facial expression. *Man* (N.S.), 4: 525–536

Greenbaum, P. E. and Rosenfeld, H. M. 1980. Varieties of touching in greetings: sequential structure and sex-related differences. *Journal of Nonverbal Behavior*, 5: 13–29

Greenspoon, J. 1962. Verbal conditioning and clinical psychology. In A. Bachrach, ed., *Experimental Foundations of Clinical Psychology*. New York: Basic Books, pp. 510–553

Gross, L. E. 1959. Effects of verbal and nonverbal reinforcement in the Rorschach. *Journal of Consulting Psychology*, 23: 6–68

Gumperz, J. J. 1964. Linguistic and social interaction in two communities. *American Anthropologist*, 66, Part 2: 137–153

1982a. *Discourse Strategies*. Cambridge: Cambridge University Press

ed. 1982b. *Language and Social Identity*. Cambridge: Cambridge University Press

Gumperz, J. and Hymes, D., eds. 1964. *The ethnography of communication*. Special Issue, *American Anthropologist*, 66 (6, Part II)

Gumperz, J. and Hymes, D., eds. 1972. *Directions in Sociolinguistics: The Ethnography of Communication*. New York: Holt, Rinehart and Winston

Gunst, V. 1982. Frieda Fromm-Reichmann: A Seminar in the History of Psychiatry. *Psychiatry*, 45: 107–115

Haggard, E. A. and Isaacs, K. S. 1966. Micromomentary facial expressions as indicators of ego mechanisms in psychotherapy. In L. A. Gottschalk and A. H. Auerbach, eds., *Methods of Research in Psychotherapy*. New York: Appleton Century Crofts, pp. 154–165

Haley, J. 1976. Development of a theory: a history of a research project. In C. E. Sluzki, and D. C. Ransom, eds., *Double Bind: The Foundation of the Communicational Approach to the Family*. New York: Grune and Stratton

Hall, E. T. 1959. *The Silent Language*. Garden City, NY: Doubleday

1964a. Silent assumptions in social communication. *Research Publications of the Association for Nervous and Mental Disease*, 42: 41–55

1964b. Adumbration in intercultural communication. In J. Gumperz and D. Hymes, eds., *The ethnography of communication*. Special Issue, *American Anthropologist*, 66 (6, Part II): 154–163

1966. *The Hidden Dimension*. Garden City, NY: Doubleday

1968. Proxemics. *Current Anthropology*, 9: 83–108

Hall, E. T. and Trager, G. L. 1953. *The Analysis of Culture*. Washington, DC: American Council of Learned Societies

Hall, P. M. and Hall, D. A. 1983. The handshake as interaction. *Semiotica*, 45: 249–264

Hare, A. P. 1962. *Handbook of Small Group Research*. New York: The Free Press

Hare, A. P., Borgatta, E. F. and Bales, R. F. 1955. *Small Groups: Studies in Social Interaction*. New York: Alfred A. Knopf

Harper, R. G., Wiens, A. N., and Matarazzo, J. D. 1978. *Nonverbal Communication: The State of the Art*. New York: John Wiley and Sons

Harris, M. 1968. *The Rise of Anthropological Theory*. New York: Crowell

Heath, C. C. 1986. *Body Movement and Speech in Medical Interaction*. Cambridge: Cambridge University Press

Heider, F. 1958. *The Psychology of Interpersonal Relations*. New York: Wiley

Heilman, S. C. 1979. Communication and interaction: a parallel in the theoretical outlooks of Erving Goffman and Ray Birdwhistell. *Communication*, 4: 221–234

Heims, S. P. 1975. Encounter of behavioral sciences with new machine–organism analogies in the 1940s. *Journal of the History of the Behavioral Sciences*, 11: 368–373

   1977. Gregory Bateson and the mathematicians: from interdisciplinary interaction to societal functions. *Journal of the History of the Behavioral Sciences*, 13: 141–159

Held-Weiss, R. 1984. The interpersonal tradition and its development: some implications for training. *Contemporary Psychoanalysis*, 20: 345–362

Heritage, J. 1984. *Garfinkel and Ethnomethodology*. Cambridge: Polity Press

Heshka, S. and Nelson, Y. 1972. Interpersonal speaking distance as a function of age, sex and relationship. *Sociometry*, 35: 491–498

Heyns, R. W. and Lippitt, R. 1954. Systematic observational techniques. In G. Lindzey, ed., *Handbook of Social Psychology*, Volume 1. Cambridge, Mass.: Addison Wesley, pp. 370–404

Hinde, R. A. and Rowell, T. E. 1962. Communication by postures and facial expressions in the rhesus monkey (*Macca mulatta*). *Proceedings of the Zoological Society of London*, 138: 1–21

Hingston, R. W. G. 1933. *The Meaning of Animal Colour and Adornment*. London: Edward Arnold

Hitchcock, R. 1891. The Ainos of Yezo, Japan. *Report of the U.S. National Museum under the Direction of the Smithsonian Institution for the Year ending June 30th, 1890*. Part 2, Washington, DC: Government Printing Office, pp. 429–502

Hockett, C. F. 1960. Ethnolinguistic implications of recent studies in linguistics and psychiatry. In W. M. Austin, ed., *Report of the Ninth Annual Round Table Meeting on Linguistics and Language Study*. Georgetown University Institute of Languages and Linguistics Monograph Series, No. 11, pp. 175–193

   1977. *The View From Language*. Athens, Georgia: University of Georgia Press

Hooff, J. A. R. A. M. van. 1962. Facial expressions in higher primates. *Symposia of the Zoological Society of London*, 8: 97–125

   1967. The facial displays of the catarrine monkeys and apes. In D. Morris, ed., *Primate Ethology*. Chicago: Aldine, pp. 7–68

1972. A comparative approach to the phylogeny of laughter and smiling. In R. Hinde, ed., *Nonverbal Communication*. Cambridge: Cambridge University Press, pp. 209–241

1973. A structural analysis of the social behaviour of a semi-captive group of chimpanzees. In M. von Cranach and I. Vine, eds., *Social Communication and Movement: Studies of Interaction and Expression in Man and Chimpanzees*. London: Academic Press, pp. 75–162

Hymes, D., ed. 1964. *Language in Culture and Society*. New York: Harper and Row

Hymes, D. 1974. *Foundations in Sociolinguistics: An Ethnographic Approach*. Philadelphia: University of Pennsylvania Press

Irvine, J. T. 1974. Strategies of status manipulation in the Wolof greeting. In R. Bauman and J. Sherzer, eds., *Explorations in the Ethnography of Speaking*. Cambridge: Cambridge University Press, pp. 167–191

Izard, C. 1969. *The Face of Emotion*. New York: Appleton Century Crofts

1979. *The Maximally Discriminative Facial Movement Coding System*. Newark, Delaware: Instructional Resources Center, University of Delaware

Jefferson, G. 1972. Side sequences. In D. Sudnow, ed., *Studies in Social Interaction*. New York: The Free Press, Collier-Macmillan Company, pp. 294–338

1973. A case of precision timing in ordinary conversation: overlapped tag-positioned address terms in closing sequences. *Semiotica*, 9: 47–96

1984. On stepwise transition from talk about a trouble to inappropriately next positioned matters. In J. M. Atkinson and J. Heritage, eds., *Structures of Social Action: Studies in Conversation Analysis*. Cambridge: Cambridge University Press, pp. 191–222

Jones, J. and von Raffler-Engel, W. 1982. Transactions at a store counter. In M. Davis, ed., *Interaction Rhythms: Periodicity in Communicative Behavior*. New York: Human Sciences Press, pp. 341–350

Jones, S. E. and Yarborough, A. E. 1985. A naturalistic study of the meanings of touch. *Communication Monographs*, 52: 19–56

Kempton, W. 1980. The rhythmic basis of interactional microsynchrony. In M. R. Key, ed., *The Relationship of Verbal and Nonverbal Communication*. The Hague: Mouton Publishers, pp. 67–75

Kendon, A. 1963. Temporal aspects of social performance in two-person encounters. Thesis submitted for the degree of Doctor of Philosophy, Oxford University

1972. Some relationships between body motion and speech. In A. W. Seigman and B. Pope, eds., *Studies in Dyadic Communication*. Elmsford, NY: Pergamon Press, pp. 177–210

1973. The role of visible behaviour in the organization of face-to-face interaction. In M. von Cranach and I. Vine, eds., *Social Communication and Movement: Studies of Interaction and Expression in Man and Chimpanzee*. New York: Academic Press, pp. 29–74

1977. *Studies in the Behavior of Social Interaction*. Lisse: Peter De Ridder Press

1978. Differential perception and attentional frame. *Semiotica*, 24: 305–315

1979. Some methodological and theoretical aspects of the use of film in the study of social interaction. In G. P. Ginsburg, ed., *Emerging Strategies in Social Psychological Research*. New York: Wiley, pp. 67–91

1980. Features of the structural analysis of human communicational behavior. In W. von Raffler-Engel, ed., *Aspects of Nonverbal Communication*. Lisse: Swets and Zeitlinger B.V., pp. 29–43

1982. The organization of behavior in face-to-face interaction: observations on the development of a methodology. In K. Scherer and P. Ekman, eds., *Handbook of Methods in Nonverbal Behavior Research*. Cambridge: Cambridge University Press, pp. 440–505

1988. Goffman's approach to face-to-face interaction. In P. Drew and A. Wootton, eds., *Erving Goffman: Exploring the Interaction Order*. Cambridge: Polity Press, pp. 14–40

Knapp, M. L., Hart, R. P., Friedrich, G. W. and Shulman, G. M. 1973. The rhetoric of goodbye: verbal and nonverbal correlates of human leave-taking. *Speech Monographs*, 40: 182–198

Knowles, E. S. 1973. Boundaries around social space: dyadic responses to an invader. *Environment and Behavior*, 4: 437–445

Komnenich, P. 1977. Decision making aspects of greeting behavior among Serbians and Montenegrins. *International Journal of Psycholinguistics*, 4: 31–49

Kraut, R. E. and Johnston, R. E. 1979. Social and emotional messages of smiling: an ethological approach. *Journal of Personality and Social Psychology*, 37: 1539–1553

La Barre, W. 1964. Paralinguistics, kinesics and cultural anthropology. In T. A. Sebeok, A. Hayes and M. C. Bateson, eds., *Approaches to Semiotics*. The Hague: Mouton, pp. 191–220

Landis, C. and Hunt, W. A. 1936. Studies of the startle pattern: III, facial pattern. *Journal of Psychology*, 2: 215–219

Leeds-Hurwitz, W. 1987. The social history of *The Natural History of an Interview*: a multidisciplinary investigation of social communication. *Research on Language and Social Interaction*, 20: 1–51

Lenneberg, E. 1971. The importance of temporal factors in behavior. In D. Horton and J. J. Jenkins, eds., *Perception of Language*. Columbus, OH: Charles E. Merrill Press

Levine, D. N. 1971. Introduction. In D. N. Levine, ed., *George Simmel on Individuality and Social Forms*. Chicago: Chicago University Press

Levinson, S. C. 1983. *Pragmatics*. Cambridge: Cambridge University Press

Lewin, K., Lippitt, R. and White, R. K. 1939. Patterns of aggressive behavior in experimentally created "social climates." *Journal of Social Psychology*, 10: 271–299

Lewis, M. and Saarni, C., eds. 1985. *The Socialization of Emotions*. New York and London: Plenum Press

Liberman, A. M. 1979. An ethological approach to language through the study of speech perception. In M. von Cranach, K. Foppa, W. Lepenies and D. Ploog, eds., *Human Ethology: The Claims and Limits of a New Discipline*. Cambridge: Cambridge University Press, pp. 682–704

Liggett, J. 1974. *The Human Face*. London: Constable

Lipset, D. 1980. *Gregory Bateson: The Legacy of a Scientist*. Englewood Cliffs, NJ: Prentice-Hall

Lockard, J., Allen, D., Schiele, B. and Wiemer, M. 1978. Human postural signals: stance, weight shifts and social distance as intention movements to depart. *Animal Behaviour*, 26: 219–224

Luchins, A. S. 1959. *Rigidity of Behavior*. Norman, OK: University of Oklahoma Press

Lyman, S. M. and Scott, M. B. 1967. Territoriality: a neglected sociological dimension. *Social Problems*, 15: 236–249

Lynn, J. G. 1940. An apparatus and method for stimulating, recording and measuring facial expression. *Journal of Experimental Psychology*, 27: 81–88

MacCannell, D. 1973. A note on hat tipping. *Semiotica*, 8: 300–312

Maclay, H. and Osgood, C. E. 1959. Hesitation phenomena in English. *Word*, 15: 19–44

Malatesta, C. Z. 1985. Developmental course of emotion expression in the human infant. In G. Zivin, ed., *Development of Expressive Behavior*. New York: Academic Press, pp. 183–219

Malatesta, C. Z. and Haviland, J. M. 1982. Learning display rules: the socialization of emotion expression in infancy. *Child Development*, 53: 991–1003

Mandelbaum, D., ed. 1951. *Selected Writings of Edward Sapir in Language, Culture and Personality*. Berkeley, California: University of California Press

Marler, P. 1979. Development of auditory perception in relation to vocal behavior. In M. von Cranach, K. Foppa, W. Lepenies and D. Ploog, eds., *Human Ethology: The Claims and Limits of a New Discipline*. Cambridge: Cambridge University Press, pp. 663–681

Matarazzo, J. D., Saslow, G. and Matarazzo, R. G. 1956. The interaction chronograph as an instrument for objective measurement of interaction patterns during interviews. *Journal of Psychology*, 41: 347–367

Matarazzo, J. D., Saslow, G., Wiens, A. N., Weitman, M. and Allen, B. V. 1964. Interviewer headnodding and interviewee speech durations. *Psychotherapy Research Theory*, 1: 54–63

McDermott, R. P. and Gospodinoff, K. 1979. Social contexts for ethnic borders and school failure. In A. Wolfgang, ed., *Nonverbal Behavior: Applications and Cultural Implications*. New York: Academic Press, pp. 175–196

McDermott, R. P., Gospodinoff, K. and Aron, J. 1978. Criteria for an ethnographically adequate description of concerted activities and their contexts. *Semiotica*, 24: 245–275

McDermott, R. and Roth, D. R. 1978. The social organization of behavior: interactional approaches. *Annual Review of Anthropology*, 7: 321–345

McDowall, K. V. 1972. Violation of personal space. *Canadian Journal of Behavioral Science*, 4: 210–217

McGrew, W. C. 1972. *An Ethological Study of Children's Behavior*. New York: Academic Press

McMillan, R. A. 1974. A method for using naturalistic video-tape recordings for the study of behavior–space relations in homes. Doctoral Dissertation, Columbia University, New York

McQuown, N. A. 1971a. Natural history method: a frontier method. In A. R. Mahrer and L. Pearson, eds., *Creative Developments in Psychotherapy*. Cleveland: Case Western Reserve University Press, pp. 430–438

ed. 1971b. *The Natural History of an Interview*. Microfilm Collection of Manuscripts on Cultural Anthropology, 15th Series, University of Chicago, Joseph Regenstein Library, Department of Photoduplication, Chicago, IL

Mead, G. H. 1934. *Mind, Self and Society*. Chicago: Chicago University Press

Miller, R. E. 1971. Experimental studies of communication in the monkey. In A. Rosenblum, ed., *Primate Behavior: Developments in Field and Laboratory Research*, Volume II. New York: Academic Press

Moerman, M. 1988. *Talking Culture*. Philadelphia: University of Pennsylvania Press

Moerman, M. and Sacks, H. 1988. On "understanding" in the analysis of natural conversation. Appendix B in M. Moerman, *Talking Culture*. Philadelphia: University of Pennsylvania Press, pp. 180–186

Moore, H. T. and Gilliland, A. R. 1926. The measurement of aggressiveness. *Journal of Applied Psychology*, 5: 97–118

Morris, D., Collett, P., Marsh, P. and O'Shaugnessy, M. 1979. *Gestures*. New York: Stein and Day

Mullahy, P. 1952. *The Contributions of Harry Stack Sullivan: A Symposium on Interpersonal Theory in Psychiatry and Social Science*. New York: Hermitage House

Neisser, U. 1967. *Cognitive Psychology*. New York: Appleton Century Crofts

Nielsen, G. 1964. *Studies in Self-Confrontation*. Copenhagen: Munksgaard

Ogden, A. 1961. Looks and glances. *Harpers Bazaar*, 84: 90–110

Ogden, C. K. and Richards, I. A. 1947. *The Meaning of Meaning*. London: Routledge

Ortega y Gasset, 1957. *Man and People*. New York: W. W. Norton

Patterson, M. L. and Edinger, J. A. 1987. A functional analysis of space in social interaction. In A. W. Siegman and S. Feldstein, eds., *Nonverbal Behavior and Communication*. Hillsdale, NJ: Lawrence Erlbaum Associates, second edition, pp. 523–562

Patterson, M. L. 1968. Spatial factors in social interaction. *Human Relations*, 21: 351–361

1973. Compensation in nonverbal immediacy behaviors: a review. *Sociometry*, 21: 351–361

Pelose, G. C. 1987. The functions of behavioral synchrony and speech rhythm in conversation. *Research on Language and Social Interaction*, 20: 171–220

Perry, H. S. 1982. *Psychiatrist of America: The Life of Harry Stack Sullivan.* Cambridge, MA: Harvard University Press

Pike, K. L. 1954–1960. *Language in Relation to a Unified Theory of the Structure of Human Behavior,* Preliminary Edition, Part I 1954, Part II 1955, Part III 1960. Glendale, California: Summer Institute of Linguistics
    1967. *Language in Relation to a Unified Theory of the Structure of Human Behavior,* second revised edition. The Hague: Mouton

Pitcairn, T. K. and Eibl-Eibesfeldt, I. 1976. Concerning the evolution of nonverbal behavior in man. In M. E. Hahn and E. C. Simmel, eds., *Communicative Behavior and Evolution.* New York: Academic Press, pp. 81–114

Pitcairn, T. K. and Schleidt, M. 1976. Dance and decision: an analysis of a courtship dance of the Melpa, New Guinea. *Behaviour*, 58: 248–316

Pittinger, R. E., Hockett, C. F. and Danehy, J. J. 1960. *The First Five Minutes: A Sample of Microscopic Interview Analysis.* Ithaca, NY: Paul Martineau, Publisher

Pomerantz, A. 1984. Agreeing and disagreeing with assessments. In J. M. Atkinson and J. Heritage, eds., *Structures of Social Action: Studies in Conversation Analysis.* Cambridge: Cambridge University Press, pp. 57–101

Post, E. L. 1965. *Emily Post's Etiquette: The Blue Book of Social Usage,* eleventh edition. New York: Funk and Wagnalls

Poulton. E. C. 1957. On prediction in skilled movements. *Psychological Bulletin*, 54: 467–478

Poyatos, F. 1983. Language and nonverbal systems in the structure of face-to-face interaction. *Language and Communication*, 3: 129–140

Rawlins, W. K. 1987. Gregory Bateson and the composition of human communication. *Research on Language and Social Interaction*, 20: 53–78

Reece, M. M. and Whitman, N. R. 1962. Expressive movement, warmth and verbal reinforcement. *Journal of Abnormal and Social Psychology*, 64: 234–236

Riemer, M. D. 1955. Abnormalities of the gaze – a classification. *Psychiatric Quarterly*, 29: 659–672

Roethlisberger, F. J. and Dickson, W. J. 1939. *Management and the Worker.* Cambridge, MA: Harvard University Press

Rosenblueth, A., Wiener, N. and Bigelow, J. 1943. Behavior, purpose and teleology. *Philosophy of Science*, 10: 18–24

Rosenfeld, H. M. 1966a. Instrumental affiliative functions of facial and gestural expressions. *Journal of Personality and Social Psychology*, 4: 65–72
    1966b. Approval seeking and approval inducing functions of verbal and non-verbal responses in the dyad. *Journal of Personality and Social Psychology*, 4: 597–605

1967. Nonverbal reciprocation of approval: an experimental analysis. *Journal of Experimental Social Psychology*, 3: 102–111

1981. Whither interactional synchrony? In K. Bloom, ed., *Prospective Issues in Infant Research*. Hillsdale, NJ: Lawrence Erlbaum, pp. 71–97

Roth, H. L. 1889. On salutations. *Journal of the Royal Anthropological Institute*, 19: 164–181

Ruesch, J. 1972. *Semiotic Approaches to Human Relations*. The Hague: Mouton

Ruesch, J. and Bateson, G. B. 1951. *Semiotic Approaches to Human Relations*. The Hague: Mouton

Rutter, D. R. 1984. *Looking and Seeing: The Role of Visual Communication in Social Interaction*. New York: John Wiley and Sons

Sacks, H. 1974. An analysis of the course of a joke's telling in conversation. In R. Bauman and J. Sherzer, eds., *Explorations in the Ethnography of Speaking*. Cambridge: Cambridge University Press, pp. 337–353

Sacks, H., Schegloff, E. A. and Jefferson, G. 1974. A simplest systematics for the organization of turn-taking for conversation. *Language*, 50: 696–735

Sandall, R. 1978. Objective graphics: ways of mapping the physical world. *Art International*, 22: 21–25

Sapir, E. 1951. The unconscious patterning of behavior in society. In D. G. Mandelbaum, ed., *Selected Writings of Edward Sapir in Language, Culture and Personality*. Berkeley, CA: University of California Press, pp. 544–559

Sartre, J.-P. 1956. *Being and Nothingness*. Translated by Hazel E. Barnes. New York: Philosophical Library

Schaeffer, J. 1970. Video-tape techniques in anthropology: the collection and analysis of data. Ph.D. Thesis, Columbia University, New York

Schaffer, H. R., Collis, G. M. and Parsons, G. 1977. Vocal interchange and visual regard in verbal and preverbal children. In H. R. Schaffer, ed., *Studies in Mother–Infant Interaction*. London: Academic Press, pp. 291–324

Schaffner, B., ed. 1956. *Group Processes: Transactions of the Second Conference*. New York: Josiah Macy, Jr. Foundation

Scheflen, A. E. 1963. Communication and regulation in psychotherapy. *Psychiatry*, 26: 126–136

1964. The significance of posture in communication systems. *Psychiatry*, 27: 316–321

1966. Natural history method in psychotherapy: communicational research. In L. Gottschalk and A. H. Auerbach, eds., *Methods of Research in Psychotherapy*. New York: Appelton-Century-Crofts, pp. 263–289

1973. *Communicational Structure: Analysis of a Psychotherapy Transaction*. Bloomington: Indiana University Press

1974. *How Behavior Means*. New York: Jason Aronson

1975. Micro-territories in human interaction. In A. Kendon, R. M. Harris and Mary R. Key, eds., *The Organization of Behavior in Face-to-Face Interaction*. The Hague: Mouton Publishers, pp. 159–173

1977. Some territorial layouts in the United States. In A. Rapaport, ed., *Mutual Interaction and the Built Environment*. The Hague: Mouton Publishers

Scheflen, A. E. and Ashcraft, N. 1976. *Human Territories: How We Behave in Space-Time*. Englewood Cliffs, NJ: Prentice Hall

Schegloff, E. A. 1972. Sequencing in conversational openings. In J. J. Gumperz and D. Hymes, eds., *Directions in Sociolinguistics: the Ethnography of Communication*. New York: Holt, Rinehart and Winston, pp. 346–380

1979. The relevance of repair to syntax-for-conversation. In T. Givon, ed., *Syntax and Semantics 12: Discourse and Syntax*. New York: Academic Press, pp. 261–288

1984. On some gestures' relation to talk. In J. M. Atkinson and J. Heritage, eds., *Structures of Social Action: Studies in Conversation Analysis*. Cambridge: Cambridge University Press, pp. 266–296

1989. Harvey Sacks' Lectures on Conversation. The 1964–65 Lectures: An Introduction/Memoir. *Human Studies*, 12: 185–209

Schegloff, E. and Sacks, H. 1973. Opening up closings. *Semiotica*, 8: 289–327

Schenkein, D., ed. 1978. *Studies in the Organization of Conversational Interaction*. New York: Academic Press

Schiffrin, D. 1974. Handwork as ceremony. *Semiotica*, 12: 189–202

1977. Opening encounters. *American Sociological Review*, 42: 679–691

1987. *Discourse Markers*. Cambridge: Cambridge University Press

Shannon, C. E. and Weaver, W. 1949. *A Mathematical Theory of Communication*. Urbana: University of Illinois Press

Shultz, J. and Florio, S. 1979. Stop and freeze: the negotiation of social and physical space in a kindergarten/first grade classroom. *Anthropology and Education Quarterly*, 10: 166–181

Shultz, J., Florio, S. and Erickson, F. 1982. Where's the floor? Aspects of the cultural organization of social relationships in communication at home and in school. In P. Gilmore and A. Glatthorn, eds., *Children in and out of School*. Washington, DC: Center for Applied Linguistics, Language and Ethnography Series 2, pp. 88–123

Sigman, S. J. 1980. *An analysis of conversational "fission" and "fusion"*. Paper presented to the 79th Annual Meeting of the American Anthropological Association, Washington, DC

1987. *A Perspective on Social Communication*. Lexington, MA: Lexington Books

Sigman, S. J., Sullivan, S. J. and Wendell, M. 1987. Conversation: data acquisition and analysis. In Charles H. Tardy, ed., *A Handbook for the Study of Human Communication: Methods and Instruments for Observing, Measuring and Assessing Communication Processes*. Norwood, NJ: Ablex Publishing Corporation, pp. 163–192

Simmel, G. 1924. The sociology of the senses: visual interaction. In R. E. Park and E. W. Burgess, eds., *An Introduction to the Science of Sociology*, second edition. Chicago: University of Chicago Press, pp. 356–361

1950. *The Sociology of Georg Simmel*, ed. K. H. Wolff. New York: The Free Press

Smith, W. J. 1968. Message–meaning analysis. In T. A. Sebeok, ed., *Animal Communication: Techniques of Study and Results of Research*. Bloomington: Indiana University Press, pp. 44–60

1969a. Messages of vertebrate communication. *Science*, 165: 145–160

1969b. Displays and messages in intraspecific communication. *Semiotica*, 1: 357–369

Smith, W. J., Chase, J. and Lieblich, A. K. 1974. Tongue showing: a facial display of humans and other primate species. *Semiotica*, 11: 201–246

Sommer, R. 1962. The distance for comfortable conversation. *Sociometry*, 25: 111–116

1967. Small group ecology. *Psychological Bulletin*, 67: 145–152

1969. *Personal Space: The Behavioral Basis of Design*. Englewood Cliffs, NJ: Prentice Hall

Soskin, W. V. and John, P. V. 1963. The study of spontaneous talk. In R. G. Barker, ed., *The Stream of Behavior*. New York: Appleton, Century, Crofts, pp. 228–281

Spitz, R. A. and Wolff, K. M. 1946. The smiling response: a contribution to the ontogenesis of social relations. *Genetic Psychology Monographs*, 34: 57–125

Stern, D. 1977. *The First Relationship*. Cambridge, MA: Harvard University Press

1985. *The Interpersonal World of the Infant: A View from Psychoanalysis and Developmental Psychology*. New York: Basic Books

Stern, D. and Gibbon, J. 1978. Temporal expectancies of social behavior in mother-infant play. In E. Thomas, ed., *Origins of the Infant's Social Responsiveness*. Hillsdale, NJ: Lawrence Erlbaum, pp. 409–429

Streeck, J. 1984. Embodied contexts, transcontextuals and the timing of speech acts. *Journal of Pragmatics*, 8: 113–137

Strodtbeck, F. L. 1951. Husband-wife interaction over revealed differences. *American Sociological Review*, 16: 468–473

1954. The family as a three-person group. *American Sociological Review*, 19: 23–29

Sudnow, D., ed. 1972. *Studies in Social Interaction*. New York: The Free Press, Collier-Macmillan Company

Sullivan, H. S. 1964. *The Fusion of Psychiatry and Social Science*. New York: W. W. Norton

Tannen, D. 1984. *Conversational Style: Analyzing Talk among Friends*. Norwood, NJ: Ablex Corporation

Thomas, D. R. 1973. Interaction distances in same-sex and mixed sex groups. *Perceptual and Motor Skills*, 36: 15–18

Thomas, S. 1980. Some problems of the paradigm in communication theory. *Philosophy of Social Sciences*, 10: 427–444

Thompson, J. 1941. Development of facial expression of emotion in blind and seeing children. *Archives of Psychology*, No. 264, 37: 1–47

Tomkins, S. S. 1963. *Affect, Imagery, Consciousness*, Volume II. New York: Springer

Trager, G. L. 1958. Paralanguage: a first approximation. *Studies in Linguistics*, 13: 1–12

Trevarthen, C. 1977. Descriptive analyses of infant communicative behaviour. In H. R. Schaffer, ed., *Studies in Mother-Infant Interaction*. London: Academic Press, pp. 227–270

   1979. Communication and cooperation in early infancy: a description of primary intersubjectivity. In M. Bullowa, ed., *Before Speech: The Beginning of Interpersonal Communication*. Cambridge: Cambridge University Press, pp. 321–347

Trevarthen, C. and Hubley, P. 1978. Secondary intersubjectivity: confidence, confiding and acts of meaning in the first year. In A. Lock, ed., *Action, Gesture and Symbol: The Emergence of Language*. London: Academic Press, pp. 183–229

Tronick, E. Z., ed. 1982. *Social Interchange in Infancy: Affect, Cognition and Communication*. Baltimore: University Park Press

Van Lawick-Goodall, J. 1968. A preliminary report on expressive movements and communication in the Gombe Stream chimpanzees. In P. Jay, ed., *Primates: Studies in Adaptation and Variability*. New York: Holt, Rinehart and Winston, pp. 313–374

Van Vlack, J. 1966. Filming psychotherapy from the point of view of a research cinematographer. In L. A. Gottschalk and A. A. Auerbach, eds., *Methods of Research in Psychotherapy*. New York: Appleton Century Crofts, pp. 14–24

Vine, I. 1970. Communication by facial-visual signals. In J. H. Crook, ed., *Social Behaviour of Birds and Mammals*. London: Academic Press, pp. 279–354

   1971. Judgement of direction of gaze: an interpretation of discrepant results. *British Journal of Social and Clinical Psychology*, 10: 320–321

   1973a. Social spacing in animals and man. *Social Science Information*, 12: 7–50

   1973b. The role of facial-visual signalling in early social development. In M. von Cranach and I. Vine, eds., *Social Communication and Movement: Studies of Interaction and Expression in Man and Chimpanzees*. London: Academic Press, pp. 195–298

   1975. Territoriality and the spatial regulation of interaction. In A. Kendon, R. M. Harris and M. R. Key, eds., *The Organization of Behavior in Face-to-Face Interaction*. Chicago: Aldine; The Hague: Mouton, pp. 357–387

Wada, J. A. 1961. Modification of cortically induced responses in brain stem of shift of attention in monkeys. *Science*, 133: 40–42

Wardwell, E. 1960. Children's reactions to being watched during success and failure. Ph.D. thesis, Cornell University, Ithaca, NY

Watzlawick, P., Beavin, J. H. and Jackson, D. D. 1967. *Pragmatics of Human*

Communication: A Study of Interactional Patterns, Pathologies and Paradoxes. New York: W. W. Norton

Webbink, P. 1986. The Power of the Eyes. New York: Springer Publishing Co.

Weisbrod, R. R. 1965. Looking behavior in a discussion group. Term Paper submitted for Psychology 546 under the direction of Professor Longabaugh, Cornell University, Ithaca, NY

Welford, A. T. 1960. The measurement of sensory-motor performance: survey and reappraisal of twelve years' progress. Ergonomics, 3: 189–230

1968. Fundamentals of Skill. London: Methuen

West, C. and Zimmerman, D. H. 1982. Conversation analysis. In K. R. Scherer and P. Ekman, eds., Handbook of Methods in Nonverbal Behavior Research. Cambridge: Cambridge University Press, pp. 506–541

Whyte, W. F. 1943. Street Corner Society. Chicago: University of Chicago Press

Wickes, T. A. 1956. Examiner influence in a testing situation. Journal of Consulting Psychology, 20: 23–25

Wiener, N. 1948. Cybernetics: or control and communication in the animal and the machine. New York: Technology Press, Wiley

Wilson, P. 1980. Man the Promising Primate: The Conditions of Human Evolution. New Haven, CT: Yale University Press

Witkin, H. A. 1949. Sex differences in perception. Transactions of the New York Academy of Sciences, 12: 23–26

Woodworth, R. S. and Schlosberg, H. 1954. Experimental Psychology, third edition. New York: Holt, Rinehart and Winston

Youssouf, I. A., Grimshaw, A. and Bird, C. 1976. Greetings in the desert. American Ethnologist, 3: 797–824

Zivin, G. 1977a. On becoming subtle: Age and social rank changes in the use of a facial gesture. Child Development, 48: 1314–1321

1977b. Preschool children's facial gestures predict conflict outcomes. Social Science Information, 16: 715–730

1982. Watching the sands shift: conceptualizing development of nonverbal mastery. In R. S. Feldman, ed., Development of Nonverbal Behavior in Children. New York: Springer-Verlag, pp. 63–98

# Index

287

# Index